Elizabeth Fries Ellet

The Queens of American Society

Elizabeth Fries Ellet

The Queens of American Society

ISBN/EAN: 9783743332232

Manufactured in Europe, USA, Canada, Australia, Japa

Cover: Foto ©ninafisch / pixelio.de

Manufactured and distributed by brebook publishing software (www.brebook.com)

Elizabeth Fries Ellet

The Queens of American Society

THE QUEENS

OF

AMERICAN SOCIETY.

BY

MRS. ELLET,

AUTHOR OF "THE WOMEN OF THE AMERICAN REVOLUTION,"
"WOMEN ARTISTS," ETC.

SIXTH EDITION.

PHILADELPHIA:
PORTER & COATES.
1873.

Entered, according to Act of Congress, in the year 1867, by
CHARLES SCRIBNER & CO.,
In the Clerk's Office of the District Court of the United States for the Southern District of New York.

PREFACE.

Some friends have objected, in advance, to the title of this volume, on the ground that the term "queens," as applied to the subjects, seems out of place in the society of a republic. But if we call to mind how continually and universally the expression is used in ordinary conversation, it must be conceded that no other would do as well. We are all accustomed to hear of any leading lady that she is "a perfect queen," the "queen of society," a "reigning belle," the "queen of the occasion," &c. The phrase is in every one's mouth, and no one is misled by it. The sway of Beauty and Fashion, too, is essentially royal; there is nothing republican about it. Every belle, every leader of the ton, is despotic in proportion to her power; and the quality of imperial authority is absolutely inseparable from her state. I maintain, therefore, that no title is so just and appropriate to the women illustrated in this work, as that of "queens."

It may be thought that too much space has been given to personal description and accounts of dress and entertainments. It should be borne in mind, that the subjects are the Flowers of the sex—choice and cultivated flowers—not representatives of womankind in general. To them especially and necessarily pertain the adornments of person and the luxury of surroundings; and in scenes of festal display they are the stars of attraction. To present them without the adjuncts and associations of dress and gayety would be fair neither to them nor the reader. There is significance, too, in the style of decoration and amusements, as well as that of daily living. The style prevalent in the early days of the republic differed widely from the present, as does that of the West and the South from ours in the metropolis and the Atlantic cities.

PREFACE.

In a country so extensive—embracing such diversities in climate, habits of life, and tone of the community—it cannot certainly be expected that society should have always and everywhere the same prevailing features. The differences are marked in different sections; and a social favorite in one might be regarded in another as entitled to no distinction. It will be obvious, therefore, how unfair it would be to measure by the same rules those who have been made unlike by diverse origin, customs, and training. There are points of similarity enough, if a broad and liberal view of other conditions be taken.

I trust the candid reader will admit that the women most prominent in our society have had better than frivolous claims to distinction; that they have possessed high moral worth and superior intellect. Many of them have devoted their influence and efforts to works of charity. It is the blessing of New York—so justly reproached as the temple of money-worship—that her most elevated society is pervaded by a noble spirit of benevolence, and the refinement of taste growing out of mental culture. A line of distinction is drawn between the class that confers honor on the country, and mere shallow and vulgar pretenders whose lavish display of wealth is their only merit. Abundant materials for the illustration of this latter class were at hand, but they have not been used.

It has seemed to me that a comprehensive view of the best society would be a valuable part of the country's history. It is curious and interesting to trace the noted families whose descendants have spread over the land, and, parting with the aristocracy derived from ancient blood, have risen to individual distinction. The limits of a single volume are too narrow to do full justice to the subject; but enough is done to show the study a worthy one.

The reader is indebted for the memoir of Mrs. Jay, to the pen of her gifted descendant, Mr. John Jay, of New York.

CONTENTS.

I.

The Early Colonial Society—In the South and the East—Leading Ladies—Prominent Families—The Virginia School of Aristocracy—Mrs. Washington—The Birthnight Ball—New York as the Capital—The President's Title—Reception of Mrs. Washington—The Inauguration—Establishment of the "Republican Court"—Presidential Receptions—Count de Moustier's Ball, &c.—New Year's Calls—Prominent Ladies—Charles Carroll's Family—Family of Thomas Jefferson—Noted Ladies 13

II.

The Livingston Family—Governor William Livingston and his Daughters—Miss Susan saving the Papers—Lady Stirling and her Daughter—Sarah's Marriage—Mrs. Jay during the gloomy Period of War—Sailing for Spain—Disasters at Sea—Correspondence—Letters of Mrs. Robert Morris, &c.—Description of Mrs. Jay—Society in Paris at the Period—Negotiation of American Commissioners for the Conclusion of Peace—Jay's Agency—Prevailing Fashions—La Fayette's Family—Intimacy with Dr. Franklin—Brilliant Circle of Celebrities around his Table—His Letters to Mrs. Jay—Mrs. Jay at Chaillot—Correspondence—Return to New York—Society there—Dinner Guests—Home Occupation—Mrs. Jay Managing the Estate—Her Character.... 41

III.

The Early Aristocracy of New England—Customs—Brissot's Observations—John Quincy Adams' Descriptions of several Belles—Mrs. Cushing—The Misses Allen—Mercy Warren—Mrs. Knox—The Sheaffe Ladies—Mrs. Adams—Her Sisters, &c.—Mrs. Smith—Her Letters on Society—John Quincy Adams' Opinion of New York Beauties—Madame de Marbois—Mrs. John Quincy Adams, &c........ 86

IV.

The Quincy Family—Marriage of Dorothy to John Hancock—Mrs. Hancock's Patriotism—Her House in Boston—Style of Living—General Washington's Visit—The Breakfast to the French Fleet—Complimentary Dinner to Mrs. Hancock by the Admiral—Anecdotes—Plate in Use—Hancock's Epicurean Taste—Breaking the China—Samuel Adams going to Jail—The Governor's Last Hours—Mrs. Hancock's Attractions—Mrs. Greene—Mrs. Wooster—Countess Rumford.................................. 113

V.

Philadelphia Society in Early Times—The Willing Family—Philadelphia the Center of Fashionable Gayety—Mrs. Bingham—Her Life abroad—Miss Adams' Letters about her—Her Home in Philadelphia—Her Country Seat—Brilliant Society—Mrs. Bingham's Taste in Dress and Entertainments—Her Beauty and Pleasing Manners—Jefferson's Letter to her—French Noblemen—The First Masquerade Ball—Judge Chase at Dinner—Illness and Departure of Mrs. Bingham—Mrs. Robert Morris............. 135

VI.

Foreign Writers on American Society—Extravagance of the Women—The Wistar Parties—The Mischianza—Fête in Honor of the Dauphin—Miss Graeme—Mrs. Bache—Miss Vining—Miss Margaret Shippen—Mrs. Arnold—Miss Franks—Lady Johnston's Interview with General Scott—Mrs. Stockton—Mrs. Rufus King—Mrs. Bruyn—Mrs. Schuyler—Mrs. Hamilton—Jerome Bonaparte's Marriage to Miss Patterson—Her after Life—Mrs. Wilson 149

VII.

The Van Cortlandt Family—Mrs. Beekman—"Castle Philipse"—The Old Dutch Church—Locality of the "Legend of Sleepy Hollow"—Region of Romance—Mrs. Gates—Mrs. Benjamin H. Field—Descended of Distinguished Families—The De Peyster Family—Its remarkable Men—Mrs. Field one of few Americans—Marriage to Mr. Benjamin H. Field—His Ancestry—"Silver Wedding"—Poem by Bishop Coxe, addressed to Mrs. Field 171

VIII.

Early Society at the South—In Charleston, South Carolina—Prominent Belles—"Moll Harvey"—Paulina the Heiress—Mrs. Rivington—Mrs. Singleton—Whig Ladies—Mrs. Brewton—"Mad Archy's" Marriage—A Brilliant Ball—Epigram—Mrs. Motte—Mrs. Gibbes—Mrs. Barnard Elliott—Mrs. William Elliott—Mrs. Lewis Morris—Mrs. Jane Elliott—Anna Elliott—Mrs. Calhoun—Esther Wake and Lady Tryon—Mrs. Wilie Jones and Mrs. Ashe—Mrs. Ralph Izard—Princess Achille Murat (*note*) 181

IX.

Belles among the Pioneers of Tennessee—Miss Hart—Miss Bledsoe—The Lady of "Plum Grove"—Mrs Sevier—Miss Sevier—The Belle of Natchez—Mrs. Iunis—Mrs. Combs—Mrs. Robertson—Mrs. Kenton—Mrs. Talbot—Miss St. Clair—Mrs. Sibley—Mrs Walworth—Mrs. Heald—Mrs. Kinzie—Mrs. Allen—Miss Trask. 195

X.

Memoir of Mrs. Polk—Early Marriage—Winters in Washington—Circles of distinguished Persons—Mrs. Polk's Dignity and Grace—Her Benevolence—Mr. Polk Governor of Tennessee—Elected President of the United States—Mrs. Polk's admirable Tact and noble Qualities—She will not have Dancing—Mrs. Maury's Account of her—Leaving the White House—Her Home in Nashville—Testimony of Respect by the Legislature and Military Companies—Mrs. Huntington of Indiana—Her Beauty and admirable Character—Mrs. "Florida White"—Mrs. Pleasants—The Daughters of Governor Adair—Mrs. Jacob Brown—La Fayette's Letter to her—Mrs. Henry Clay—Mrs. Joshua Francis Fisher—Miss Sallie Ward—The Belle of the Southwest—Her Father—Mrs. Robert J. Ward—Early Training—Rare Gifts of the young Girl—Popular Admiration—Presentation of Flags to the Louisville Legion, &c.—The Greeting on their Return—Mrs. Johnston—A Fancy Ball Dress—Mrs. Hunt's Beauty and imperial Elegance—Taste in Dress—Mrs. Hunt's Charity—Her Elevation of Mind—Her splendid Home in New Orleans—A Masquerade Ball—Domestic Retirement............................. 213

XI.

PAGE

Memoir of Mrs. Madison—Her Family—Her Beauty and Fascinations—Her first Marriage and Widowhood—Her Marriage to Mr. Madison—Hospitality at Home—The new National Capital reclaimed by Mrs. Madison—Her elegant and liberal Style of Entertainment—The Presidential Election—The Inauguration Festivities—Danger of the Capital in 1814—Mrs. Madison's Letter—Her noble Conduct—Celebration of Peace—Mrs. Madison's Mountain Home—Letter from Judge Johnson—Montpelier—The aged Mother-in-law—Mrs. Madison's Letter—Her Return to Washington—Loss of Fortune—Her Last Days—Anecdotes—Eleanor Parke Custis—Mrs. Mary Custis—Mrs. Marshall—Mrs. Sitgreaves—Mrs. Wallace.................................. 238

XII.

Mrs. J. P. Van Ness—A distinguished Belle and Heiress—Her Marriage—Splendid House in Washington—Elegant Hospitality—Brilliant Circle—Her Personal Attractions—Her Piety and Charity—Marriage of her Daughter to Arthur Middleton—Death of Mrs. Middleton—Mrs. Van Ness's Retirement from Society—Founding of the Orphan Asylum—Her Burial with Public Honors—Mrs. Woodbury—Mrs. McLane—Miss Butt—Mrs. Edward Livingston—Miss Cora Livingston—Mrs. Thomas Barton—Evening Scene at the White House—Mrs. Andrew Jackson—Pure Morals and Taste in Society.. 264

XIII.

Mrs. J. J. Roosevelt—Her Mother, Mrs. Cornelius P. Van Ness—The Governor's hospitable Home in Vermont—Residence in Madrid—Miss Cornelia Van Ness—A brilliant Belle in Washington—In Spain with the Ambassador—Her Admission to the exclusive Circles of the Spanish Grandees—Favor shown her by the King and Queen of Spain—Her Marriage in Paris—La Fayette bestows the Bride—Return to America—Letter of La Fayette—Mrs. Roosevelt helps to reform a Social Usage in Washington—Tributes in her Album—Her Correspondence with distinguished Persons—Her Leadership of Society in New York—Superintendence of the "Knickerbocker Kitchen," &c.—Lady Ouseley—Her Stay in Washington.. 281

XIV.

Mrs. Winfield Scott—Scott's and Washington Irving's Tributes to William C. Preston of South Carolina—The Preston Family—Mrs. William Preston—Mrs. Merrick—Anecdote—Mrs. William C. Preston—Baron Raumer and the Peacock—Mrs. Preston in Columbia, South Carolina—Her Illness and Death—Mrs. Renwick —Celebrated by Burns—The Blue-Eyed Lassie of Lochmaben— Picture of her New York Life—Her House Washington Irving's "Ark"—Mrs. John C. Stevens—Her Masquerade Ball—Mrs. Parish—Mrs. Hickson Field—Mrs. Redfield—Mrs. Leavenworth. 295

XV.

Memoir of Mrs. Harrison Gray Otis—Her Widowhood—Return from abroad—Her Devotion to Works of Charity—The Mount Vernon Ball—Washington's Birthday made a Public Holiday through the Influence of Mrs. Otis—Her Receptions and Soirées—Her commanding Position—Her Relinquishment of Social Honors to take Charge of the Enterprise for the Benefit of Poor Soldiers and their Families—Extracts from Reports—Her Perseverance and Benevolence—The Swedish Compliment to her—Successful Closing of the House—Tributes to Mrs. Otis—Her Portrait in the "Gallery of Fallen Heroes"—Her patriotic Liberality—Miss Marshall—Mrs. Derby—Mrs. Wallace—Mrs. William H. Prescott— Miss Harriet Preble 311

XVI.

Memoir of Mrs. Crittenden—Her Family—Early Marriage—Her Daughters—Stay in Washington—"The Belle of the Capital "— Mrs. Ashley the Center of a Brilliant Circle—Residence in St. Louis in her Widowhood—Education of her Daughters—Winters in Washington—Always a Favorite in Society—Her Tact, Grace, and generous Kindness—Marriage to Hon. J. J. Crittenden—Appearance in Washington—Address to her at the National Hotel —Her Removal to New York—Miss Lane—Miss Fendall—Miss Morgan—Mrs. McLean—Mrs. Slidell—Her Appearance at a Ball, &c.—Mrs. A. G. Brown, of Mississippi—Mrs. A. V. Brown, of Tennessee—Entertainment at her House—Mrs. Calhoun—Miss Dahlgren—Mrs. Pringle—Mrs. Duval, of Louisiana—Prominent Richmond Ladies—Mrs. Reverdy Johnson—Mrs. Douglas—Mrs. Gaines—Mrs. Thornton. 327

XVII.

Ladies prominent in Benevolent Enterprise—Mrs. James W. White—Her Family—Her Mother—"The sweet Song" of her Girlhood—Daniel Dickinson's Letter—Her Marriage—Mr. White's Family—"Castle Comfort"—Perfect Domestic Management—A happy Home—Instruction of her Children—Their Musical Talent—Mrs. White's noble Works—The first Great Fair—The first private Charity Soirée—Fair in the Academy of Music—Letter of the Archbishop—Method of Home Education—Home Amusements—Drawing-room Operas—Mrs. White's Correspondence and Influence—Señora del Bal—Her great Work in Santiago—Origin of the Idea of the "Nursery and Child's Hospital"—Charity of Mrs. Thomas Addis Emmet and Mrs. Cornelius Dubois—Erection of the Building—Fashionable Entertainments for its Benefit—Other fashionable Charities—Mrs. Dubois—Mrs. Emmet 342

XVIII.

Memoir of Mrs. Rush—Her Education—Dr. James Rush—She takes the Lead in Philadelphia Social Life—Her splendid Home—Enlarged Hospitalities—Description of her—Acknowledged the Queen of Society in Philadelphia—Parties and Receptions—Celebrities shown—Musical Character of the Receptions—Mrs. Rush's Estimate of Intellect—Her Disregard of Conventional Distinctions—Her Life at Saratoga Springs—A Fancy Ball—The Succession in Seats next her at Table—Conditions imposed—Her Dresses—Her last Ball at Home—The Robbery of her Jewels—Her last Summer at Saratoga—Illness and Death—Mrs. MacGregor—Mrs. Daniel Webster—Mrs. Henry D. Gilpin—Brilliant in Washington Society as Mrs. Johnston—Her Marriage to Mr. Gilpin—Their Tour in Europe—Attentions received in London—Hospitalities extended by Persons of Rank and Literary Repute—Mrs. Gilpin's Tour on the Continent—Ascent of the Nile—Visit to Asia Minor—Turkey—Greece—Acquaintance with the Earl of Carlisle—Mrs. Gilpin's Home in Philadelphia—Her Musical Receptions—Her Hospitality and Charities 363

XIX.

Mrs. Coventry Waddell—Her Family—Her Marriage—Mr. Waddell's noble Ancestry—"Murray Hill" Hospitalities, and brilliant Parties at this Villa—Tributes of Foreign Visitors—Mrs. Waddell at Saratoga—Ball at Murray Hill—Fancy Dresses—Complimentary

Letter of Washington Irving—Ball at Murray Hill—Mr. Thackeray's Letter—Mrs. Waddell's playful Wit—Loss of Fortune—Cheerfulness in Adversity—Home in the Highlands—Suburban Residence near New York—Mrs. Wadsworth—Mrs. Montgomery Ritchie—Miss Schaumburg—Her Ancestors—Her Gifts in Vocal Music and Poetry—A Belle in Philadelphia Society—Admired by the Prince of Wales—Her wonderful Dramatic Talent—Performances at the Amateur Theater for Charity—Ristori's Surprise and Delight 382

XX.

Memoir of Madame Le Vert—Her extraordinary Popularity—Cause of such universal Admiration unmixed with Envy—Her warm and kind Heart—Her Family—Childhood of Octavia—Visit to La Fayette—Classic and Scientific Studies—Miss Walton a great Linguist—Friendship with Washington Irving—Marriage—Friendship with Lady Emmeline Stuart Wortley—Her Poem addressed to Madame Le Vert—Visit to England—Distinguished Attentions to Madame Le Vert—Invitation to a Court Ball before her Presentation—A Star in the Court Circle—Presentation at the French Court, &c.—Return to Mobile—Her crowded Receptions—Miss Bremer's Tribute—Description of a Ball at her House in Mobile—Madame Le Vert in Washington—At Newport—At Saratoga—Years of Trial at the South—Bereavements—Visit in New York—In Washington—Return to her Birth-place—In New Orleans—Devotion of her Servants.—MRS. ACKLEN—Her Loveliness and Virtues—Marriage and Widowhood—"Bellemonte"—The most beautiful Home in the Southwest—Her Charity and Hospitality—Her Marriage to Dr. Cheatham.—Mrs. Stanard of Richmond—Miss Emily Mason of Kentucky—Presides at the Governor's House in Detroit—A Celebrity in New Orleans, &c.—Loss of Fortune—The Market Farm—Rural Life—Seizure of her Home—Suspected as a Spy—Her Benevolent Labors in the Hospitals and for Southern Girls—Rosa Vertner Jeffrey................ 396

XXI.

Memoir of Mrs. Frémont—Her peculiar Influence—Her Maternal Ancestry—Colonel McDowell's eminent Position—Region in Virginia where the Family was settled—Early Customs—Contempt of mere Moneyed Aristocracy—The leading Families opposed to Slavery—Established Order of Society—Thackeray's

Types of the best Class—Absence of deceptive Display—Character of the true "Virginia Gentleman"—Colonel Benton's Family—In connection with leading Families of the State—Mrs. Albert Sidney Johnston—Colonel Benton's Family in Washington—In St. Louis—In New Orleans—The Changes in Travel, and varied Experiences—Mrs. Benton's Washington Coteries—She gives Freedom to her Slaves—Miss Benton's early Studies and Society Experiences—Marriage to Mr. Frémont—Share in his Western Adventure—The Flatteries of Society in Washington—Detention at Panama—Mrs. Frémont's Residence in California—The practical Evidence of her Example said to influence the Decision for Freedom—Her Experiences in Western Life—The honest Spaniards—Mrs. Frémont's Visit to Europe—Privileged at the English Court—Scene in Paris at the Restoration of the Empire—Scene at the Court of St. James—The Campaign of 1856—Again in Paris—Count de la Garde's Album left to Mrs. Frémont—Letter of Queen Hortense—Mrs. Frémont at St. Louis during the War—Her Removal to New York—Her Country Seat on the Hudson—Her Home Life and Instruction of her Children—Her active Charities and Aid to Benevolent Associations—The Brown Locks suddenly silvered—Mrs. Frémont's brilliant Wit and Humor—Her prepossessing personal Appearance 428

XXII.

Mrs. Hills—The American Improvisatrice in Music—Lydia Maria Child enchanted by her Playing—Mrs. Osgood's Impromptu Lines—Mrs. Girard's Introduction of Morning Receptions—Mrs. Hills' "Mission"—Remark of Willis—Improvisation—Her Concerts at Dr. Ward's Theater—Mrs. John Schermerhorn—Miss Minnie Parker—Miss Hetty Carey—Miss Lillie Hitchcock—Mrs. Harvey—Miss Breckenridge—Mrs. William Schermerhorn—Her Fancy Ball—Mrs. Hamilton Fish—Mrs. Auguste Belmont—Brown, the Sexton and Manager of Entertainments—Poetical Tribute to him—Present Leaders in Boston—The Ladies prominent in Fashionable Life not merely Frivolous, but Women of superior Intellect and Culture—Ball in Fifth Avenue—Presidential Reception—New Fashion at Delmonico's—Recent Changes in Social Life—"Fast" People—The "Shoddy" and "Petroleum" Element—Those who scatter Money merely for Display not worthy to be named—The Ball Season of 1866—"Fast" Ladies—Pure Aristocracy in New York 449

THE QUEENS OF AMERICAN SOCIETY.

I.

ANY view of society in the United States must, of necessity, take in a variety of aspects. During the existence of the Republic, there has been no period when its social condition was like that of a compact nation which had been a unity in its origin, growth, and development. In the early colonial days, the leading society in the North, in the East, and in the South was composed of diverse elements; in each section differing from that of others. Virginia—the first colony that could boast an aristocracy—traced her proud and gentle blood to ancient families of England; in Pennsylvania, and farther south, the best society came of that stock of continental Protestantism—the French and Flemish refugees—whom the bigotry of Philip the Second in one century, and of Louis XIV. in the next, drove from their homes and places of worship, to seek, in the wild solitudes of a new world, "freedom to worship God." To these, in Pennsylvania, were added the Quakers, who came to the country with William Penn. In New England, the Puritan element mingled with an aristocracy created by prosperity and growing wealth. Thus the social phases presented had various aspects, modified, in the progress of years, by the various modes of living. The unity of feeling produced by the Revolution caused some change and assimilation, so far as the great cities were concerned; in other portions of the Union social differences not only continued to exist, but developed into more marked peculiarities. We cannot help observing this in the most general survey.

About the middle of the last century we find a ruling class in families of wealth and distinction living hundreds of miles apart. We note this when we read of George Washington being entertained at the house of Beverley Robinson, and being captivated by the charms of his host's fair sister-in-law, Mary Philipse. She was the daughter of the lord of the old manor of Philipsborough, who owned an immense estate on the Hudson. Her marriage afterwards with Captain Roger Morris, and the confiscation of that portion of the Philipse estate, led to the formation of a home of another character. Both Mrs. Morris and her sister, Mrs. Robinson, who shared in the outlawry and attainder, were leaders in the society of that period, and remarkable for graces and accomplishments.

About 1749 Mrs. Jeykell was leading lady of the ton in Philadelphia, pre-eminent in beauty and fashion. She was the grand-daughter of the first Edward Shippen, and married a brother of Sir Joseph Jeykell, secretary to Queen Anne.

The first dancing assembly, said to have been held in Philadelphia in 1748, had its subscription list mostly filled with names of English families attached to the Church of England. The list was under the direction of John Inglis and other gentlemen, and each subscription was forty shillings. The custom was universal among men, of wearing the hair tied up with ribbon, in a long bunch, in a form called a queue. Gentlemen's coats were made of cloth or velvet, of all colors; the collar being sometimes of a different hue from the coat. In the Supreme Court the Judges, in winter, wore robes of scarlet faced with black velvet; in the summer, full black silk gowns.

Agnes, Lady Frankland, was the wife of Sir Charles Henry Frankland, Baronet, who was buried alive at the great earthquake at Lisbon; and being rescued through the efforts of the young girl, married her in 1755. Lady Frankland came to America after his death in 1768, and was allowed an escort to Boston by the Provincial Congress, and to take "seven trunks, beds and bedding, boxes, crates, a basket of chickens, some ham and veal, two barrels and a hamper, two horses and chaises, one phæton, and small bundles."

The biography of Catalina Schuyler, written by Anne McVickar, well known as Mrs. Grant, is an interesting memorial of early times. Catalina was the niece

of the first Colonel Philip Schuyler. She was born in
1702, and married her cousin, Philip Schuyler. Her
house, near Albany, was a fine building, with large
latticed portico with seats. The birds had their nests in
the trees, and were so tame they would run across the
table with insects or crumbs for their young. The Hudson
river was in front, and on its brink, under elm and
sycamore trees, ran a road to Saratoga and the Lakes.
The French Canadian prisoners usually called the good
lady "Madame Schuyler," and she was "Aunt Schuyler"
to the country people. She kept a liberal table, and
had much influence in the primitive society of the country,
though old-fashioned in her manners. Her superior
mind and education, her virtues of character, and her
majestic grace, commanded general respect. British
officers of rank and merit were fond of visiting her.
She read a great deal; and Milton and the Scriptures
were her constant companions. When she laid down
the book she always took up her knitting. The grave
of her husband was on the grounds near the house, and
she was accustomed to sit near it.

The fringe of civilization on the colonial seaboard in
1770 and 1771 was very narrow, for though across the
continent scattered military settlements extended to the
Ohio, a hostile Indian population was not farther than
the Susquehanna and the Lehigh from Philadelphia,
then but a large village, with village habits and modes
of life. For all articles of luxury, and even many of
necessity, the colonies were dependent on the "Old

Country;" and the few ships which periodically crossed the Atlantic were freighted with hats, shoes, pins, needles, and clothing of all kinds. Mrs. Reed, writing to her brother, in 1772, sends to England for "bowed cap-wires, quilted caps," and a gown to be dyed "any color it will take best." The literary taste of the period was the same prevalent in England, when the "Idler," the "Rambler," "Thomson's Seasons," or "Young's Night Thoughts," and their contemporary books, formed the current literature. In religious history, the time was that of the supervening of enthusiastic devotion upon the formalism of the Church of England; of the diffusion of the spirit that animated Wesley and Whitefield to lift a banner alien to old forms, and rally round it the humble and the poor.

One of the most prominent Maryland families was that of Fitzhugh. It was ancient and honorable in England. The first settler in America was William Fitzhugh; he made a home in Westmoreland County, Virginia, and married Miss Tucker. From him descended all the Fitzhughs in Virginia, Maryland, and Western New York. William was an eminent lawyer, and managed land causes for the great landholders. He was counselor for the first Robert Beverley, and transacted business for Lord Culpepper.

Martha Washington is venerated as the earliest representative among the ladies prominent in our republican society. She belonged to the Virginia school of aristocracy. The original settlements of that colony were agricultural, and the early settlers brought with them the feelings and habits of their native country. The extensive landed proprietors formed a population thinly scattered over a wide surface, and lived in almost patriarchal fashion. Their lands had a multitude of hands for cultivation; but the only produce the Virginia gentry chose to deal in, was tobacco. They exercised boundless hospitality; the gentlemen welcomed each other's visits and traveled in something like feudal state. The slavery question was never agitated. Thus, in the second or third generation, a class of "first families" was built up, and the best education was limited to them; for there were no schools for the masses. There existed, therefore, a broad line of distinction between those wealthy proprietors and the common people. The planters had their tenants and slaves, and lived luxuriously. The emigration of the cavaliers, in the days of Cromwell, did not lessen the supremacy of this landed aristocracy; and the public offices, in most cases, passed into their hands; the peasantry being retainers to their patrons. There were scarcely any towns, and the establishments of the gentry were like little villages, in which they and their vassals dwelt. Some, indeed, were needy potentates, living in a rough manner, and attended by domestics in ragged liveries; but all kept open house, were habitually idle, and loved field-sports like gentlemen of good lineage. They were "horse-racing, cock-fighting Virginia squires." Visiting was done in ponderous emblazoned coaches. The hospitable board was loaded with terrapins, shad, salmon, wild geese, pigeons, plover, canvas-back ducks, venison, and every variety of bread, with "that delicious hotch-potch," gumbo, and other country dainties. The laced lappets of sleeves were turned up to carve, and guests were pressed to demolish the various meats and wash them down with cider, ale, brandy, and Bordeaux wine.

Twenty-one counties in Virginia, comprising nearly a quarter of the State, are said to have once belonged to one family—that of Fairfax. Every acre was confiscated, after the Revolution, because of loyalty to Great Britain. Many battles of the late civil war were fought on the old Fairfax domain.

Robert Carter, called "King Carter," was a representative and agent of the Culpepper and Fairfax families. The Jacquelines were of Huguenot descent. The first of the name came from Kent, in England, 1697, married Miss Carey, and settled at Jamestown. The Ambler family came also from England, and was much noted in Virginia. Mrs. Edward Carrington was Jacqueline's grand-daughter. Thorpe is another noted name, dear to philanthropy as friendly to the Indians and early colonists.

A curious incident of Bishop Clagget's consecration of the old St. Paul's Church, in Alexandria, is traditional. As he walked to church, in his robes and mitre, the boys ran alongside, admiring his peculiar dress, which his gigantic stature and Herculean form set off. His voice matched his frame in irrepressible strength. As he entered the church, amid profound silence, and uttered the opening words of the service, a young lady, turning suddenly and seeing his huge form thus arrayed, fell into violent convulsions and was taken out.

The name of Barradale is memorable in law, as well as of ancient respectability. Bray and Nelson are also remembered. When the British were about landing from James River, and Yorktown lay exposed, General Nelson sent his wife and infant to the upper country. Near Williamsburg she met a company of armed youths, marching to encounter the enemy. As they halted and presented arms, she saw two of her own sons, boys who had escaped from preparatory school. She ordered them into her carriage, and sent them back to Philadelphia.

The first wife of Governor Page was Frances Burwell, of the Isle of Wight. She was said to have no enemies, and to know no competition but how to out-do others in kindness and good offices. In the proud mansion of his forefathers, this patriot soldier had on his walls the portrait of Selim, an Algerine negro, among those of his family.

The name and blood of the Custis family was intermingled with those of the best families of Northampton and Accomac. John Custis appears earliest on record, in 1640. John Custis the fourth, educated in England, received the Arlington estate from his grandfather, removed to Williamsburg, and married the daughter of Colonel Daniel Parke. He was father to the first husband of Martha Washington.

So many biographies of Mrs. Washington have been published, that any sketch of her life would be superfluous. As a belle at the colonial court in Williamsburg, as a beautiful young widow reigning among the chivalrous Virginians, as the wife of the Commander-in-chief and the President of the new nation—her benign aspect is familiar. It will be remembered that she was accustomed to join General Washington in camp, traveling with postillions in white and scarlet liveries. During the six years that elapsed before Washington was chosen to the Presidency she remained at Mount Vernon, dispensing its ample hospitalities with gracious tact and the dignity of a Virginia matron. Brissot wrote: "Every thing about the house has an air of simplicity; the table is good, but not ostentatious; and no deviation is seen from regularity and domestic economy. She superintends the whole, and joins to the qualities of an excellent housewife the simple dignity which ought to characterize a woman whose husband has acted the greatest part on the theatre of human affairs."

At a brilliant entertainment given in the camp near Middlebrook, in celebration of the anniversary of the American alliance with France, Mrs. Washington, Mrs. Greene, Mrs. Knox, and many other distinguished ladies were present, forming "a circle of brilliants." The *fête* was opened by the discharge of cannon; there was a dinner, and dancing and fireworks followed in the evening. The adornments and illuminations were cheap;

the company consisting of hardy soldiers and lively belles.

At a subscription ball in Philadelphia, the master of ceremonies distributed partners by lot. The dances related to politics. One was called "The Success of the Campaign;" another, "The Defeat of Burgoyne;" another, "Clinton's Retreat," &c. A young lady who in talking forgot her turn in the figure, was sharply reproved by a manager. "Take care, Miss!" he cried. "Do you think you come here for your own pleasure?"

The Birth-night Ball was instituted at the close of the war. Its first celebration was at Alexandria, and it became general in all the towns. Among the brilliant illustrations of a birth-night were groups of young ladies, wearing in their hair bandeaux or scrolls embroidered in ancient and modern languages with the motto: "Long live the President." The last celebration was attended by Washington, in Alexandria, February 22, 1798.

General Washington came to Annapolis in December, 1783, after his adieu to the army in New York. Generals Gates and Smallwood, with a large concourse of distinguished citizens, met and escorted him to the hotel, amid the firing of cannon, the display of banners, and other manifestations of popular respect. A dinner was given to him by the members of Congress, at which two hundred persons were present; and he attended a grand ball in the State House, which was brilliantly illuminated. Washington opened the ball with Mrs. James Macubbin, one of the most beautiful women of the time.

Mr. Noah Webster visited Mount Vernon in 1785, when the old mansion of the retired chief was crowded with a succession of guests. He mentioned that the last course at dinner consisted of pancakes, with a bowl of sugar and one of molasses. Webster refused the molasses: "Enough of that in my own country," he said. General Washington then told the story of a hogshead of molasses upset in a wagon and stove in, at Westchester; and some Maryland troops being near, the soldiers running to fill their hats and caps.

The court end of New York before the Revolution had been Pearl Street, between Coenties Slip and the neighboring streets. Wall Street became a rival seat of fashion, surperseded by Park Place. "Few Americans," says Mr. Jay, "as they pass the northwest corner of Wall and Broad Streets, now faced by the Custom House on one side, and Broad Street with its throng of brokers on the other, recall the memorable historic scenes associated with the spot where stood the old Federal Hall, adorned with the portraits of Louis XVI. and Marie Antoinette, presented by the French monarch—portraits that graced the chambers where assembled the first Congress under the new Constitution. Washington Irving was one of the latest survivors of the throng that, in 1789, witnessed from the balcony of the Hall the inauguration of the first President, and whose acclamations greeted the announcement by Chancellor Livingston: 'Long live George Washington, President of the United States!' It should not be forgotten by

New Yorkers that on the same spot were heard, in the Senate, the voices of John Langdon, Oliver Ellsworth, Charles Carroll, Richard Henry Lee, and Ralph Izard; and, in the Chamber of Representatives, the voices of Elbridge Gerry, Roger Sherman, Jeremiah Wadsworth, Elias Boudinot, Frederick A. Muhlenberg, James Madison, and that greatest of American orators, Fisher Ames."

A ball was given at the Assembly Rooms, on the east side of Broadway, above Wall Street (New York was then the capital), on the 7th May, 1789, to celebrate the inauguration. The members of Congress and their families were present, with the ministers of France and Spain, distinguished generals of the army, and persons eminent in the State. Among the most noted ladies were Mrs. Jay, Mrs. Hamilton, and Mrs. Montgomery, the widow of the hero of Quebec. A specialty at this ball was the presentation by the committee, to each lady, of a fan made in Paris, the ivory frame containing a medallion portrait of Washington, in profile. These fans were presented to the ladies as each couple passed the receiver of tickets. It was of this ball that an account was published by Jefferson in his "Ana," upon insufficient authority. Washington danced in two cotillions and a minuet. Colonel Stone, in describing this ball, says: "Few jewels were then worn in the United States, but in other respects the costumes were rich and beautiful, according to the fashions of the day. One favorite dress was a plain celestial-blue satin gown, with a white satin petticoat. On the neck was worn a very large Italian gauze handkerchief, with border stripes of satin. The head-dress was a puff of gauze in the form of a globe, the head-piece of which was composed of white satin, having a double wing in large plaits, and trimmed with a wreath of artificial roses, falling from the left at the top to the right at the bottom in front, the reverse behind. The hair was dressed all over in detached curls, four of which, in two ranks, fell on each side of the neck, and were relieved behind by a floating *chignon*."

Some of the ladies wore hats of white satin, with plumes and cockades. A plain gauze handkerchief, sometimes striped with satin, was worn on the neck, the ends tied under the bodice.

In the evening of the inauguration, the house of Count de Moustier—near Bowling Green, in Broadway— was brilliantly illuminated, the doors and windows displaying borderings of lamps that shone on paintings suggestive of the past, present, and future in American history. There were large transparencies over the front of the house, said to be painted by Madame de Brehan, sister to the Count.

The subject of the President's title had caused much discussion in society. Madison recommended that he be spoken of simply as "The President," or "The Chief Justice;" McKean proposed "His Serene Highness," without the "most," as a title that had not been appropriated in Europe. General Muhlenberg thought Washington would like the title "High Mightiness," used by the Stadtholder of Holland. The General, dining with Washington, observed on the subject: "If the office could always be held by men as large as yourself or Wynkoop, it would be appropriate; but if by chance a president as small as my opposite neighbor were elected, it would be ridiculous." He therefore voted against any title.

More than a month after the inauguration, Mrs. Washington set out for New York with her grandchildren, Eleanor Custis and George Washington Parke Custis, traveling in her private carriage, with a small escort on horseback. She was received at Hammond's Ferry by a deputation of citizens; and fireworks, a supper, and a serenade celebrated her arrival. Her dress was entirely of American manufacture. Information being sent to Philadelphia that she would breakfast in Chester, two troops of dragoons, under Captains Miles and Bingham, left town early, with a numerous cavalcade of citizens, and halted at ten miles distance to await her appearance. The military formed and received her with honors, the procession defiling on either side for her carriage to pass. At Darby, seven miles from Philadelphia, she was met by a brilliant company of ladies in carriages, who escorted her to Gray's Ferry, on the Schuylkill. At that favorite resort a collation was prepared, at a fashionable inn, for more than a hundred persons.

Mrs. Robert Morris, who was to entertain Mrs. Washington, here took a seat in her carriage, resigning her own to young Custis. About two o'clock the procession entered High Street, amid the ringing of bells, the firing of thirteen guns, and shouts of joy from the people. Mrs. Washington thanked them, and dismissed her escort. The doors of Mrs. Morris were thronged with visitors next day.

Such a reception may have recalled to the memory of Mrs. Washington the disaffection shown her on an earlier visit to Philadelphia, during the war, when she was waited on with a request that she would *not* attend a ball in preparation.

Mrs. Morris accompanied her when she left Philadelphia. The party slept at Trenton, and at Elizabethtown were the guests of the venerable Mr. Livingston. The President left New York at five o'clock, in his barge, manned by thirteen pilots in rich white dresses, to meet his wife. A crowd gathered on the wharves to greet the returning vessel, and a salute of thirteen guns was fired as it approached the Battery.

The winter of 1787-88 had been remarkably gay in New York. William Livingston, in a letter written in March, 1787, alludes to the extravagance and dissipation of fashionable life in that city. "My principal secretary of state," he says, "who is one of my daughters, is gone to New York, to shake her heels at the balls and assemblies of a metropolis which might as well be more studious of paying its taxes than of instituting expensive diversions."

The residence of President Washington was on the

spot now known as the corner of Cherry Street and Franklin Square. The house had plain furniture. The family plate had been melted and renovated. The state coach was the finest carriage in the city, and was drawn by four horses; by six, when it conveyed the President to Federal Hall. The coach-body was in the shape of a hemisphere, cream-colored, and ornamented with cupids supporting festoons, with borders of flowers around the panels.

The principal ladies of New York, at the time the "Republican Court" was established there, were Mrs. George Clinton, Mrs. Montgomery, Lady Stirling, Lady Kitty Duer, Lady Mary Watts, Lady Temple, Lady Christiana Griffin, the Marchioness de Brehan, Madame de la Forest, Mrs. John Langdon, Mrs. Tristram Dalton, Mrs. Knox, Mrs. Robert R. Livingston, of Clermont, the Misses Livingston, Mrs. Thompson, Mrs. Gerry, Mrs. McComb, Mrs. Edgar, Mrs. Lynch, Mrs. Houston, Mrs. Provost, Mrs. Beekman, the Misses Bayard, &c.

Mr. Wingate describes the dinner given at Washington's house the day after his wife's arrival, as the least showy of any he ever saw at the President's table. The Chief said grace and dined on boiled leg of mutton. After dessert one glass of wine was offered to each guest, and when it had been drunk, the President rose and led the way to the drawing-room. Two days afterwards Mrs. Washington held her first levee, the President continuing to receive every Tuesday afternoon. Mrs. Washington received from eight to ten every Friday evening. The levees were numerously attended by all that was fashionable, elegant, or refined in society; but "there were no places for the intrusion of the rabble in crowds, or for the mere coarse and boisterous partisan, the vulgar electioneerer, or the impudent place-hunter, with boots, frock-coats, or roundabouts, or with patched knees and holes at both elbows. On the contrary, they were select and more courtly than have been given by any of the President's successors." Mrs. Washington was careful, in her drawing-room, to exact those courtesies to which she knew her husband entitled. "Democratic rudeness had not then so far gained the ascendency as to banish good manners." "None were admitted to the levees but those who had either a right by official station or by established merit and character; and full dress was required of all."

The journals of the day especially noted a magnificent ball given by Count de Moustier at his house. A lady said she heard the Marchioness declare she had exhausted every resource to produce an entertainment worthy of France, and Elias Boudinot calls it "a most splendid ball indeed. After the arrival of the President, a company of eight couples formed, and, entering the room, began a curious dance called *en ballet*. Four of the gentlemen were dressed in French regimentals, and four in American uniforms; four of the ladies had American flowers with blue ribbons round their heads, and four had red roses and the flowers of France."

"Three rooms were filled, and the fourth was elegantly set off as a place for refreshment. A long table crossed this room in the middle, and the whole wall inside was lighted up, and covered with shelves filled with cakes, oranges, apples, wines of all sorts, ice-creams, &c. A number of servants behind the table supplied the guests with every thing they wanted from time to time, as they came in to refresh themselves, which they did as often as a party had done dancing, making room for another set. We retired about ten o'clock, in the height of the jollity."

The anniversary of the Declaration of Independence was celebrated by a brilliant ball, at which Mrs. Washington and the principal ladies of "her court" were present.

At the Presidential receptions Washington wore "his hair powdered and gathered behind in a silk bag. His coat and breeches were of plain black velvet; he wore a white or pearl-colored vest and yellow gloves, and had a cocked hat in his hand, with silver knee and shoe buckles, and a long sword, with a finely-wrought and glittering steel hilt. The coat was worn over this and its scabbard of polished white leather." He never shook hands at these receptions, even with intimate friends. Visitors were received with a dignified bow, and passed on. At Mrs. Washington's levees he appeared as a private gentleman, with neither hat nor sword; conversing without restraint, and generally with ladies.

Private theatricals were sometimes given at Washington's house. President Duer enacted Brutus, in "Julius Cæsar," before him in the attic of the Presidential mansion, young Custis taking the part of Cassius.

At one of Mrs. Washington's Friday evening drawing-rooms, owing to the lowness of the ceiling, the ostrich feathers in the head-dress of Miss Mary McEvers, a distinguished belle in New York, took fire from the chandelier, to the general confusion and alarm. Major Jackson, aid-de-camp to the President, flew to the rescue, and, clapping the burning plumes between his hands, extinguished them. This lady married Edward Livingston, the minister to France.

At Mrs. Washington's drawing-rooms, "Mrs. Morris always sat at her right hand; and at all the dinners, public or private, at which Robert Morris was a guest, that venerable man was placed at the right of Mrs. Washington." At the age of thirty-six, Robert Morris had married Miss White, the sister of Bishop White. She was described as "a lady of elegant accomplishments, rich, and well qualified to carry the felicity of connubial life to its highest perfection."

Mrs. Washington was accustomed to speak of her days of public life in New York and Philadelphia as her "lost days." She preferred home comforts and seclusion. Contrasting the pictures, Mrs. Carrington wrote to her sister, a short time before Washington's death, describing his wife's room at Mount Vernon: "On one side sits the chambermaid with her knitting; on the other a little colored pet learning to sew. A decent-looking old woman is there, with her table and shears, cutting out the negroes' winter clothes; while the good old lady directs them all, incessantly knitting herself. She points out to me several pairs of nice colored stockings and gloves she has just finished, and presents me with a pair half done, which she begs I will finish, and wear for her sake."

Loving such simple, domestic employments, and wearied with the glare, no wonder the illustrious lady was restive under the etiquette of public life.

The custom of calls on New Year's day was introduced by the Dutch and the Huguenots. The President received calls on the first of January, 1790. At Mrs. Washington's levee the visitors were seated, and tea and coffee were handed, with plain and plum cake. The company was expected to retire early. "The General retires at nine, and I usually precede him," the lady would say.

To an inquiry by the President whether such observances were casual or customary, it was answered that New Year's visits had always been kept up in the city. Washington remarked that the favored situation of New York would in time attract numerous emigrants, who would gradually change its ancient customs and manners; but, he added, "whatever change takes place, never forget this cordial and cheerful observance of New Year's day."

Curwen, in his Journal, gives, as the origin of the

custom of offering New Year's presents, the tradition that Tatius, King of the Sabines, was presented with boughs from the forest of the goddess Strenia, in token of good-will, and consecrated the holiday to Janus. The people sacrificed to Janus, and brought presents of dates, figs, honey, &c., covered with leaf-gold.

Of New York, Brissot wrote: "The inhabitants prefer the splendor of wealth and the show of enjoyment to a simplicity of manners and the pure pleasures resulting from it. The expenses of women cause matrimony to be dreaded by men." But when Oliver Wolcott, in 1789, was appointed Auditor of the Treasury, he wrote to Ellsworth about the cost of living, and was informed that a thousand dollars a year ought to supply him and his family. "The example of the President," said his correspondent, "and his family, will render parade and expense improper and disreputable."

Among the ladies most intimate with Mrs. Washington, beside Mrs. Knox, Mrs. Hamilton, Mrs. Morris, and Mrs. Powell, were Mrs. Bradford, Mrs. Otis, and Miss Ross. Mrs. Otis was the wife of the Secretary of the Senate, and mother of the great Senator, Harrison Gray Otis, who married in Boston, May, 1790, Miss Sally Foster, daughter of a prominent merchant. She was remarkable for beauty of person and grace of demeanor, vivacity of wit, and powerful intellect. She was prominent in metropolitan society during the administration of Washington. Mrs. Stewart, also noted in the same circle, was the wife of General Walter Stewart; and

Miss Ross was the beautiful daughter of a Senator from Pennsylvania.

Mrs. Bradford was the only child of Elias Boudinot, and married William Bradford, afterwards judge of the Supreme Court of Pennsylvania. Her house was always the elegant abode of the most cordial hospitality. Her graces of person were so remarkable, that even at the age of four-score her appearance was strikingly prepossessing, and her carriage was stately as ever. Her suavity of manner and kindness of heart were also memorable. Mrs. Wallace, the wife of a nephew of Mr. Bradford's, thus described her:—

"Mrs. Bradford is one of the finest models of mild and courtly dignity this country can exhibit. Early accustomed to the best society, of a family and connections holding rank and offices of trust and honor—her happy and much caressed girlhood was passed in intercourse with persons long since the boast of the brightest days of American refinement and patriotism. With her husband she commanded a sphere of extensive influence, the just desert of their united excellencies, and lived more than ten years in the full possession of every earthly enjoyment. Well for them they lived as Christians ought to live, in constant remembrance of their accountability to God! for in the height of distinction their well-planned schemes of happiness were laid in the dust by the death of Mr. Bradford. For many years afterward Mrs. Bradford maintained a position of useful-

..ness, dispensing elegant hospitality to her numerous relatives and friends."

This lady, Mrs. Hamilton, and the younger Mrs. Charles Carroll, were the last survivors of the ladies of the Republican Court. Mrs. Carroll was Harriet Chew, daughter of Benjamin Chew, and was married after the retirement of Washington to Mount Vernon. One of her sisters married Henry Philips; another, Colonel John Eager Howard, of Baltimore, coming to live in Philadelphia in 1796. These ladies were great favorites with Washington, and were belles in society. Julia Seymour was another celebrated beauty. Miss Mary Ann Wolcott, also distinguished for charms of person, was married to Chauncey Goodrich, of New York. Mrs. Wolcott, of Connecticut, had less beauty, but was noted for graceful manners, and few could be compared with her for culture, intelligence, and refinement. The British minister remarked to Tracy at a dance: "Your countrywoman, Mrs. Wolcott, would be admired even at St. James's."—"Sir," replied the senator, "she is admired even on Litchfield Hill." A member of Congress called her "a divine woman;" another, "the magnificent Mrs. Wolcott;" and some compared her to Mrs. Bingham.

The family of Charles Carroll had been settled in Maryland ever since the reign of James the Second. They were among the wealthiest in the Union, and stood at the head of the landed aristocracy, which was naturally in alliance with the Government. Yet Carroll was among the first to sign the Declaration of Independence. "There go millions of property!" was the comment; and when it was said, "You will get clear; there are so many of the name," he added to his signature, "of Carrollton." He was senator from Maryland. He had "one fair daughter," Polly, who was married in 1786 to Richard Caton, an Englishman. In 1809 two of her daughters were the reigning belles of Baltimore and Washington. The eldest had a romantic history. She was married, when very young, to Robert Patterson, a wealthy merchant. Traveling in Europe, she attracted the attention of Sir Arthur Wellesley, afterwards the Duke of Wellington. He was so captivated with her, that he followed her over half the European continent, causing some scandal, notwithstanding her prudence, by his unguarded devotion. After Mrs. Patterson's return to Maryland, her admirer kept a diary for her amusement, and sent her letters. After she became a widow she revisited London; but the future hero of Waterloo was then a married man. He introduced to her his elder brother, the Marquis of Wellesley; the great statesman whose outset in life was marked by a cordial support of American Independence. He was Viceroy of Ireland. He married Mrs. Patterson, while Sir Arthur continued her warm friend. The Marchioness of Wellesley died at Hampton Court in December, 1853. One of her sisters was the wife of Colonel Harvey, aid-de-camp to Lord Wellington at the battle of Waterloo; and, being widowed, married the Marquis of Cærmarthen, afterwards Duke of Leeds. Another daughter of Mrs. Caton married Baron Stafford; another, Mr. McTavish, of Baltimore.

In 1796, General Washington received as a guest, at Mount Vernon, Don Carlos Martinez, Marquis d'Yrujo, the newly arrived Spanish ambassador, who had succeeded Jaudennes. The Marquis had not been long in Philadelphia before he fell in love with Sally, the daughter of Thomas McKean, Chief-Justice of Pennsylvania. Miss McKean, a celebrated beauty, became the Marchioness d'Yrujo. Her son, the Duke of Sotomayer, who was born in Philadelphia, became the Prime Minister of Spain.

Henry Wansey, in his Travels, also speaks of the simple manners of Washington and his family. He breakfasted with them, June 8, 1794, and Mrs. Washington made the tea and coffee. There were plates of sliced tongue, dry toast, and bread and butter.

The wife of Thomas Jefferson was Mrs. Martha Skelton, a rich widow, twenty-three at her second nuptials. She was of good family, beautiful, accomplished, and greatly admired. The story went, that two, among the many suitors for her hand, going severally to her house on the same errand, to learn their fate from her decision, met in the hall, where they heard her playing on the harpsichord and singing a love-song, accompanied by Jefferson's voice and violin. Something in the song or the manner of the singing satisfied both wooers of the folly of their hopes, and they withdrew. The statesman was fond of the violin. When his paternal home was burned he asked, "Are all the books destroyed?"—"Yes, massa," was the reply, "dey is; but we saved de fiddle."

Thomas Jefferson kept open house, it is said, and a liberal table. His eldest daughter, Martha, was born in 1772. John Randolph called her "the sweetest young creature in Virginia." She was intrusted in Paris to the care of Mrs. Adams, and pleased every one by the good feeling and kindness expressed in her conversation. Mrs. Smith wrote: "Delicacy and sensibility are read in her every feature, and her manners are in unison with all that is amiable and lovely." While Martha was at school in Philadelphia, 1783, boarding with Mrs. Trist, her father wrote: "With respect to the distribution of time, the following is what I should approve: From eight to ten, practice music; from ten to one, dance one day and draw another; from one to two, draw on the day you dance, and write a letter next day; from three to four, read French; from four to five, exercise yourself in music; from five till bedtime, read English, write, &c. Communicate this plan to Mrs. Hopkinson, and, if she approve of it, pursue it."

Miss Jefferson was educated in Philadelphia and in Europe. She married Thomas Mann Randolph, of Tuckahoe, "a gentleman of genius, science, and honorable mind," who afterwards filled a dignified station in the General Government, and the highest in his own State. They lived in Virginia.

Mrs. Graydon was born in the island of Barbadoes,

but came very young to Philadelphia. Dr. Baird called her "the finest girl in Philadelphia, having the manners of a lady bred at court." After her marriage to Mr. Graydon, their house was the resort of numerous distinguished guests, who were hospitably entertained. Among the foreigners were, Baron de Kalb; Lady Moore, the wife of Sir Henry Moore; and her daughter, Lady Susan O'Brien; and her husband, Major George Etherington; Sir William Draper, and others. During the War of the Revolution, Mrs. Graydon went from her home in Reading to Philadelphia, to solicit the release of her son Alexander from Sir William Howe. She met with many curious adventures,* but succeeded in her object.

Margaretta Faugeres, the daughter of Mr. Bleecker, was distinguished in New York fashionable society, after the war, as a highly gifted and accomplished woman. She died at twenty-nine.

The daughters of Henry White, who married Miss Van Cortlandt, were greatly admired; the family holding a high position among loyalists before and during the Revolutionary war. They lived in Wall Street, near Broadway. One of the Misses White was dowager Lady Hayes, and the widow of Peter Jay Monroe. Mrs. White possessed great wealth, "and her recollections of New York society were curious." I find thus quoted an old citizen's reminiscences:—

"You must remember the Misses White, so gay and

---

* Women of the American Revolution.

fashionable; so charming in conversation, with such elegant figures! I remember going one night, with Sir John Temple and Henry Remsen, to a party at their house. I was dressed in a light-blue French coat, with high collar, broad lapels, and large gilt buttons; a double-breasted Marseilles vest, nankeen-colored cassimere breeches, with white silk stockings, shining pumps, and full ruffles on my breast and at my wrists, together with a ponderous white cravat with a pudding in it, as we then called it. I was considered the best dressed gentleman in the room. I remember to have walked a minuet with much grace with my friend Mrs. Verplanck, who was dressed in hoop and petticoats; and, singularly enough, I caught cold that night from drinking hot port-wine negus, and riding home in a sedan-chair with one of the glasses broken."

II.

The Livingstons in America, at the time of the Revolution, according to Mr. Theodore Sedgwick, in his life of Governor Livingston, were descended from Robert, the second son of the fourth Lord Livingston of Scotland, whose daughter was in attendance upon the Scottish Queen at the French Court. At a later day the seventh Lord Livingston was made Earl of Linlithgow, and the earldom continued in the family for five generations. Robert was born in 1654, emigrated to America 1674, and married, about 1683, Alida, widow of the Reverend, sometimes called Patron Nicholas Van Rensselaer, and daughter of Philip Pieterre Schuyler. The patent of the Manor and Lordship of Livingston granted to Robert bears date the 22d of July, 1686, and comprised from one hundred and twenty thousand to one hundred and fifty thousand acres on the Hudson River. His son, Philip Livingston, who succeeded to the manorial estate, born at Albany in 1686, and prominent in the history of the Colony, married Catherine Van Brugh, daughter of Peter Van Brugh, of Albany, of the Dutch family of Van Brugge, of whom was Carl Van Brugge, Lieutenant-Governor under Peter Stuyvesant in 1648.

Among the children by this marriage were Robert, who succeeded to the manor as the last lord—the Revolution breaking the entail; and Peter Van Brugh, merchant, of New York, who married Mary Alexander, sister of Lord Stirling, both adhering to the British during the war; with Philip, the signer of the Declaration of Independence; John, merchant, of New York; William, Governor of New Jersey; Sarah, wife of Alexander, Lord Stirling; Alida, who married, first, Henry Hausen; and secondly, Martin Hoffman; Catharine, who married John L. Laurence, and Henry.

William Livingston, born 1723, married, in 1745, Susannah French, of New Brunswick, a grand-daughter of Philip French, an English gentleman.*

Governor Livingston's political principles were decidedly Republican, and he declined to give to his country-seat at Elizabethtown any name more aristocratic than "Liberty Hall." He was a man of marked ability, decided in his views, and fearless in their expression; a

---

* Mr. French at one time owned a tract in New Jersey, comprising what is now New Brunswick. Miss French was grand-daughter on her mother's side to Anthony Brockhold, Lieutenant-Governor of the Colony of New York under Andross, 'and subsequently its chief magistrate. Philip French, of England, married a daughter of Frederick Philipse, or, as formerly written, Flypsen, a Protestant refugee from Bohemia, where his father had lost his life. The other children of Philipse were Eva (who married Jacobus Van Cortlandt, and became the mother of Mary Van Cortlandt, wife of Peter Jay, and mother of John Jay) and two sons, Frederick and Adolphus. A grandson, also named Frederick, and the inheritor of the manor of Philipsburgh, joined the Tories in the Revolution, and his estate was confiscated.

forcible writer, and exhibiting at times great power of satire.

Sarah Van Brugh, his fourth daughter, born in August, 1757, inherited some of his finest traits, intellectual and moral, which were developed by a very careful education, while with the father's stern patriotism and resolution she blended features of gentleness, grace, and beauty peculiarly her own. The delicate sensibility occasionally exhibited in her letters seems to have come from her mother.

The family of Governor Livingston was a large one, and besides sons, who died young, there were four other daughters: Susan, who married John Cleve Symmes; Kitty, who married Mathew Ridley, of Baltimore; Judith, who married John W. Watkins; and Mary, who married James Linn.

When the Governor's house was forcibly entered at night by British soldiers, in February, 1779, not finding him, they demanded his papers. Miss Susan Livingston had been prepared for this visit, and quietly assented, claiming only safety for a box containing "her private property." The officer set a guard over it, while the library was ransacked, and the men filled their foraging bags with worthless law papers, and then quitted the house. The box thus saved contained the Governor's correspondence with Congress, the Commander-in-Chief, and State officers.

In one of Livingston's letters to the Earl of Stirling, he says he has intrusted to his daughter Catherine his dispatches to his correspondents in Spain. General Washington's complimentary note to this lady was first published in "The Women of the American Revolution."

The sister of Governor Livingston, Sarah, married the Earl of Stirling, whom she accompanied to camp when he served in the American Army. She visited New York while it was in possession of the British, to see her daughter, Lady Catherine Alexander, whose husband was neutral in politics. Lady Stirling was a strong patriot, and would not avail herself of Sir Henry Clinton's permission to take any thing out of the city.

Lady Catherine Alexander was the daughter of Lord Stirling, and was married at Baskenridge, New Jersey, to Colonel William Duer, in 1779. She was very beautiful, and much admired in society.

On the 28th of April, 1774, Sarah Livingston, then in her eighteenth year, was married at Elizabethtown to John Jay, a young lawyer in his twenty-ninth year, of a Huguenot family, which, by intermarriage with the Bayards and Van Cortlandts, had become connected with the prominent families of the province. Mr. Jay, up to this time, had held no public office, excepting that of Secretary to the Royal Commission for settling the boundary between New York and New Jersey. Before the honeymoon, however, was complete, in May, 1774, Jay was called to take part in the first movements of that Revolution which was to result in the birth of a new Republic, and from this date the private life of Mrs.

Jay was so shaped and controlled by public events that it is hardly possible to give even a sketch of her career without occasionally referring to the history of the country. Mr. Jay's public duties as member of the New York Provincial Congress and of the Committee of Safety, and in other important capacities, kept him constantly separated from his young wife, who passed the greater part of the time at the residence of her father, with occasional visits to her husband's parents at their country place at Rye, Westchester County, New York. Her husband wrote to her from Philadelphia:— "I am much obliged to you for being so mindful of my good mother." The letters of Mr. Jay's father, Peter Jay, frequently show the fondness of the old people for their youthful daughter-in-law; and one of his notes about this time, from Rye to his son at Philadelphia, thus mentions a passing visit from the Commander-in-Chief: "General Washington, and several gentlemen with him, called here about ten o'clock last Tuesday morning. They stayed about an hour with me and refreshed themselves, then set off again on their journey, and appeared much pleased with the reception they had met here. * * General Washington told me you were well."

The progress of the war brought to the Americans living near New York increased hardship and anxiety, and added to the trial already suffered by Mrs. Jay of being separated from her husband. He had written to her in December, 1776—"I begin to wish for the holi days as much as a school-boy ever did;" and soon a rumor reached him that the British, after landing at Staten Island, had marched to Elizabethtown. It proved to be an exaggeration, and he wrote to his wife— "I much commend the coolness and presence of mind with which you received the alarm." A concentration of American troops in New Jersey presently tended to the safety of the Livingston country-seat.

Peter Jay the elder wrote this year to his son from Rye—"When you write to Sally, remember our love to her, and that she must every day give your little boy (Peter Augustus) a hearty embrace for us. We long to see them both again here, but despair of its being soon, in these unhappy times. I am, dear Johnny, your affectionate father." Later, Mr. Jay thought it best to send his wife and son to Fishkill for greater safety, and the family from Rye removed also to the same place. Among the pleasant country-seats where Mrs. Jay passed a part of her time was Mrs. Livingston's, at Rhinebeck; and Mr. Jay, in writing to her at this place, 12th of September, 1778, remarks—"As I always wish you to be with me, I hope an opportunity will soon offer, though I confess I am the less anxious, as you can't fail of being happy in so agreeable a family." In December of the same year, after Mr. Jay's election as President of Congress, his wife wrote him—"I had the pleasure of finding by the newspapers that you are honored with the first office on the continent. * * * * Had you consulted me, as some men have their wives about public measures, I should not have been Roman matron enough to have given you so entirely to the public."

Notwithstanding this disclaimer of Roman heroism, Mrs. Jay's letters, during the most gloomy and anxious periods of the war, show the cheerfulness with which the patriotic women of the day, however carefully nurtured, endured the trials and privations demanded by their country. During this year, the fashionable gayeties which the war had interrupted were resumed at Philadelphia, after its occupation by General Howe. The British officers devoted themselves to amusements, enacting plays three times a week—the drop-curtain having been painted by Major André. It was wittily said, that "it was not Howe who had taken Philadelphia, but Philadelphia which had captured Howe." A more moderate cheerfulness was found at times in the American camp; and Miss Kitty Livingston, writing from Raritan, General Greene's quarters, February 22, 1779, to Mr. Jay, at Philadelphia, says: "Your favorite beauty, Miss Helena Morris, is sitting by me, and desires her compliments. * * * It is very gay at camp, at present. The Troy, the Princeton, and the Baskenridge beauties are all here."

Mrs. Jay writes the same month, from Persipiney, of a grand dinner and entertainment at General Knox's head-quarters, with fireworks; and a note dated March 11th, announcing "four approaching marriages in Cousin Livingston's family," shows that the war at that moment interrupted but slightly the old order of events. These gayeties, however, were exceptional.

On the 10th of October, 1779, Mr. Jay, having been appointed Minister to Spain, sailed in the Congressional frigate, *The Confederacy*, accompanied by Mrs. Jay, her brother, Colonel Brockholst Livingston, afterwards a judge of the Supreme Court of the United States, as his private secretary, and by Mr. Carmichael, a member of Congress, as his public secretary.

On the 7th of November, the vessel was disabled by a sudden gale, and a letter from Mrs. Jay to her mother gives a graphic sketch of their troubles; within a half hour, she writes—" We had been deprived of nothing less than our bowsprit, foremast, main-mast, and mizzen-mast, so that we were in an awkward situation, rendered still more so by a pretty high southeast wind and a very rough sea. However, our misfortunes were only begun. The injury received by our rudder the next morning served to complete them. * * *

"Let my dear mamma imagine the dangerous situation of more than three hundred souls, tossed about in the midst of the ocean in a vessel dismasted and under no command, at a season, too, that threatened approaching inclemency of weather."

By the aid of a temporary mast constructed of spars the frigate reached St. Pierre, on the north side of Martinico, on the 18th of December, narrowly escaping capture from a fleet of six English ships of the line off

Port Royal, on the south side of the island, for which some of the passengers had wished the captain to steer.

At St. Pierre they were received with warm hospitality, and the Governor placed at their service the French frigate *Aurora*, in which they embarked for Toulon, on the 28th of December.

The *Aurora* was chased by a British man-of-war, and cleared for action, but outsailed her pursuer, and put into Cadiz for intelligence. It was found that the naval superiority of the enemy in the Mediterranean was so great as to render it unsafe for her to proceed to Toulon.

At Cadiz they received every attention from Count O'Reilly, the Governor of Andalusia, who invited them to his house, and treated them with great cordiality. Hence they proceeded to Madrid, where they lived for a time in the Street of St. Mattes, near St. Barbary, the former residence of the Saxon minister.

Of the many letters written to them by their friends in America, but a small number came safely to hand, some being captured by hostile cruisers, and others arrested by the Spanish post-office. Dispatches rarely reached them safely except by Government cruisers or private hands.

Extracts from a few of them may here be interesting, as illustrative of the character of their writers and of persons and events at home.

Governor Livingston, Trenton, 17th of March, 1780, wrote to Mr. Jay, at Madrid:—

"Heaven grant that you, and all the cargo shipped on board the *Confederacy*, in which I have so great an interest, may be safely arrived at Madrid before this reaches that metropolis. I have suffered much for poor Mrs. Jay, though I have been greatly comforted to hear that she bore the terrors of the ocean with so much magnanimity. Her letters from Martinique are safely arrived."

Mr. Jay from Ilfonso wrote, 18th of September, to Miss C. Livingston :—

"You are really a charming correspondent, as well as a charming every thing else. We have more letters from you than from all our friends in America put together. I often wish you with us for our sakes, and as often am content that you are not, for yours. We go on, however, tolerably well, flattering ourselves that we shall not be long absent, and anticipating the pleasures we are to enjoy on our return; among them, that of your being again with us is, I assure you, not the least."

Trenton, April 26, 1780, Miss Kitty Livingston wrote to Mrs. Jay, at Madrid :—

"MY DEAR SISTER:—

"Last Monday I left Philadelphia, under the escort of General Schuyler, Mr. Mathews, and Mr. Peabody, the committee from Congress to General Washington. * * * * * * *

"Mr. Witherspoon is establishing your character for the greatest philosopher of the age. You would have saved me, and all your friends, no small degree of uneasiness, had you mentioned in your letter to mamma (and that is all that has reached us of your whole family) how little you had been affected with the accident and other disagreeable circumstances attending your voyage. * *

"The minister, Don Juan, and M. Marbois, are on their return from camp. He contributed not a little to the pleasure of Philadelphia last winter, and is much esteemed there. He is one of the best and most cheerful tempers in the world."

Again, May 23, 1780 :—

"Lady Mary and Mr. Watts have rented Mrs. Montgomery's farm for two years. Cousin Nancy Browne is one of their family.

Colonel Lewis has purchased a house in Albany; one of the girls lives there with Gittey. He and Robert have each presented Cousin Livingston with a grand-daughter. The Chancellor's is a remarkably fine child. Mrs. L. never looked so well as she did the last winter, and was much admired in Philadelphia. She and Mrs. Morris were inseparable. She was also a first favorite of Mr. Morris. His esteem I think very flattering. Robert is in Congress, and I believe is at present there. She is to accompany him in the fall. General and Mrs. Schuyler are at Morristown. The General is one of the three that compose a committee from Congress. They expect to be with the army all summer. Mrs. Schuyler returns to Albany when the campaign opens.

"Apropos, Betsey Schuyler is engaged to our friend Colonel Hamilton. She has been at Morristown, at Dr. Cochrane's, since last February. Morristown continues to be very lively. The fate of Charlestown still depending—and Mrs. P. is said to be making a match with her daughter and her husband's brother. She has absolutely refused to let her go to her relations, and to let her choose a guardian. Colonel Burr and she are not on speaking terms."

In July, 1780, she writes to Mrs. Jay:—

"Do you know I am trading on your stock of firmness; and if you are not possessed of as much as I suppose you to have I shall become bankrupt, having several wagers depending that you will not paint nor go to plays on Sundays. The Chevalier is not to be convinced that he has lost his bet till Mr. Carmichael informs him you do not use paint. Mr. Witherspoon informs me that he was questioned by many, at Martinique, if you did not. (Mrs. Jay had a most brilliant complexion.) Mr. Bingham makes very honorable mention of you and Mr. Jay to your friends at Philadelphia.

"In our last distresses from the invasion of the British troops, Mr. and Mrs. Morris sent for me to come and live with them. It was exceedingly friendly; and it is certainly no small alleviation to our infelicities to have such friends as can feel for us, and by their kind endeavors soothe our troubled bosoms to peace and tranquillity. They have at present a delightful situation—Springsberry. Mr. Morris has enlarged the buildings and converted the greenhouse into a dining-room, which far exceeds their expectations in beauty and convenience."

Mrs. Jay, writing from Madrid, December 1, 1780, in reply to this letter:—

"The bets depending between you and the Chevalier I hope are considerable, since you are certainly entitled to the stake, for I have not used any false coloring, nor have I amused myself with plays or any other diversions on Sundays."

Mrs. Morris wrote from New Jersey to Mrs. Jay, September 6, 1780:—

"Yesterday we were informed from camp of the death of your cousin, William Alexander Livingston, who received his death from a Mr. Steaks, in a duel. Also, was buried at the same time, in like circumstances, a Mr. Peyton, from Virginia. You may judge how fashionable dueling is grown, when we have had five in one week, and one of them so singular that I cannot forbear mentioning it. It happened between two Frenchmen, who were to stand at a certain distance, and, marching up, were to fire when they pleased. One fired and missed, the other reserving his till he had placed his pistol on his antagonist's forehead, who had just time to say, 'Ah, Mon Dieu, pardonnez-moi!' at the same time bowing, whilst the pistol went off, and did no other mischief than singeing a few of his hairs."

Susan Livingston wrote in October, from Rhinebeck, to Mrs. Jay:—

"I ought to conclude, and beware the third page, as they say a woman can't write more than two pages without scandal. You must be more or less than woman, for you have written thirteen pages without scandal—witness your letter that we call the Confederacy."

"We are in such high spirits about our public affairs that I must tell you a little about it."

The letter then gives an account of a brilliant naval

victory, and their hope of hearing presently of the surrender of Lord Cornwallis.

Mrs. Robert Morris wrote from Philadelphia, July 12, 1781, to Mrs. Jay:—

"Kitty and myself often avail ourselves of the pleasure memory affords us, in the recollection of the many happy days spent together in this city. The Chevalier de la Luzerne, M. de Marbois, and Mr. Holker, expect great pleasure at your remembrance of them, and request your acceptance of their best wishes. The Chevalier acquiesces in the loss of his bet, presented Kitty with a handsome dress cap, accompanied with a note acknowledging your firmness. Mr. Morris's friends here, and, indeed, all who know him, were exceedingly shocked at his irreparable misfortune—the loss of his leg. * * * I never knew an individual more sympathized with."

During a part of the time, Mr. Jay was compelled to follow the court to Ilfonso, and leave his wife behind, attended by his youthful nephew, Peter Jay Munro, of whom Mr. Jay wrote to his father, "Peter has masters both for his head and heels." Mrs. Jay writes, 24th April, "We have had a charming winter—clear, mild, sunshine almost every day;" but of her sketches of society in Madrid we have no note. Her sister Susan, referring to the new circles around her, writes, July 18, 1787:—

"I wonder whether my dear sister appears as sweet, amiable, and beautiful to the signoras as she does to her own countryfolks."

Mrs. Jay's person, conversation, and character at this period were thus alluded to by Mrs. Janet Montgomery, in a letter to Mrs. Mercy Warren:—

"You speak of my dear friend, Mrs. Jay. We have heard from her at Hispaniola, where she was obliged to put in after the storm, in which she had like to be taken. When she arrives at Paris I expect to hear from her; if in the descriptive way, it shall be entirely at your service. She is one of the most worthy women I know; has a great fund of knowledge, and makes use of most charming language; added to this, she is very handsome, which will secure her a welcome with the unthinking, whilst her understanding will gain her the hearts of the most worthy. Her manners will do honor to our countrywomen, and I really believe will please, even at the Court of Madrid."

Mrs. Montgomery evidently thought, as did the Americans generally, that Spain was about to recognize our independence and lend us the assistance we required. She did neither the one nor the other. The little money she loaned us was given grudgingly, and with the attempt to attach unreasonable, if not impossible, conditions to her grants. As Mr. Jay declined to accept the courtesies of the Court, except as the minister of an independent nation, it is probable that Mrs. Jay never appeared at the Royal assemblies.

Of the characteristics of Mrs. Jay's personal appearance, glimpses are occasionally given in the family correspondence. In March, 1776, her husband, describing a very beautiful country-girl whom Colonel Morris and he had met at an inn near Gray's Ferry, and who, from her exquisite complexion, they had called "the conch-shell beauty," said: "Her teeth were as good, and her eyes of the same color and almost as fine as those of my fair correspondent. Colonel Morris thought she bore a great resemblance to the lady who will open this letter, and I assure you his opinion was not ill-founded."

Nearly twenty years afterwards, in April, 1794, Mr. Jay, then Chief Justice, writing to his wife, and referring to her eyes, says: "Tell me if they are as bright as ever."

Lady Strangford, *née* Philipse, a cousin of Mrs. Jay, with whom she had been intimate, and whose husband had married her when in orders, and had afterwards succeeded to the title, occasionally corresponded with Mrs. Jay in after years, sending her souvenirs of affection —in one case a ring, and in another a cross. Although her father was a tory, and his estate at Philipsburgh had been confiscated, Lady Strangford retained a touching devotion to America.

"I have," she writes, in a letter from England, "a warm and affectionate regard for every thing American; and though fate has rendered me stationary here, my own dear country can never be forgotten by me." In another, she says: "Though so long departed from America, I have the liveliest attachment to whatever relates to it, and feel inexpressibly interested in its welfare. And now one word of my girls. They are both good and handsome as I could wish, and my eldest is particularly elegant. I fancy her, my dear cousin, very like you in feature and complexion."

Congress having associated Mr. Jay with Dr. Franklin, Mr. Adams, and Mr. Laurens, in a commission to negotiate a peace, Dr. Franklin requested his presence in Paris; and on the 23d of June, 1782, after a tedious journey from Madrid, Mrs. Jay, with her husband and child, arrived at the Capital. The Doctor had written in April, "Let me know by a previous line if you conclude to come, and if, as I hope, Mrs. Jay will accompany you, that I may provide for you proper lodgings."

Their first quarters were in the Hotel d'Orleans, Rue des Petits Augustines, where the Commissioners frequently assembled; and again at Passy, where they lived with Dr. Franklin, in a mansion which is still standing, and occupied as a pension for girls. Once again, in November, 1783, they removed to a house, a very charming one, from Mrs. Jay's description of it, at Chaillot "sur la Chaussée de Versailles, près de la Carrière de la Conférence."

Rarely has the French capital, during its checkered history, been more the centre of interest to Europe and to the world. The peace between America and England, of which Franklin and Jay were to arrange the preliminaries—of their associates, Adams being in Holland, Jefferson in America, and Laurens in London, just released from the Tower—was the initial step towards a peace between England and Holland; and to those who did not dream of the dark shadow gathering over France, it must have seemed an auspicious omen for the young Republic of the New World, that its birth was to restore, on sea and land, the broken repose of the older nations.

Did our space permit, we should be tempted to blend with this sketch something more than a mere glance at the historic memories of the period connected with the peace negotiations, in which Mrs. Jay was almost a participant, from her intimate association with the negotiators, who frequently met at her apartments. There is no page certainly in our foreign diplomacy to which the intelligent American reader will ever recur with more national pride and interest than that which records the progress and result of these negotiations, in view of the fact that the American Commissioners began their work fettered by the resolution of Congress peremptorily instructing them to take no step without the knowledge and concurrence of the French ministers, and to be governed by their opinion and advice.

The illness of Dr. Franklin threw the chief responsibility upon Jay, and the first advice given by the French minister, that they should treat under a British Commission that recognized us not as an independent nation, but as British colonies or plantations, decided Jay to disregard, from that moment, the order of Congress, as no longer applicable to the situation. Promptly acting on this resolution, without further consultation with the French Court, he demanded, as indispensable, a new commission; to which the British Cabinet consented, allowing Jay to dictate its form.

The importance to England of a definite settlement with her late colonies in advance of her final negotiation with the European allies, gave to the American Commissioners a position of advantage, to which Jay's sternness and resolution, backed by the approval of Adams and Franklin, gave immense strength. The terms they demanded relating to the fisheries, the Mississippi, and the boundaries, while of immense importance to the United States, were regarded, under the circumstances, as of minor significance by the English ministry in their settlement of the European question; and such was the address and decision of the American Commissioners, that they obtained all they demanded, and far more than they had dared to hope for.

The preliminary articles were signed on the 20th of January, 1783. On the 3d of September, when France and Spain had settled their respective terms, the definitive treaties were signed, and Count de Vergennes entertained the diplomatists at a grand dinner at Versailles. On this conclusion of a general peace, England, France, Spain, and Holland, by a series of mutual concessions, on the principle of restitution and compromise, returned in great part to the *statu quo*. The United States alone, which, in the view of England and France, had entered the council-chamber as English "colonies or plantations," whose independence was to be granted by treaty stipulation, and which, to their surprise, had refused to take the first step except as a sovereign nation, and on an equal footing, came forth from that chamber endowed with the fisheries, the Mississippi, and a vast extent of territory to the north, the west, and the south, whose cession quieted forever all rival claims from Canada, France, or Spain, and gave to the infant Republic boundaries imperial in their grandeur.

In America, no one had ventured to hope for boundaries so magnificent. Governor Livingston wrote to Jay, Burlington, 20th of May, 1783, "The treaty is universally applauded." Hamilton wrote to him "The New England people talk of making you an annual fish-offering;" and John Adams said, of the title of "Le Washington de la Négociation," which had been bestowed upon him, "I sincerely think that it belongs to Mr. Jay." Years later, Mr. Adams, when President, wrote to Mr. Jay (November 24, 1800), "Among the very few truths in a late pamphlet, there is one that I shall ever acknowledge with pleasure, viz., 'that the principal merit of the negotiations for peace was Mr. Jay's.'"

More than half a century after the negotiations, the British Minister, Mr. Fitzherbert, who had become Lord St. Helens, after reading the life of Jay, wrote: "I can safely add my testimony * * * that it was not only chiefly, but solely, through his means that the negotiations of that period, between England and France, were brought to a successful conclusion."

Mrs. Jay wrote to Mr. Jay, January 21, the day after the signing of the provisional articles:—

"I long, my dear, to embrace you now as a deliverer of our country, as well as an affectionate and tender husband."

The scenes and the society amid which Mrs. Jay lived for nearly two years, presented a brilliant contrast to the trials and hardships to which she had been subjected by the war at home, as well as to her more retired life during their residence at Madrid.

Mr. Jay's health having become impaired, he went for a while to England, to try the Bath waters; and on his return, in January, 1784, with improved health and spirits, the last months of their stay in Paris were devoted to the enjoyment of its polished society.

History has made us familiar with the Paris of that period; so interesting, as presenting the last pictures of the pride and splendor that were still unconscious of the impending revolution. Marie Antoinette, now in her twenty-ninth year, still justified by her grace and beauty the magnificent apostrophe of Burke. In a letter to Mrs. Robert Morris, 14th of November, 1782, Mrs. Jay thus describes the Queen—after whom was named one American town, Marietta, in Ohio:—

> She is so handsome, and her manners are so engaging, that, almost forgetful of Republican principles, I was ready, while in her presence, to declare her born to be a queen. There are, however, many traits in her character worthy of imitation, even by Republicans; and I cannot but admire her resolution to superintend the education of Madame Royale, her daughter, to whom she has allotted chambers adjoining her own, and persists in refusing to name a governess for her. The Duchess of Polignac is named for that office to the Dauphin. I have just been interrupted by a visit from the Princess Mazarin, who informed me that the Count d'Artois was expected here in eight days hence, and the Prince, her husband, soon after; so that I conjecture the siege of Gibraltar is to be abandoned."

The fantasies of fashion, says a court historian, revealed the spirit of France as capricious and changeable. The queen and her intimate friends, especially the Comtesse Diane de Polignac and the Marquise de Vaudrienne, changed the mode day by day. The women wore the hair most fantastically raised in a pyramid, and this high edifice was crowned with flowers, as if it were a garden. Mrs. Jay wrote to Mrs. Morris:—

"At present the prevailing fashions are very decent and very plain; the gowns most worn are the robes à l'Anglaise, which are exactly like ye Italian habits that were in fashion in America when I left it; the Sultana is also à la mode, but it is not expected that it will long remain so. Every lady makes them of slight silk. There is so great a variety of hats, caps, cuffs, &c., that it's impossible to describe them. I forgot that the robe à l'Anglaise, if trimmed either with the same or gauze, is dress; but if untrimmed must be worn with an apron, and is undress. Negligées are very little in vogue. Fans of eight or ten sous are almost the only ones in use.

"At the Marquis de la Fayette's table I had the pleasure of hearing you, my dear Mrs. Morris, mentioned in terms the most grateful imaginable."

Among the first to congratulate Mrs. Jay on her arrival at Paris were the Marquis and the Marchioness de la Fayette. A note from the Marquis bears date the 25th June, and the Marchioness offers to Mrs. Jay her "tender homage." Some two years later, on leaving Paris, Mr. Jay wrote to la Fayette: "I shall never think of France without recollecting your friendly attention to Americans and American affairs."

The two circles of society where Mrs. Jay was entirely at home in Paris were those which were to be found in the hotels of la Fayette and Franklin.

"La Fayette and his companions had left the country," says the author of Memoirs of Marie Antionette, "Frenchmen, but came back Americans. They set out in quest of danger and military glory only, but brought back systems and patriotic enthusiasm. They appeared again at court, boasting of the scars and wounds received in the cause of liberty, and wearing with their dress the emblems of republican decorations."

This feeling was not confined solely to France. While the princes of Germany lent themselves to the purposes of Great Britain, the better mind of Germany sympathized with the American people, and our rising empire was not altogether overlooked in the thought of Goethe, Lessing, Schiller, and Kant.

The acquaintanceship of Mrs. Jay and Madame de la Fayette soon ripened into friendship, and their letters are marked by a tone of sincere regard and affection, and indicate a degree of intimacy between these youthful mothers closer than that which usually characterized the courtly circle that lent brilliancy to the Hotel de Noailles. The kind devotion of Madame de la Fayette to Mrs. Jay was extended to her children, and in the invitations to dinner the latter was sometimes prayed to bring Mademoiselle, her daughter (Maria), to see Madame de la Fayette's little family. Mrs. Jay's letters in reply refer gracefully "to the pleasure it will give her daughter to wait upon the charming little Miss Virginia." There is reason to believe that both enjoyed these domestic scenes more than the *salon* where they were surrounded by the elegance, wit, and beauty of the ancient *régime*, whose splendor was presently to disappear forever.

Miss Adams, the daughter of John Adams, writing from Paris in 1785, said:—

"Every person who knew her when here bestows many encomiums upon Mrs. Jay. Madame de la Fayette said she was well acquainted with her and very fond of her, adding that Mrs. Jay and she thought alike, that pleasure might be found abroad, but happiness only at home, in the society of one's family and friends."

Among the souvenirs presented by Madame de la Fayette to Mrs. Jay were two arm-chairs, embroidered by her own hands. One of these is now in the possession of Mrs. Henry E. Pierrepont, of Brooklyn, a granddaughter of Mrs. Jay.

Did space permit, we might give some interesting extracts from Mrs. Jay's correspondence with her husband while in England and her friends in America. One of his first letters from London says: "The doctor advises me to be as idle as possible, but so agreeable an employment as that of writing to you can hardly be a trespass on that injunction." Another, dated Bath, 22d December, gives an account of the celebrated Lady Huntington, her chapel, and its fine music, her cheerful conversation and pleasant recollections of Lord Bolingbroke, Lord Bath, Lord Bathurst, Lord Chesterfield, Pope, and other celebrities of her earlier years.

To Dr. Franklin, now in his seventy-sixth year, Mrs. Jay was indebted for uniformly kind attentions; and if the circle she met at the Hotel de Noailles was marked by its aristocracy of rank, that which surrounded the venerable philosopher at Passy was no less celebrated for happily blending the choicest and most opposite elements of the world of learning, wit, and fashion. Retaining, at that advanced age, a singular gayety and spirit, having lost, according to Mr. Adams, neither his love of beauty nor his taste in judging of it, he was constantly surrounded by savans, statesmen, and sprightly women, who flocked to pay their affectionate homage to the "Sage," as Mirabeau afterwards apostrophized him, "whom two worlds alike claimed, and for whom the history of science and the history of empires were disputing." The Paris of that day teemed with celebrities; among whom to Franklin, as the philosopher who had snatched the lightning from heaven and the sceptre from tyrants, the historians of the period assign the first place.

There was Mesmer, with his fascinating doctrine of the influence of the planets and the mysterious harmonies of ideas and forms, censured by the Academy, but popular in the salon. There were Lavoisier, exciting wonder by his application of chemistry; Buffon, the naturalist; Bailly, the astronomer; Legendre, the mathematician; and Darcet, the chemist. There was Guillotin, the philanthropic physician to the king, who, to alleviate the horrors of capital punishment, recommended the use of the machine which has perpetuated his name in connection with scenes which cannot be recalled without a shudder. There was Cagliostro, with his filters, talismans, and amulets, exhibiting, in the language of a French chronicler, an audacity that only superstition could authorize. There was Montgolfier, with his balloons, creating, on his first ascension, a furor of excitement; and Jean Gaspar Lavater, the youthful pastor of Zurich, calm and reflective, the author of sacred songs and Helvetique chants, challenging the admiration of the world by deducing traits of character from the physiognomy. The painters of the period included Greuze, Vernet, Doyen, Ménageot, David, and Le Brun; and the musicians, Mozart, Grétry, Delaysac, and Gluck.

There seems to have been a theatre, and a good one, at Passy, for Mrs. Jay writes, in 1782, "The queen has recently returned to Versailles, after a residence of eight or ten weeks at Passy. While there, I used sometimes to have the pleasure of seeing her at the plays."

Among the more intimate friends of Franklin were Turgot, the Abbé Raynal, Rochefoucault, Cabanes, Le Roy, Mabley, Mirabeau, D'Holbach, Marmontel, Neckar, Malesherbes, Watelet, and Mesdames de Genlis, Denis, Helvetius, Brillon, and La Reillard.

Such were the types of the brilliant circle that surrounded the Doctor's table or enlivened his evenings, and for their benefit he kept a printing-press in his house, for the convenient circulation among them of his "bagatelles." Of his genial, pleasant humor, his letters and those of Mrs. Jay afford abundant evidence. One of them (June 18, 1780), sending his portrait to Mrs. Jay at Madrid, thus pleasantly refers to his own celebrity:—

"Mrs. Jay does me much honor in desiring to have one of the prints that have been made here of her countryman. I send what has been said to be the best of five or six, engraved by different hands from different paintings. The verses at the bottom are truly extravagant. But you must know that the desire of pleasing by a perpetual use of compliments in this polite nation has so used up all the common expressions of approbation that they have become flat and insipid, and to use them almost implies censure. Hence, music, that formerly might be sufficiently praised when it was called *bonne*, to go a little farther, they called *excellente*, then *superbe*, *magnifique*, *exquisite*, *céleste*, all which being in their turn worn out, there remains only *divine*, and when that is grown as insufficient as its predecessors, I think they must return to common speech and common sense, as from vying with one another in fine and costly paintings on their coaches, since I first knew the country, not being able to go further in that way, they have returned lately to plain carriages, painted without arms or figures, in one uniform color."*

Here is one of the Doctor's little notes:—

"Dr. Franklin regrets exceedingly that his health does not permit the honor and pleasure of waiting upon Mr. and Mrs. Jay, according to their obliging invitation.

"He hopes Mr. and Mrs. Jay will condescend to indemnify him for the loss he sustains, by honoring him with their company at dinner on Saturday next. The Doctor would be happy to see Mr. Munro at the same time. Passy, 9th October, 1782."

Mrs. Jay's almost romantic devotion to her husband could hardly escape notice and comment in the Parisian circles, where she was known as "la belle Américaine;" and an incident to which it led on one occasion, in an assemblage at Passy, interesting from its connection with the Doctor's development of magnetism, and charm-

---

* Another of the Doctor's presents to Mrs. Jay—a tea-kettle of Sèvres china—is preserved in the family of Dr. John C. Jay, at Rye.

ingly illustrative of the man, is thus related in a letter from Mrs. Jay at Chaillot to Mr. Jay at Bath, November 18, 1783:—

"Dr. Franklin charges me to present you his compliments, whenever I write to you, but forbids my telling you how much pains he takes to excite my jealousy at your stay. The other evening, at Passy, he produced several pieces of steel; the one he supposed you, at Chaillot, which, being placed near another piece, which was to represent me, it was attracted by that, and presently united; but when drawn off from me, and nearer another piece, which the Doctor called an English lady, behold, the same effect! The company enjoyed it much, and urged me to revenge; but all could not shake my confidence in my beloved friend. The Doctor has just sent me word that he'll drink tea with me this evening, notwithstanding the storm."

An extract from Mr. Jay's reply to this letter is, in its turn, characteristic. He writes to Mrs. Jay from Bath:—

"It gives me pleasure to hear that our friend the Doctor is in such good spirits. Though his magnets love society, they are nevertheless true to the pole, and in that I hope to resemble them."

A letter from Mrs. Jay to her husband, a few days later, dated Chaillot, 2d of December, gives a full description of the first ascent, at Paris, by Messrs. Charles and Robert, of Montgolfier's, balloon, which created a great sensation. It landed some nine leagues distant, and the Dukes of Chartres and Fitz James, following by relays, arrived in time for its descent. The letter closes thus:—

"If I had four balloons to make a Mercury of a common messenger, you should not be twenty-four hours without hearing from us."

After Mrs. Jay's return to America, Dr. Franklin's letters show the strong attachment he had conceived for her and her children. He wrote to Mrs. Jay from Passy, 8th of February, 1785:—

"I received, by the Marquis de la Fayette, your kind letter of the 13th of December. It gave me pleasure on two accounts, as it informed me of the public welfare and that of your, I may almost say our, dear little family, for since I had the pleasure of their being with me in the same house I have ever felt a tender affection for them, equal, I believe, to that of most fathers."

Again, the Doctor writes to Jay, at New York, from Passy, 10th of May, acknowledging the resolution of Congress permitting his return:—"Next to the pleasure of rejoining my own family will be that of seeing you and yours well and happy, and embracing my little friend,* whose singular attachment to me I shall always remember. Be pleased to make my respectful compliments acceptable to Mrs. Jay, and believe me ever, with sincere and great respect and esteem, &c."

After Franklin's return to America, Jay welcomed him in a cordial letter. He says, in reference to the Doctor's proposed visit to New York:—

"Mrs. Jay is exceedingly pleased with this idea, and sincerely joins with me in wishing to see it realized. Her attachments are very strong, and that to you being founded on esteem, and the recollection of kind offices, is particularly so. I suspect your little friend has forgotten your name. Your name is familiar to her, as indeed it will be to every generation."

Soon after, Mr. Jay left his wife at Passy, attended

---

* Maria, afterwards Mrs. Banyer.

by his nephew, P. J. Munro, in order that he might try the Bath waters, she moved her little family to the house at Chaillot, which Mr. Jay had engaged for her, and she thus describes it in a letter to him, November 6, 1783:—

"Everybody that sees the house is surprised it has so long remained unoccupied. It is so gay, so lively, that I am sure you'll be pleased. Yesterday the windows were open in my cabinet while I was dressing, and it was even then too warm. Dr. Franklin and his grandsons, and Mr. and Mrs. Coxe and the Miss Walpoles drank tea with me likewise this evening, and they all approve of your choice. As the sky is very clear and the moon shines very bright, we were tempted to walk from the saloon upon the terrace, and while the company were admiring my situation, my imagination was retracing the pleasing evenings that you and I have passed together in contemplating the mild and gentle rays of the moon."

Mrs. Jay's family now embraced two daughters. Her husband, in announcing to his brother Frederick the birth of the last (26th of August, 1783), said: "She is to be baptized this morning, by the name of Anne. I wish we could as easily give her the virtues as the name of our amiable sister."

Those who were so fortunate as to have known personally the late Miss Anne Jay, or who are familiar with the extent of her charities and the beauty of her life, will not think that her father's wishes were unaccomplished.

We find a mention in one of Mrs. Jay's letters of having met at dinner, at the Marquis de la Fayette's, 20th October, 1783, the younger Pitt, who, accompanied by Mr. Wilberforce and Mr. Elliot, was making a hurried tour through France.

Governor Livingston writes to Mrs. Jay, from Elizabethtown, 8th of January, 1783:—

"I long to see you both, and my dear little French granddaughter Maria. My sweet little Peter is now standing at my elbow. He is really, and without flattering, one of the handsomest boys in the whole country."

November 12th, Mrs. Jay, at Chaillot, writes to her husband, at Bath:—

"I hope the weather is fine in England, for we have a most enchanting autumn here. You'll be pleased with our situation here when you return, for which I most ardently long, though I would not have you leave England until you have given it a fair trial. My little Nancy is a perfect cherub, without making the least allowance for a mother's partiality."

Mrs. Jay left Paris with her husband and children for Dover on the 16th of May, 1784, and landed at New York on the 24th of July, after an absence of more than four years and a half.

Mr. Jay had, the autumn before, written from Passy to his old friend, Peter Van Schaick: "I have asked leave to become a simple citizen, and to return home next summer;" but Congress, having heard from Dr. Franklin of his anticipated return, appointed him, in advance of his arrival, to the office of Secretary for Foreign Affairs, which has been described as "unquestionably the most prominent and responsible civil office under the Confederation." There was then no President of the United States, and the Secretary had charge of the whole foreign correspondence as well as of that between the General and State Governments. In this position, the entertaining of the foreign ministers, officers of Government, members of Congress, and persons of distinction, was an important incident, and Mrs. Jay's domestic duties assumed something of an official character.

Her long residence near European courts, and her recent association with the brilliant circles of the French capital, assisted her to fill with ease the place she was now to occupy, and to perform its graceful duties in a manner becoming the dignity of the republic to whose fortunes she had been so devoted.

We have no record relating to the entire period during which she presided over the entertainments given by her husband as Secretary for Foreign Affairs; but by a happy chance her "Dinner and Supper List for 1787 and '8" has been preserved, and the names which the list furnishes, together with the memoranda afforded by occasional private correspondence, and the published notes of European travelers touching that interesting period, help to give a picture, that already possesses an historic interest, of the social circles of New York during its brief existence as the National capital under the Articles of Confederation, and for two sessions of the first Congress under the Constitution.

The society of New York at that time, despite the comparative insignificance of the city in extent and population, and all that it had suffered during the war, presented more strikingly than in after years, when domestic and foreign emigration had made it a common centre, those distinguished characteristics derived from its blended ancestry and colonial history, that are still discernible in the circles of the Knickerbockers, and which recall alike to Americans and Europeans the earlier traditions of the National metropolis. While here and there might be found members of a family which, misled by mistaken convictions, had, during the war, sided with the mother country, or had timidly endeavored to preserve an inglorious neutrality, the tone of society was eminently patriotic, and worthy of the antecedents of an ancestry representing, in the words of an English historian, "the best stock of Europe who had sought homes in the Western World, and in whose forms of Government, charter, provincial and even proprietary, may be discerned the germs of a national liberty." With the culture and refinement of a class thus descended was blended that love of country which lends dignity to wealth and respectability to fashion.

The bar of New York gave to the salons of the day a list of names never since surpassed in our juridical history, in James Duane, Richard Harrison, Aaron Burr, Alexander Hamilton, Morgan Lewis, Robert Troup, Robert R. Livingston, Egbert Benson, John Watts, Governeur Morris, Richard Varick, James Lansing, and Josiah Ogden Hoffman and James Kent, both in their youthful vigor, the last of whom had been admitted in 1785, and was just commencing the career that gave him while yet living a world-wide reputation. The

Church furnished, of the Presbyterians, Dr. Rogers and Dr. John Mason; and of the Dutch Reformed Church, Dr. John H. Livingston and Dr. William Linn. Among the Episcopal clergy, the chief was the "easy, good-tempered, gentlemanly, and scholarly Dr. Provoost, Bishop of New York—a chaplain of Congress, and a welcome guest at the dinner-table of his friends." The Doctor had been devoted to the American cause, and was in every respect a most estimable and agreeable person; and, in addition to his classic, ecclesiastical, and Hebrew lore, he is said to have been familiar "with the Greek, Latin, French, German, and Italian languages." It is even affirmed that, as a literary recreation—and the circumstance seems more significant in view alike of his Episcopal duties and the times—he had made a new poetical translation of Tasso. The medical profession was represented by Dr. Charlton, Dr. Samuel Bard, Dr. John Bard, Dr. Wright Post, Dr. Bailey, Dr. Kissam, and Dr. Jones.

To the older families of New York mentioned in Mrs. Jay's invitation list, among whom were prominent those of Beekman, Bronson, Clinton, Clarkson, Cruger, Sterling, De Peyster, Livingston, Morris, Rutherford, Schuyler, Van Horn, Van Cortlandt, Van Rensselaer, Verplanck, and Watts, were now added, by the presence, first, of the Congress under the Confederation, and then under the Constitution, some of the most eminent of the statesmen and generals of "the old thirteen" who had helped to vindicate the independence and lay deep the foundation of the country. Among the names on Mrs. Jay's list may be found those of John Langdon, Paine, and Wingate; Roger Sherman and Benjamin Huntington, of New England; Elias Boudinot and Cadwallader, of New Jersey; Robert Morris, of Pennsylvania; George Read, of Delaware; Charles Carroll, of Maryland; Mr. Grayson, Theodoric Bland, and James Madison, of Virginia; Pierce Butler, Ralph Izard, Daniel Huger, and Thomas Tudor Tucker, of South Carolina; and William Few, of Georgia.

These gentlemen were, in many cases, accompanied by their families, representing in part the higher circles of New England, Philadelphia, Baltimore, and the South; and to these was added the small circle of diplomats accredited to the United States, and occasionally European travelers, attracted by the rising greatness of the young Republic. The letters of the day which have been preserved, both of Americans and Frenchmen, allude frequently to the grace, beauty, and attractiveness of many women then in society. Among them were Lady Mary Watts and Lady Kitty Duer, daughters of Lord Stirling, and cousins of Mrs. Jay; Mrs. Ralph Izard, grand-daughter of the Huguenot Etienne de Lanci; Mrs. Alexander Hamilton, daughter of General Schuyler; Mrs. Beekman (Miss James Kettletass); Mrs. Theodore Sedgwick (Miss Pamela Dwight); Miss Wolcott, of Connecticut, afterwards Mrs. Chauncey Goodrich; and to New York came also, occasionally, the belles of other cities, especially of Philadelphia. Mrs

Jay's dinners and receptions at this time are thus alluded to by Mrs. Wm. S. Smith, in a letter to her mother, Mrs. John Adams:—

"Mrs. Jay gives a dinner almost every week, besides one to the *corps diplomatique* on Tuesday evening; Miss Von Berckel (daughter of the Dutch Minister) and Lady Temple see company on Thursday; Mrs. Jay, Mrs. De la Forest, the wife of the French Consul; on Friday Lady Christiana, the Presidentess (of Congress); and on Saturdays, Mrs. Secretary ——."

Again, on the 20th of May, Mrs. Smith writes to her mother:—

"Yesterday we dined at Mrs. Jay's, in company with the whole *corps diplomatique*. Mr. Jay is a most pleasing man, plain in his manners, but kind, affectionate, and attentive; benevolence is stamped in every feature. Mrs. Jay dresses showily, but is very pleasing on a first acquaintance. The dinner was à *la Française*, and exhibited more of European taste than I expected to find."

On referring to Mrs. Jay's list, it appears that the guests at the dinner referred to by Mrs. Smith on the 20th of May, 1788, were as follows:—

The President of Congress, Mr. Griffin; Lady Christiana Griffin, his wife, belonging to a noble family in Scotland; Count de Moustier, the French Minister; his sister, the Marchioness de Brehan; Mr. Otto, afterwards Count de Mosloy, who had succeeded M. Marbois as Chargé d'Affaires, and had married a Miss Livingston; Comte de Brehan; Don Diego Gardoqui, the Spanish Minister; M. Von Berckel, the Dutch Minister; his daughter, Miss Von Berckel; Sir John Temple, the British Consul General; and Lady Temple, who was the daughter of Governor Bowdoin of Massachusetts; General Armstrong, Mr. Arthur Lee, Mr. and Lady Mary Watts, Mr. and Mrs. Watts, Mr. Bingham, Colonel William S. Smith and Mrs. Smith, Mr. Daniel McCormick, Mr. Kean.

Among the distinguished foreigners on Mrs. Jay's list, is found the name of M. Brissot de Warville, well known from his work on America, written on his return to Europe, and for his prominent and tragical connection with the Girondists of the French Revolution. He dined at her table on the 2d of September, 1788, with the following guests:—

Mr. and Mrs. Pintard, Mr. and Mrs. Rufus King, Mr. and Mrs. Montgomery, Mr. and Miss Von Berckel, Mr. Otis, Mr. Dane, Mr. Gerry, Mr. Sedgwick, Mr. Gilman, Mr. Wingate, Mr. Wadsworth, Mr. Huntington, M. de la Valle, and M. de Saussure.

M. Brissot de Warville had brought to Mr. Jay, from La Fayette, a letter commending him as a writer on the side of liberty, and as one of the founders of the society in behalf of the blacks; and another from the Chevalier Burgoyne, the minister from Saxony to Paris. His character and life have been cleverly drawn; among others, by Lord Brougham, and also by Grace and Philip Wharton, in their "Queens of Society," under the heading of his friend, the unfortunate Madame Roland.

The inauguration, by the new Government, under the National Constitution, in the spring of 1789, was heralded by the arrival of Vice-President Adams, after an almost triumphal progress from Boston. He was conducted in state, by the civil dignitaries and military officers, through a multitude of people, to the house of John Jay, in the lower part of the city.

On the 23d of March General Washington arrived, by the Bay, attended by the heads of departments, and escorted by a fleet of boats and sloops; and in the evening the city was brilliantly illuminated, and there was a display of fire-works. On the 13th of April he was inaugurated, at Federal Hall.

Mr. Jay's duties as Chief Justice carried him, this year, on the New England circuit, in the course of which, especially at Boston, he was received with cordial hospitality.

A letter to him from Mrs. Jay gives a pleasant picture of her home occupation, and a glimpse also of Mrs. Washington:—

"Last Monday the President went to Long Island to pass a week there. On Wednesday, Mrs. Washington called upon me to go with her to wait upon Miss Von Berckel, and on Thursday morning, agreeable to invitation, myself and the little girls took an early breakfast with her, and then went with her and her little grandchildren to breakfast at General Morris's, Morrisania. We passed together a very agreeable day, and on our return dined with her, as she would not take a refusal. After which I came home to dress, and she was so polite as to take coffee with me in the evening. * * * If you see Mrs. Langdon, pray thank her for her very polite attention. Governor Langdon was well last evening, when I was honored with his company."

Another letter says:—" Our friends Mr. and Mrs. Hamilton left New York last Wednesday; they dined with me on Sunday and Tuesday." Mrs. Jay mentions also having entertained Mrs. Iredell, her daughter, and Mr. and Mrs. Munro, and adds:—" My endeavor has been to show my affection for you by my attention to your friends."

In the spring of 1784 Mrs. Jay suffered a trial in the separation from her husband, who was sent by Washington as special ambassador to England, where he negotiated with Lord Grenville the treaty which bears his name, and which subsequently encountered, at the hands of the Democratic party, a vigorous but unsuccessful opposition.

Congress was sitting in Philadelphia when Mr. Jay advised his wife of the President's decision. Her reply, dated April, shows how deeply she was affected by it:—

"The utmost exertion I can make is to be silent; excuse me if I have not philosophy. * * * Should you leave me I must entreat you to permit your son to accompany you. It would give him infinite pleasure and me great consolation. * * *

"Adieu, my best beloved, absent or present, I am wholly yours.   SA. JAY."

Another of her letters, about this time, closes:— " Farewell, my best beloved. Your wife till death, and after that a ministering spirit."

Mr. Jay acceded to his wife's wish, and their son, Peter Augustus, then in his nineteenth year, accompanied his father. Soon after they had sailed, a violent storm occurred at New York, to which Mrs. Jay thus alludes, in a letter dated the 2d of May:—

"Oh, my dear Mr. Jay, how greatly do circumstances alter our ideas of things. I've known the time when in your company I have enjoyed a storm like this. At present I cannot, nor would I wish to describe the painful fancies it gives birth to. I know you disapprove the anticipation of evils, but indeed, my best of husbands, such a storm as this is enough to prostrate one's reason. At this season of the year it is so unusual. The poplars this morning were on the ground, and the cherries, still unripe, were blown from the trees before the dining-room window into the stable-yard. Frank has raised the poplars. When I droop who shall raise me, if the wide ocean should swallow up my husband and child?"

Mrs. Jay's letters to her husband, during his absence, are in great part devoted to his domestic affairs at home, of which she assumed the chief charge, assisted occasionally by his nephew, Peter Jay Munro. They are full, practical, and exact, giving the particulars of moneys paid in and reinvested, by the advice of friends, in the National Bank and stocks, with quotations of their rise, and the sale of lands, the progress of the mill and dam, then being built on the Jay estate at Bedford, and matters of more minute importance, in which Mr. Jay was sure to feel an interest.

In one of Mr. Jay's letters to his wife, he says:—

"Thanks for your many affectionate letters and unceasing attention to our mutual concerns. I frequently anticipate with satisfaction the pleasing moment when I shall again take my place by our own fireside, and with William on one knee and Sally on the other, amuse you with a variety of information."

Mrs. Jay was accustomed to ride on horseback, and her care in regard to her horses is occasionally exhibited in her letters. She writes to Mr. Jay, October 11, 1794:—

"Last Tuesday J. Lyon came to town on business, and brought the carriage horses. They are lean and entirely unbroke, even to a wagon. I was advised to send for Swan, a person who is said to understand breaking horses. He has undertaken it, and if he succeeds is to receive £6, but is not to be paid any thing if he does not. Frank attends him daily with the horses, for Swan says that the coachmen of this city require as much breaking as the horses."

A fortnight later, she writes that—

"The young horses have become gentle and tractable under the tuition of Mr. Swan and your man Frank. I have rode out with them, and last evening paid some visits in town. They stood very quietly; and, what to me was of equal consequence, they did not, like a former pair, *stand longer* than I wished."

The horses in question had exposed Mrs. Jay to vexations, with a mention of which she had avoided annoying her absent husband. She had been disappointed at the delay of Mr. Jay's agent at Bedford in breaking them for her use, and had sent him by his son a mild message on the subject, which by some persons had been maliciously distorted into a notice that he should never be pardoned, and that Mr. Jay would require him to quit the farm on the 1st of May following. This untrue statement induced a hasty and ill-tempered letter, dated the 10th of November, to Mrs. Jay, written under extreme irritation. Its tone may be gathered from a single line: "Madam, although I am your servant, I am not your slave." The next day brought a more civil letter, making an offer of potatoes, turnips, &c., but no apology for the first. Mrs. Jay's reply exhibits at once the force and dignity of her character, as well as her womanly tact and skill of expression.

After declining the vegetables, with thanks, she proceeded:—

"I could wish, Major, your letter of the 11th had been unaccompanied by the one of the 10th, as I am convinced you have yourself too much sensibility to reflect, without regret, on having wounded the feelings of a lady who has invariably treated you with cordiality and politeness."

After stating distinctly what she had said, the letter concludes:—

"That, sir, is the whole of what I told your son. Mr. Jay or the farm were not mentioned, and the word pardon neither entered my thoughts nor escaped my lips. I leave you, sir, to judge whether my observations merited the strictures you thought proper to make. Though Mr. Jay could not but be aware of the many inconveniences, injuries, and anxieties, that would be the consequence of his acceptance of a mission three thousand miles from his family, yet I am well convinced asperities from you, sir, to his solitary wife never entered his calculations. It is unnecessary, Major, to trouble you with further observations. Should Mr. Jay's labors abroad be again blessed to his country, the sacrifice his long absence costs his family shall be submitted to without murmuring.

"SA. JAY."

In one of her letters, Mrs. Jay tells Mr. Jay, that, in consequence of his prolonged absence, she had resolved, upon her own responsibility, to send their daughter Maria to the Moravian school for girls at Bethlehem, Pennsylvania, under the charge of Mr. and Mrs. Adams. Their friends, Mr. and Mrs. Arden, had already two daughters at the establishment. This was the most celebrated of the schools for girls, "where, in nun-like seclusion, were educated a large proportion of the belles who gave the fashionable circles of New York and Philadelphia their inspiration during the last twenty years of the century." When first visited by Mr. Adams, he found one hundred and twenty living under the same roof, and in a letter to his daughter he compared it to a nunnery. Mrs. Jay's daughter Anne afterwards joined her sister at Bethlehem, and both retained in after life pleasant recollections of the days passed there.

On the 28th of May, 1795, Mr. Jay returned from England, and learned that during his absence he had been elected Governor of the State, the result having been declared but two days before his arrival. He landed at the Battery, in the presence of a large concourse of citizens, who welcomed him with bells and cannon, and attended him to his house in Broadway. This popular applause was presently succeeded by vehement abuse, by the Democratic party, of "that damned arch traitor, John Jay;" and Mrs. Jay had the opportunity of observing both sides of a political career, when she found her husband burned in effigy at Philadelphia, and when Hamilton, defending the treaty, was answered with stones.

Mr. Jay was a second time elected Governor, and the State Government, which had sat in New York, was, during his first term, removed to Albany. Mrs. Jay's health, in 1796, sent her to Lebanon Springs, which had already a high reputation. She was accompanied by her daughter Maria, and her letters show the enjoyment and benefit she received from the waters, aided by a simple country life and mountain air.

The State Government had made no provision for a Governor's residence at Albany, and it was not until 1797-'8 that Mrs. Jay permanently assumed the charge of her husband's house, and presided over the reunions of the descendants of the Dutch Huguenot and English colonists, whose devotion to freedom had given to New York its proud position in the country; while the wealth and importance derived from stately manors, miles in extent, and but recently invested with almost baronial privileges, blended with the simplicity of the young Republic, social features that had something of the dignity and grace usually associated with ancient aristocracy.

In 1801, at the conclusion of his second term as Governor, Mr. Jay retired from public life, declining a reappointment as Chief Justice, tendered him by President Adams, and with his daughter Anne he repaired to his farm at Bedford, where the improvements of the old dwelling-house were not yet completed. Mrs. Jay's health forbade her coming until the mechanics had all departed; and while staying at Oakhill, May 27, 1801, she wrote to Mr. Jay:—

"Say every thing to our dearest daughter (Anne) that a fond and delighted mother could express. Thank her for her charming letter. No cordials could have so salutary an effect on my spirits as the dear letters I receive from you both. I have perused and reperused them twenty times at least."

A little later she wrote from Rye, October 6, to Mr. Jay:—

"I have been rendered very happy by the company of our dear children, but could we have been together it would have heightened the satisfaction, every word and every look of our dear little boy (William). Your brother himself frequently exclaimed, you are a dear little dog. Banyar and his little wife (Maria) are an amiable couple, and I often, I should say daily, bless God for giving us such amiable children. May they long be preserved a blessing to us and to the community."

Mrs. Jay wrote on her arrival at Bedford: "I can truly say I have never enjoyed so much comfort as I do here." Her enjoyment, however, of the calm pleasures of domestic life, surrounded by her children, was destined to be but brief. Within twelve months she died, after a short illness, on the 28th of May, 1802.

The character of Mrs. Jay is in part exhibited by the brief extracts given from her letters. However much of its equanimity was due to the example and influence of her husband, her letters show that, with a singular delicacy of feeling and sensibility of organization was combined a strength of mind based upon Christian principle, which enabled her to face danger without fear and to endure hardships and disappointments without a murmur. "You have a soul," wrote Mrs. Morris, in 1780, to Mrs. Jay, "superior, I know, to this. You look forward, doubtless, to events like my misfortunes with the eye of a philosopher and the mind of a Christian."

Her biography and correspondence, should it be published, would illustrate in no slight degree the early days of the Republic, and disclose the temper of the men and the women whose virtue secured the independence of their country, and whose characters and accomplishments sustained its dignity at home and at the courts of Europe. If to Sarah Livingston Jay belonged beauty, elegance, and accomplishments; if, from the charms of her manners or the vivacity of her conversation, combined with the accidents of birth and position, there is assigned her a prominent place among American women, she is entitled to regard on far better grounds than simply as a "Queen of American Society." Her memory may be cherished as that of one who exhibited from her youth, amid trial and hardship, a steadfast devotion to her country; who, amid the gay society of Paris and New York, preserved unimpaired her gentleness, amiability, and simplicity; and who, throughout her life, fulfilled with Christian fidelity and womanly affection the duties of a daughter, sister, wife, and mother.*

---

* Mrs. Jay left five children: Peter Augustus, born at Elizabethtown, 24th of January, 1776; Maria, born at Madrid, 20th of February, 1782, died 21st of November, 1856; Anne, born at Passy, 13th of August, 1783, died 13th of November, 1856; William, born at New York, 16th of June, 1789, died 14th of October, 1858; Sarah Louisa, born at New York, 20th of February, 1792, Died 22d of April, 1818. Governor Jay long survived his wife, and died at Bedford, 17th of May, 1829.

III.

In the country's early days, New England had her acknowledged aristocracy, and Massachusetts boasted the most finished school of refined manners. Her public officers, clericals, and most wealthy persons constituted her gentry, or the upper classes, in all the towns; in the country, those who held large landed estates, who were representatives, or held high civil or military offices, were regarded as members of the aristocracy. Habits and dress plainly denoted rank in life. One who was a gentleman usually went abroad in a wig, white stock, white satin embroidered vest, black satin small-clothes, with white silk stockings and fine broadcloth or velvet coat. At home, he wore a velvet cap, sometimes over a fine linen one, instead of a wig; a gown of colored damask lined with silk in place of a coat, and leathern slippers.

In most genteel families, a tankard of punch was prepared every morning, and visitors during the day were invited to partake of it; the master frequently taking the vessel from the cooler, drinking first from it himself, and handing it to his guests.

Dinners and suppers were frequently interchanged. The fashionable hour was never later than three o'clock, and the table groaned with the dainties provided. The evening amusements were dancing and cards. Dramatic entertainments were prohibited by law; but concerts were in vogue, and in Boston gentlemen in private life performed vocal and instrumental music for the amusement of their friends. The dancing was conducted with a severe regard to propriety. The modern objectionable waltzes were unknown; the stately minuet, with its high-bred, formal courtesy, was varied by the contradance; and cotillions did not come into favor till brought by French refugees from the West Indies.

Glimpses of the social life of Boston at the close of the war may be found in the memoirs of the Marquis de Chastellux, who went the rounds of fashionable gayety in 1782. The city was the home of the Winthrop families, noted as founders of the colony; there were the Cushings, Quincys, Bowdoins, Danas, Prescotts, &c., and more real respectability was to be found there than in almost any other town of its population. The Marquis noticed the prevalence of a "tone of ease and freedom;" but thought the gentlemen awkward dancers, particularly in minuets. The women were well dressed, but with less elegance than in Philadelphia. He took tea at Bowdoin's, and was at supper with a select party of twenty; noticing especially the host's beautiful granddaughter, the eldest child of Lady Temple—"an angel in the disguise of a young girl." Elizabeth Temple, the daughter of Sir John Temple, and grand-daughter of Governor Bowdoin, in whose family she was brought up, was married in 1786 to Thomas Lindall Winthrop. During the years of the war, she had been in the habit of seeing Franklin, La Fayette, and the principal French and American officers. She was the reigning belle of Boston. La Fayette was her ardent admirer, and often called to see her. Her husband, Governor Winthrop, possessed an ample fortune, and they lived in style, exercising a generous hospitality, and receiving at their table most strangers of consideration who came to the vicinity. This lady was the mother of Robert C. Winthrop.

Lady Temple, the wife of Sir John, was a daughter of Governor Bowdoin. The Marquis de Chastellux said, in 1782: "If I do not place Mrs. Temple in the list of handsome women, it is not from want of respect, but because her figure is so distinguished as to make it unnecessary to pronounce her truly beautiful."

Jean Pierre Brissot de Warville was also intimate with the fashionables of Boston. He "hopes the Boston women may never, like those of Paris, acquire *la maladie* of perfection in music, which is not to be attained but at the expense of the domestic virtues." The ladies, he said, had "the liberty of Geneva, in the days of the republic, when vows of love were believed, and the women were occupied in rendering their husbands happy." At that time, Frenchmen were inquisitive and intelligent speculators on our resources, government and society. Brissot afterwards appeared in Paris in Quaker costume, and was the first to introduce the fashion of wearing the hair without powder. "The Bostonians," he said, "unite simplicity of manner with that French politeness and delicacy which renders virtue more amiable. Music, which their teachers formerly proscribed as a diabolical art, begins to make part of their education."

On the road to New York he marveled at "supper, cider, tea, punch, and all for fourteen pence a head. Breakfast, coffee, tea, boiled and roast meat, tenpence each. On the road you often meet those fair Connecticut girls, driving a carriage, or alone on horseback, galloping boldly; with an elegant hat on the head, a white apron and a calico gown." This leads to comments on the general innocence of manners.*

Sullivan says: "An important person in the fashionable world was Mrs. Haley, sister of the celebrated John Wilkes, who came over and purchased a house in Boston, in 1785. She was, at the time, rather advanced in life,

---

* A curious anecdote of the misfortune of a veteran gallant—Jeremiah Smith, of New Hampshire—who "had dabbled in love many times," and at last became a Benedick, illustrates the dress of the times. On his way to the bride's house, he lost his trunk with his wedding suit, and had to stand up in his traveling clothes. His biographer gives a list of the articles:—"A light-colored broadcloth coat, with pearl buttons; breeches of the same cloth; ditto, black satin; vest, swansdown, buff, striped; ditto, moleskin, cheque figure; ditto, satin figured; ditto, Marseilles, white; ditto, muslinet, figured; under vest, faced with red cassimere; two ditto, flannel; one pair flannel drawers; one ditto, cotton; one pair black patent silk hose; one ditto, white ditto; one ditto, striped; ten or a dozen white silk hose; four pairs gauze ditto; a towel; six shirts; twelve neckhandkerchiefs; six pocket handkerchiefs, one a bandanna; a chintz dressing-gown; a pair of silk gloves; ditto, old kid—all valued at two hundred dollars."

and of singular personal appearance, but was extremely prepossessing in manner. She afterwards married a gentleman who was the uncle of a celebrated Scotch reviewer, and her house became a place of fashionable resort."

The sympathy of a portion of the people with French Jacobinism was shown in observances by no means in good taste.

A "civic feast" was given in Boston, in honor of the success of the French Revolution. "A whole ox, skinned and dressed, with head and horns entire, and eyes protruding from the sockets, was turned on a great wooden spit before a furnace. When sufficiently roasted, it was placed on a sledge or carriage, propped up, and drawn through the principal streets, followed by two cartloads of bread and two hogsheads of punch. An immense concourse attended. A table was laid in State Street for the feast intended for the friends of liberty. The cutting up and distribution became ridiculous, then riotous. The roasted fragments were hurled into the air, and at the female spectators on the balconies and at the windows. A pole fifty or sixty feet high was raised in Liberty Square, surmounted with the horns of the ox, and stood several years. This feast took place on the day Louis XVI. was guillotined."

Elsewhere the same spirit was exhibited by a part of the democracy. M. Genet, the first minister of the French Republic, on entering the house of the President, and seeing there a bust of Louis XVI., complained of it as an insult to France. At a dinner at which Governor Mifflin was present, a roasted pig received the name of the murdered king, and the head severed from the body was carried round to each of the guests, who, after placing the liberty cap on his own head, pronounced the word "Tyrant," and proceeded to mangle with his knife that of the luckless creature doomed to be served for so unworthy a company.

M. Genet first landed in Charleston, where his reception and his journey to Philadelphia were triumphal; for, notwithstanding the President's proclamation of neutrality, the sympathy for the French was irrepressible. "Aristocrats" were denounced; the common expressions of the *sans-culottes* were adopted in society, and the title "Citizen" became common. Genet married Cornelia Tappan Clinton, the daughter of the Governor of New York. One of her sisters was Madame Campan, noted for her ability and her intimate relations with the royal family of France; another was the beautiful Madame Auguie, mother-in-law of Marshal Ney. Madam Genet's home was at Greenbush, near Albany.

John Quincy Adams wrote, in January, 1789, of Miss Aleny Ellery: "She is, unfortunately, somewhat deaf, but is uncommonly sensible, and (what I am grieved to say is still more uncommon in this country) her mind is much improved by reading, so that she can entertain a company with a large variety of conversation without having recourse to the stale and trivial topics of commonplace, or to the ungenerous and disgraceful topic of scandal. She is not handsome, and is, I suppose, twenty-seven years old; yet, were she in company with twenty of the most beautiful young ladies in the State, and in this company I had to choose my seat, it should certainly be by her side. I have been endeavoring, my sister, ever since I returned from Europe, to find a female character like this, united to great beauty of person; and I begin to have the same prejudice against a beauty as you have expressed in one of your letters against handsome men."

At a ball, he wrote: "It fell to my lot, at first, to dance with the handsomest lady in the company. I endeavored to enter into conversation with her; but, to every thing I could say, the only answers were, 'Yes,' 'No,' 'I think so,' 'Indeed.' I was soon tired of her, and concluded she was too much occupied in thinking of herself to give any of her attention to other people."

Dr. Abner Hersey, of Barnstable, Massachusetts, was accustomed to rail at the fashions of the day. He lived on milk and vegetables, and wore a coat made of tanned calf-skins. The widow of his brother once proposed to visit him. He wrote: "Madam, I can't have you here; I am sick, and my wife is sick; I have no hay or corn for your horses; I have no servants; and I had rather be chained to a galley-oar than wait on you myself." It was this eccentric man who founded the professorship of Theory and Practice of Medicine in Harvard University.

Chastellux mentions an entertainment given by Mrs.

Cushing, where Mrs. Bowdoin was a guest, and the supper was on the table four hours after dinner.* Mrs. Cushing was the wife of Judge Cushing, of the Supreme Court, and often traveled with her husband. Mrs. Pinckney wrote to her, July 5, 1795: "Mr. Izard contrived to overset his chair and himself on his journey home, and dislocated his arm. He says the accident could not have happened had he taken Mrs. Izard with him, and that it was in consequence of thinking of politics instead of the road. So you see, my dear madam, in what a variety of ways your traveling with Mr. Cushing is beneficial to him."

John Adams wrote, in 1774: "We breakfasted with Mr. Isaac Low, a gentleman of fortune and in trade. His lady is a beauty." Mrs. Low was the daughter of Cornelius Cuyler, Mayor of Albany, and was greatly admired in New York society for her personal attractions and her amiable character. She died in London, at the age of eighty.

The eldest Miss Allen was one of the most splendid beauties in the country. She became Mrs. Greenleaf. Mrs. Adams mentions the sisters and the Misses Chew among "a constellation of beauties." Mrs. Theodore Sedgwick, of New England, had a charming face and an air of elegance and refinement. She was Miss Pamela Dwight.

---

* "The aliments," he says, "behave with the American stomach as we do in France on paying visits; they never depart till they see others enter."

In point of influence, Mercy Warren was the most remarkable woman who lived in the days of the American Revolution. She was the daughter of James Otis, of Barnstable, in the old colony of Plymouth. The Otis family came to this country about 1630, and first settled in Hingham. Mercy was born in 1728, and passed her youth in retirement, her studies being directed by the parish minister, who directed her attention especially to history. At the age of twenty-six she married James Warren, a merchant, and resided on a farm. Here she continued her literary pursuits, and amused herself by writing poetry. Her active and powerful mind entered with deep interest into political affairs, and she maintained a rich correspondence with some of the leading spirits of the Revolutionary era. Samuel and John Adams, Jefferson, Knox, and others, wrote to her, and consulted her in regard to important matters. Her close friendship and correspondence with Mrs. Adams continued unchanged through a long and eventful life; the sister of Mrs. Adams, Mrs. Shaw, was also warmly attached to her. During the years preceding the war, Mrs. Warren's house was the resort of much company; and, as she said, "by the Plymouth fireside were many political plans originated, discussed, and digested." During the war she lived part of the time in Milton; and wherever she was, the friends of her country were always welcomed to shelter and hospitality. Washington, Lee, Gates, and other distinguished officers, were frequently her guests; also Mrs.

Washington; and her social influence and literary abilities were alike directed to the advancement of her country's cause. She wrote poems, tragedies, political letters, and a history of the war, in which her pen did justice to those distinguished by merit. Her letters to the widow of General Montgomery and other eminent women have been quoted in another work,* in which an extended memoir is given.

Mrs. Warren invited Mrs. Washington to her house, and paid her many attentions on her visit to head-quarters in Cambridge. In a letter to Mrs. Adams, Mrs. Warren describes one of these visits to Mrs. Washington, and a drive in her chariot to see the enemy's deserted lines and the ruins of Charlestown. Speaking of Mr. Custis, she says: "His lady, a daughter of Colonel Culvert, of Maryland, appears to be of an engaging disposition, but very delicate in health. She is pretty, genteel, easy, and agreeable; but a kind of languor about her prevents her being as sociable as some ladies."

One of Mrs. Warren's intimate friends was Hannah Winthrop, the wife of Dr. Winthrop, of Cambridge. The two ladies corresponded under the signatures of "Honoria" and "Philomela;" the last name being given to Mrs. Warren for her powers of song. Her usual poetic signature was "Marcia." Other correspondents were Mrs. Montgomery and the celebrated Mrs. Macaulay.

* Women of the American Revolution.

Mrs. Warren is described by Rochefoucault, in his "Travels in the United States." "Although seventy years of age, she was," he says, " truly interesting; for, lively in conversation, she has lost neither the activity of her mind nor the graces of her person." As a writer, she was in advance of the age. Her portraiture of Mr. Adams, in her history, gave offense to the great statesman; but, after a sharp correspondence, all was reconciled, and Mrs. Adams sent her a ring with her own and her husband's hair.

Seldom has a woman, in any age, acquired such ascendency by the mere force of a powerful intellect, and her influence continued to the close of life.

———

The Duc de la Rochefoucault Liancourt said of Mrs. Knox: "Seeing her in Philadelphia, you think of her only as a fortunate player at whist; at her house in the country, you discover that she possesses sprightliness, knowledge, a good heart, and an excellent understanding." Her father, Thomas Flucker, was the last Secretary of the Province of Massachusetts Bay. He married Hannah, the daughter of General Waldo, proprietor of the Waldo Patent, in Maine. The portions of this domain belonging to Mrs. Flucker and her two brothers were afterwards confiscated. Flucker's high position gave his daughter, in girlhood, the advantages of the best society in Boston. Entitled, as she was, to a brilliant match, it was mortifying to her parents that their lovely and accomplished daughter should bestow her affections upon an obscure young man; one, too, who favored the rebellion of the colonies against the mother country. The maiden found that her marriage with Henry Knox would separate her from her dearest relatives, but love triumphed in the struggle, and she cast her all on the die that was to decide the nation's fate.

After her marriage, Mrs. Knox found herself in the midst of new surroundings. She was much in the society of Mrs. Washington, and even more constantly in camp with the army. Her influence was shown in the deference uniformly paid to her. She was at Mount Vernon during the siege of Yorktown, soothing the grief of Mrs. Washington, in bereavement, by her affectionate sympathy. After the close of the war, General and Mrs. Knox returned to Boston, where they found great changes in society. She used to say, "The scum had all risen to the top." The prominent loyalists had fled the country. Knox took charge of the War Department under the old Confederation, and they removed to New York. They found a disposition general to welcome the new era with social festivities. Mrs. Washington was sovereign of the new court, and Mrs. Knox, her intimate friend and close neighbor, occupied a high post of honor.

The removal of the capital to Philadelphia was the signal for hilarity and rejoicings in the latter place. It was said that the influence of Robert Morris had led to this removal, and he was caricatured in New York by pictures exhibiting the great financier carrying off the body of Congress on his back, with the motto, "Stick to it, Bobby." The world of fashion seemed to have run mad. All kinds of entertainments became popular, and ladies prominent as leaders were emulous in gayety and splendor. Mrs. Knox made her house the resort not only of fashionable people, but of the intellectual and cultivated. Her tact and talent in the management of life "at the court" were of essential service to Mrs. Washington, who relied on her guidance. The French Revolution brought an accession of many illustrious visitors, in princes and nobles driven from their own land. The house of General Knox was hospitably open to them, and some were entertained as his cherished guests. The Duc de Liancourt passed several seasons with them at their beautiful home in Maine. In his destitution of proper apparel he was heard to exclaim: "I have three dukedoms on my head (beating it with violence), and not one coat to my back!" The suit was immediately supplied from the wardrobe of the General, and the kindness was gratefully remembered when the nobleman was restored to favor and wealth. Another visitor, both in Philadelphia and Maine, was the celebrated Talleyrand. La Fayette visited General and Mrs. Knox in Boston, and stood godfather to their son.

On the retirement of General Knox, in 1795, they finally quitted Philadelphia. Mrs. Knox was the only one of her family entitled to inherit property in the United States, and one-fifth of the large tract of land in Maine, the "Waldo Patent"—originally owned by her grandfather, General Waldo—belonged to her. General Knox bought a tract of equal extent from another branch of the family, and determined to establish a new home on this noble estate. At Thomaston, at the head of St. George's River, he built a splendid mansion; a palace in dimensions, and called a "chateau" by his French visitors. It was furnished with luxurious taste; the outhouses comprised every convenience; and a vast amount of expenditure rendered "Montpelier" really a princely abode. Here the retired soldier exercised unbounded hospitality; receiving the great, patriotic, and distinguished of the land, and frequently entertaining total strangers, who came with real or assumed claims. Louis Philippe and his two younger brothers, the Duc de Montpensier, the Comte de Beaujolais, and Duc de Charolais were often welcome visitors at the house of Knox, in Boston, where he and Mrs. Knox were accustomed to spend their winters. The daughter of Mrs. Knox remembered the princes' expressions of anxiety about their mother and sister, still in the power of French Jacobins. One day when they came to dinner she saw them, with apparent joy, tear the tri-colored cockade from their hats, and trample them under foot. News had just come of the escape of their relatives into Spain; and they would no longer keep terms with the wretches who bore sway in their native country!

The hospitality dispensed at Thomaston was such as the country has seldom seen. It was not unusual to order an ox and twenty sheep killed on Monday, to be consumed by guests in the course of the week, and to have a hundred beds made daily. Their daughter, Mrs. Thacher, wrote to the author of this volume:—

"My mother, I think, was never more entirely satisfied with her situation. Her greatest trouble was, that the retirement she anticipated was far from being realized. My father's hospitable propensities still induced him to open his doors to all who were disposed to visit him; and, as every thing that could interest or amuse was liberally provided, we were often favored much longer than was desirable with the company of guests who were entire strangers, and had no possible claim. It was to some such visitors as these, I doubt not, that my mother may have appeared distant and haughty. Such instances I well recollect, particularly when these unasked visits were unreasonably prolonged; but those whom she liked, or was at all interested in, would have given her a far different character."

It was in the second summer of Mrs. Knox's residence in Maine that a party from Philadelphia, consisting of Mr. and Mrs. Bingham, their two daughters, Miss Willing, the sister of Mrs. Bingham, said to have been sought in marriage by Louis Philippe, the Viscount de Noailles, the brother-in-law of La Fayette, and one of the most polished nobles of the French Court—Mr. Richards, an English gentleman, and Mr. Baring, afterwards Lord Ashburton, passed six weeks at Montpelier. The gentlemen made extensive excursions through the adjacent country, and Messrs. Bingham and Baring were induced to purchase a million of acres on the Kennebeck, and a tract somewhat smaller east of the Waldo Patent. The wilds of Maine were thus enlivened by the most brilliant of the society of the national capital their companionship solacing the depressed spirits of Mrs. Knox, who suffered many sorrows in the loss of children. After the death of her husband her days were spent in retirement. She died in June, 1824, at the age of sixty-eight.

Justice has not been done to Mrs. Knox, either by chroniclers of the times or by contemporaries who were not admitted to intimacy, and failed, in consequence, to perceive that she had a heart full of warm sensibilities. She had a mind of a high and powerful cast, with such qualities as make a deep and abiding impression, and her influence was marked on all who approached her. But some called her dignity hauteur, and gave the name of boldness to the independence of a calm and lofty spirit. She gave a decided tone to the manners of the day in general society, and the deference shown her by General and Mrs. Washington sanctioned the homage paid to her superior intellect.

Mrs. Knox was a remarkably fine-looking woman. Without being tall, her dignity of manner gave her a commanding appearance; and she had a blooming complexion and brilliant black eyes. Stuart, who painted the General, attempted a portrait of her, but became dissatisfied, rubbed it out, and would never resume the work.

The daughters of William Sheaffe, of Boston, were noted for beauty and fashion. A romantic incident is remembered of Captain Ponsonby Molesworth, a nephew of Lord Ponsonby, landing at Boston, in command of British troops, and halting opposite the house of Mr. Sheaffe. Susanna Sheaffe and her sisters were in the balcony or piazza. Captain Molesworth, struck with the girl's beauty, exclaimed, "That girl seals my fate!" She was at the time about fifteen. The Captain obtained an introduction, visited her, and proposed marriage, but the father refused his consent. The young lady agreed to an elopement, and, accompanied by her governess, fled with her lover to Rhode Island, where they were married. They afterwards went abroad.

Margaret Sheaffe married John R. Livingston, then a Boston merchant, and died in Boston, 1784, at the age of twenty-four. "So handsome no one could take her picture." La Fayette visited and admired her. He said once to her lover, "Were I not a married man I would try to cut you out." After his return to France, the Marquis sent her a "satin cardinal, lined with ermine, and an elegant silk garment to wear under it." The relic was long preserved.

Helen, another daughter, "like a rosebud just opening to view," married James Lovell, afterwards an officer in the naval service. At thirteen she wrote a poem in answer to the question, "What is religion?" She died in Boston, 1802, at the age of thirty-three. Her daughter, Mrs. Loring, resides at Brookline, Massachusetts. Lady Temple was very intimate with the ladies of the Sheaffe family. William Sheaffe was nephew and heir to Major-General Sir Roger Hale Sheaffe, Baronet.

Abigail Adams was descended from the genuine stock of the Puritan settlers of Massachusetts. She was the daughter of Rev. William Smith—pastor during forty years of the Congregational church at Weymouth, in the colony of Massachusetts Bay—and of Elizabeth Quincy, born in 1744. In October, 1764, she married John Adams, then a young lawyer of Braintree, afterwards the second President of the United States. She passed with her family through the horrors of war and many scenes of distress, after peace leaving her modest home to accompany Mr. Adams on his mission as the first representative of the United States at the British Court. She passed some years abroad, visiting France and the Netherlands; and her letters to her sister are a faithful transcript of life in the Old World. She bore an important part in the nation's early history, while sustaining its social fame. Her republican simplicity of manners was compensated by habitual elevation of demeanor, which commanded the highest consideration; and her close observation, clear judgment and discrimination, enabled her to exercise an influence widely acknowledged. When Adams entered on the Vice Presidency, and when afterwards he became Chief Magistrate of the nation, the worthy partner of his honors added grace and dignity to her elevated position. One chief charm of her conversation was the perfect sincerity apparent in all she said. By her cheerful, affectionate sympathy and buoyant spirit, her sensibility, tact, and practical knowledge of life, she sustained her husband in the severest cares and labors of his station, disarmed the demon of party spirit, calmed the agitation of discord, plucked out the root of bitterness, and healed the wounds of political animosity. She was, indeed, fitted for eminent usefulness as the companion of one great statesman and the guide of another. After the President's retirement to private life, she continued to feel a deep interest in public affairs, as is shown in her correspondence with Mercy Warren. Mrs. Adams's exemplary deportment, during the twelve years of her husband's connection with the American government, and her well-known devotion to him, with her superior mental endowments, gave her a ruling social influence founded on universal esteem. She always maintained a liberal hospitality, was faithful and warm in her friendships, kind and benevolent to the poor, and a bright example of womanly and Christian virtues. During her later years, she lived in rural seclusion at Quincy, and died at the age of seventy-four, October, 1818.

Mrs. Adams thus described her residence on Richmond Hill: "The avenue to which is interspersed with forest trees, under which a shrubbery rather too luxuriant and wild has taken shelter. In front of the house the noble Hudson rolls his majestic waves, bearing on his bosom innumerable small vessels. Beyond the Hudson rises to view the fertile country of the Jerseys, covered with a golden harvest, and pouring forth plenty like the cornucopia of Ceres. On the right hand an extensive plain presents us with a view of fields covered with verdure and pastures full of cattle. On the left the city opens upon us, intercepted only by clumps of trees and some rising ground. In the background is a large flower-garden, inclosed with a hedge, and some very handsome trees; on one side is a grove of pines and oaks fit for contemplation."

The mother of Mrs. Adams was the daughter of Hon. John Quincy, of Braintree. She possessed great dignity, combined with benignity of character. She had three celebrated daughters. The eldest, Mary, in 1762 married Richard Cranch, Judge of the Court of Common Pleas in Massachusetts; the youngest, Elizabeth, married Rev. John Shaw, of Haverhill, and after his death Rev. Stephen Peabody, of Atkinson. These ladies were handsome, with polished and courtly manners, and superior powers of conversation; for they had high culture and were well read in the English classics. Mrs. Shaw's house, at Haverhill, was the centre of an elegant circle of society for many years after the Revolution; the resort of the most cultivated residents of Boston and the vicinity; and light and joy were liberally dispensed by the accomplished mistress. As Mrs. Peabody she corresponded with Mrs. Warren, and with her brother-in-law,

John Adams. Her manuscript journal describes a dinner on bacon and eggs on the road to Plymouth, a quilting by the daughters of the house, and her reading to them from her book, "Zulima the Coquette," " Virtue and Constancy Rewarded," &c.

Abigail, the daughter of John and Abigail Adams, was married in London, 1786, to Colonel William S. Smith, then Secretary of Legation. She returned to the United States in May, 1788.

She describes the Marchioness de Brehan, sister of the French Minister, as "the oddest figure eyes ever beheld; she speaks English a little, and is very much out of health." Madame de Brehan wrote with spirit, and was an accomplished artist. She painted portraits of Washington, one of which he presented to Mrs. Bingham. Jefferson wrote to her, on her quitting Paris for the United States: "The imitations of European manners which you will find in our towns, will, I fear, be little pleasing. I beseech you to practice still your own, which will furnish them a model of what is perfect. Should you be singular, it will be by excellence."

Mrs. Smith wrote of Mrs. Clinton: "Mrs. Clinton is not a showy, but a kind, friendly woman. She has five daughters and one son; the second daughter is as smart and sensible a girl as ever I knew; a zealous politician and a high anti-Federalist.

"You would not be much pleased with society here. It is quite enough dissipated. Public dinners, public days, and private parties, may take up a person's whole attention. The President of Congress gives a dinner one or two or more days every week, to twenty persons—gentlemen and ladies. Mr. Jay, I believe, gives a dinner almost every week."

The dignity of office was then maintained by forms designed to inspire respect, and special regard was paid to the wives of men who had deserved much of their country. The widows of Greene and Montgomery were always handed to and from their carriages by the President himself, the secretaries and gentlemen of his household performing those offices for the other ladies.

These New York gayeties, in 1788, had been increased by numerous weddings in fashionable circles. Miss Montgomery, in her "Reminiscences," relates an anecdote of a wedding at the Rutgers' Mansion. Her grandfather, who was to sail at daylight, was persuaded to stay to the wedding-supper. He took his departure after eleven o'clock, a servant being ordered to conduct him through a huckleberry swamp on the way to his lodgings. He declined the service, but the moon going down, he lost his way, and wandered all night among thorns and briers, emerging at dawn with his clothes nearly torn off. This swamp was long ago the centre of the city.

The correspondence of John Quincy Adams with his sister gives an amusing picture of the times. Before her marriage he visited the family of Colonel Smith, at Jamaica, Long Island. There were six daughters. "Sally is tall, with a fine shape, blue eyes, and much vivacity." "She has," he says, "the ease and elegance of the French ladies, without their loquacity." This lady married his brother, Charles Adams, a few years later. He mentions also a "celebrated beauty, Miss Ogden, who resembles the handsome Mrs. Bingham, of Philadelphia; also a Miss Von Berckel, who complains of not understanding our language." "Lady Wheate is one of the most celebrated belles of the city. About two years ago she married Sir Jacob Wheate, a British officer between sixty and seventy—she not yet sixteen. Sir Jacob, before he had been married a week, went to the West Indies, and there died, leaving her a handsome fortune. It is said she is soon to wed Sir Francis Cochrane, son of Lord Dundonald, a Scotch nobleman.

"Miss Sally Smith was with Lady Wheate, having spent nearly a week with her. I am vastly pleased with this lady; the contrast between her manners and those of Lady Wheate is greatly in her favor, and very striking."

He wrote of Lady Duer, whom Adams met at a dinner at General Knox's:—

"Lady Duer is not young or handsome; but she would not have been thought old by a man over eighteen, and she had been, if she was not then, one of the sweetest looking women in the city.

"Miss Sears is very pretty, and has the reputation of being witty and sharp. I am sure she does not look *méchante.*" After a passage of more than twelve weeks from Amsterdam, the daughter of Mr. Von Berckel arrived in Philadelphia, and the Minister went out to meet her. Adams had seen her in Holland. "The young ladies here are very impatient to see her, and I dare say, when she comes, reflections will not be spared on either side. The beauties of New York will triumph; but, I hope, with moderation." "Oh, that our young ladies were as distinguished for the beauties of their minds as they are for the charms of their persons! But alas! too many of them are like a beautiful apple that is insipid to the taste!"

M. de Marbois, French Chargé d'Affaires in 1784, had married Miss Moore. General Washington wrote to congratulate him on his union, alluding to "the accomplishments of the lady, and her connections." Their daughter, born in New York, married the Duke de Plaisance, the son of Le Brun, one of Napoleon's colleagues in the Consulate. Madame de Marbois was a spruce, pretty little woman; she spoke French habitually, and had none of the rigid notions of the Quakers, among whom she was born. John Quincy Adams writes, in 1785, after a visit to her house on Long Island: "Madame de Marbois may be called a pretty little woman; she was a Quaker, but appears not to retain any of the rigid tenets of that sect."

The wife of John Quincy Adams was Louisa Catherine, daughter of Joshua Johnson, of Maryland. She was born in London, in 1775, and spent her early years in England and France. Her father's house in London was the general resort for Americans. She was married to Mr. Adams in July, 1797. He had been resident Minister at the Hague. After the elder Adams became President his son was Minister to Berlin, where his young wife performed her part in the higher circles of social and political life. She proved quite competent to sustain honors with dignity, and her good humor and conciliating manners made friends. In 1801 she returned with Adams to the United States; and, as he was Senator, their winters were passed in Washington, while their summers were spent in Boston. In 1808, Adams was appointed by Madison the first accredited Minister to Russia; and his wife was the first lady presented at that Court as the representative of American female manners and character. The impression she made was eminently favorable. While Adams was at Ghent, to negotiate a mediation between England and the United States, Mrs. Adams passed the winter alone at St. Petersburgh. In the spring she set off to travel by land to Paris, to join her husband. The dangers of the journey were great, in a small carriage, with only her son, eight years of age, besides menials. The carriage got buried in a snow-drift as night was coming on, and the servants were compelled to rouse the peasants to dig it out. They heard tales of robbery and murder at every stopping-place, and were cautioned as to the character of the servants. A Polish cap worn by one nearly caused a riot. The hostility shown was so alarming, Mrs. Adams was obliged to dismiss her attendants and hire others to go on. Then they became entangled with the wild soldiery, elated by news from Napoleon, on their way to Paris to prepare, under his inspection, for the field óf Waterloo. These troops requiring demonstrations of political faith, Mrs. Adams appealed to the commander of the detachment, and by his advice fell back till the last of the soldiers had passed. She then diverged into another road, and by a circuit avoided another meeting. Her calmness and presence of mind were of essential service in these trying situations. She arrived safely in Paris, March, 1815, very shortly before the memorable arrival of Napoleon and flight of the Bourbons. She had opportunities for seeing every thing at the beginning of the celebrated "hundred days."

When Mr. Adams was appointed Minister to England, she quitted France for their sweet and modest country-seat near London. After his eight years' absence, Adams returned to America in 1817, and she resumed the habits of republican life, unspoiled by court customs, and unawed by civil or military supremacy. The society in Washington was then on a most agreeable footing; it was "the era of good feelings," and the relenting of national animosity, and the ascendency of polished urbanity. Mrs. Adams presided with ease and graceful courtesy for eight years in the house of the Secretary of State. Her sprightly conversation and capacity for enjoyment produced a benign and enlivening effect in the circles where she moved. When the contest for the election of President began, she retired, in a measure, from society, and continued in seclusion till called to do the honors of the Executive mansion as the wife of the President. Her manners were elegant, though her tastes were extremely simple. The failure of her health made it necessary for her again to seek retirement, and she was no longer seen in fashionable circles, though she still presided at public receptions. When Mr. Adams's term expired, her retirement became complete; the remainder of life being devoted to the cares of her family and the practice of homely domestic virtues.

IV.

The Quincy family can be traced back for more than six centuries. Supposed to be of Norwegian origin, it received its territorial appellation from the village of Quincy, in Normandy. Robert de Quincy came from Normandy to England with William the Conqueror. As a feudal baron, after the conquest he held an eminent position. His grandson was created Earl of Winchester by King John, about 1207. He attended the call of the convention between King John and the barons, which resulted in extorting from the monarch the grant of Magna Charta; thus helping to establish the earliest basis of English constitutional liberty. The title of Winchester soon became extinct for lack of male heirs, but the daughters married into illustrious families in England. Edmund Quincy came to Boston with the Reverend John Cotton, in 1633. His name and his wife's are on the record of the first church established— the "Old South." His son Edmund inherited and settled upon his father's estate at Mount Wollaston, afterwards Braintree, now Quincy. His grandson, John Quincy, was one of the most distinguished public characters of the period, serving, in succession, as a representative of Braintree and a member of the Executive

Council, forty years. His patrimonial estate passed to the possession of his great grandson, John Quincy Adams. Edmund, the uncle of John, was also eminent in public life, and became judge of the Supreme Court in 1718. He was appointed by the General Court of Massachusetts their agent at the court of Great Britain in the controversy between the provinces of Massachusetts Bay and New Hampshire, and died while employed on the mission, in 1738. The General Court, in acknowledgment, made a donation of a thousand acres of land in the town of Lenox, Berkshire County, to his heirs. His eldest son, Edmund, who lived on the ancestral estate at Braintree, was the father of Dr. Jacob Quincy, and Dorothy, the subject of this sketch. Some of the family removed to Portland, Maine. Dr. Quincy's eldest daughter married Hon. Asa Clapp, and her daughter was the wife of Hon. Levi Woodbury, Secretary of the Treasury of the United States. The celebrated philosopher and rhapsodist, Thomas de Quincy, was of this family, and boasted, even in the ears of George III., of his ancient and honorable blood.

Sullivan pronounced John Hancock "one of the greatest men of his age." The honor which encircled his name received added lustre from his wife. She was a leader of taste and fashion in the best circles of society. The daughter of Judge Edmund Quincy, she was born in 1748. In 1775, Dorothy Quincy was married to John Hancock, then Governor of Massachusetts, afterwards President of the first Congress. The wedding took place at the country-seat of Thaddeus Burr, in Fairfield, Connecticut.* Mr. Hancock had gone thither for safety, and was in concealment with Samuel Adams, a price having been put upon their heads by the King of England. It was not deemed safe for Mr. Hancock to return, that the marriage might take place in Boston. Their meals were privately conveyed to them, and they were kept in strict seclusion. After a time, they were permitted to sit down to the dinner table with the members of the family, in expectation of a comfortable repast. Before they had realized the anticipated pleasure, a farmer from the neighborhood came in, greatly excited, and requested the Rev. Mr. Clark (at whose house the fugitives were staying) to lend him his horse and chaise to go after his wife, as "the British were coming." This news in a moment scattered the whole party. Adams and Hancock were hurried away to their hiding-place; and Mrs. Hancock used to say it was always a matter of wonder to her what became of that dinner, for none who sat down to it ever tasted it. The alarm was occasioned by a false report; but there was a time when the leaden balls of the enemy reached the house that sheltered them. A fortnight after the birth of her first child, Mrs. Hancock was conveyed on a bed, with her baby, to her carriage, to travel from Boston in

---

* I am indebted for the reminiscences in this sketch to Miss Martha A. Quincy, of Boston, the grand-daughter of Mrs. Hancock's youngest brother, Dr. Jacob Quincy, and the companion of Mrs. Hancock during the last ten years of her life. Her reminiscences were a contribution to Mrs. Lincoln Phelps' volume entitled "Our Country."

the winter to Philadelphia, in company with her husband, then chosen President of the first Congress. She often spoke of his reluctance, from natural modesty, to accept the office. While he hesitated, one of the members clasped him around the waist, lifted him from his feet, and placed him in the chair of state.

While Mrs. Hancock was in Philadelphia, her husband came to her room one day, saying he had a secret to communicate, which must be faithfully kept. It was that he had that day received a letter from home, stating that it was thought it would be necessary to burn the city of Boston, to prevent its falling into the hands of the enemy; and, as his wealth was centered there, he was asked if he would be willing to sacrifice all his property for such an object. He immediately replied that he gave his full consent to commit his property to the flames, if the good of the people demanded it. This, Mrs. Hancock answered, was rather a disagreeable secret. Her husband acknowledged that it would reduce them to beggary. But his purpose was fixed—he wished his possessions to be devoted to the best interests of his country.

His wife was at this time just preparing to attend a Quaker meeting for the first time. This terrible announcement, or the thought of what might be the result, did not overcome her even so much as to deter her from the proposed attendance upon the meeting. She often told her friends how the room was crowded when she arrived at the place, and how the painful secret weighed upon her as she sat there three hours, waiting to hear what she supposed would be a speech, from which she hoped mental relief for the time. But no relief came; for no utterance broke the silence before the time for parting. On further consideration, the inhabitants of Boston deemed it unnecessary to burn the town.

At the time when the "continental money" was nearly worthless, Governor Hancock's sympathies led him to continue taking the bad paper of those who presented it, until his friends saw that he would soon dispose, in this way, of his whole fortune. They told his wife that the "money-trunk" must be removed from the house, or she and her child would be penniless. It was removed without consulting the Governor. At that time he resided in the then magnificent mansion built by Thomas Hancock, and left at his death to his adopted nephew, John Hancock. It was situated on Beacon Street, opposite Boston Common, and was the finest residence in the town. In 1863, this house, built in 1737, was taken down. It was held to the last year by the family.

Hancock lived in luxurious style. He was noted for his hospitality, and kept an open house and a sumptuous table for his friends. La Fayette, on his first visit to this country, accepted an invitation to spend some time in his house. The Marquis General was much attached to Mrs. Hancock, and, on his second visit to America, she was the first lady on whom he called. Many spoke of the interesting interview between "the once youthful chevalier and the splendid belle." It is probable that few if any, in his day, surpassed Mr. Hancock in his style of living. His equipage 'was a carriage and four horses; his coach being fitted up in good taste, with brilliant plate-glass and handsome ornaments, suitable both for traveling and parade. Thirteen servants and a goodly number of horses were attached to the service of the Governor's family. His wife had a pretty pony, with a light, drab-colored saddle-cloth, highly embroidered. Hancock gave every Saturday what was called a "salt-fish dinner;" an elaborate affair, duly prized in those days. Prince Edward of England, while traveling in this country, called upon Mrs. Hancock, and made himself very agreeable, telling her that he was said to resemble some noted personage, and asking her what she thought of his "red whiskers." His friends regretted that she did not, as it was Saturday, give him an invitation to her "fish dinner." All classes were entertained; the veterans, the clergy, the gay, the gifted, and those who had no superior claims.

Brissot wrote of John Hancock: "He shows himself the equal and the friend of all. I supped at his house with a hatter, who appeared to be in great familiarity with him. Mr. Hancock is amiable and polite when he wishes to be; but they say he does not always choose it. He has a marvelous gout, which dispenses him from all attentions, and forbids the access to his house." Sullivan, in his "Letters on Public Characters," expresses his opinion that so much gout was caused by the general

MRS. JOHN HANCOCK.

practice of drinking punch in the mornings as well as evenings. The tankard was prepared early, and visitors, during the day, were invited to partake of it. The usual dinner-hour was one or two; and the suppers were abundant in good things. The evening amusements were cards and dancing; concerts were attended, theatres were prohibited. We may gather some idea of the manner of living by the fact that, when going to visit a niece of his wife in Portsmouth, New Hampshire, Hancock traveled with a coach and four, two outriders, a postillion, coachman, and footman,—the servants in livery,—besides seven horses. At the end of the first day's journey they reached Marblehead; arriving at Portsmouth, sixty miles from home, on the second day. At another time they were a fortnight traveling from Boston to Philadelphia, in similar style. Once, when journeying on this route, Mrs. Hancock found, after stopping over night at a certain place, that her horses were so jaded they could not proceed the next day. On inquiry, it was ascertained that they had been taken in the night and used on a pleasure excursion in honor of St. Patrick's day.

Governor Hancock was a great sufferer from the malady aforementioned. At one time, when he returned from public business, he was so ill that he was taken from his carriage in the arms of his servants, and laid upon the sofa till the tailor who had made the new suit of clothes he had on could cut them off, so that he could be carried with less pain to his sleeping-room. At another time, when suffering in a similar way, he went as usual to the State House, which was then at the head of State Street, to attend to his appointed duties. Coming out, he was surrounded by an admiring multitude, who, after he had entered the carriage in which his wife had come to meet him, began to remove the four horses, with the design of drawing him themselves to his home in Beacon Street. Four hundred men were already forming in procession with this intent. The Governor was overcome by this demonstration of public respect, and being so ill he could not speak for himself, he requested his wife, who was noted for her personal beauty, to address the crowd from the carriage window, and say to them that the Governor was overwhelmed by the honor they desired to confer upon him; that he gratefully acknowledged the kindness of feeling that prompted the act; but he must beg them, on account of his present weak state, to permit him to be taken by his horses as rapidly as possible to his home. His request was granted.

Mrs. Hancock often related the circumstances of his severe attack of gout at the time when General Washington was expected to make his first appearance in Boston. The General had accepted an invitation to dine that day with the Governor. It had been represented to Washington that etiquette demanded that the Governor should be at the entrance of the town to welcome him. This was expected; and when the General had been delayed two hours—waiting, in a cold wind, with delicate health—Hancock not appearing, he asked if there were no other entrance to the town by which he could speedily reach his lodgings. Being answered in the negative, he ordered the cavalcade to move on at a quick pace, proceeding directly to the place of his abode. Meanwhile, Governor Hancock was patiently keeping back his dinner, in continual expectation of the arrival of the distinguished guest. Soon the report reached the house, and was whispered about, explaining why he had not come.

The next day the Governor ordered his carriage, and, with limbs wrapped in red baize, he was placed in it, in order to call on the General. When he arrived at Washington's lodgings, he was carried in the arms of his servants to the head of the stairs, and thence he crawled on his hand and knees into the presence of the Commander-in-Chief. The General, seeing him in this position, was moved to tears. All difficulties being soon removed, kindness and cordiality were reciprocated.

Mrs. Washington and Mrs. Hancock were friends. The first would say to the latter: "There is a great difference in our situations. Your husband is in the cabinet, but mine is on the battle-field." Persons of eminent position in other countries, as well as his own, were often favored guests in Governor Hancock's family. While the French fleet was in Boston Harbor, Count d'Estaing and some other persons of rank, with their life-guards, visited the Governor. Hancock sent a note to the Admiral of the fleet, inviting him to breakfast, with thirty of his officers. The Admiral accepted the invitation, but sent a request to the Governor to permit him the pleasure of bringing all his officers, including the midshipmen. This request was granted, but not without some solicitude as to the possibility of accommodating three hundred officers and providing for their entertainment. In those days, there were not the facilities of confectioners, and other resources of the present time. It was summer, and carts and wagons were pressed into the service to bring from the surrounding country the various fruits of the season.

It was found that milk sufficient for the demand could not be obtained, even from the whole vicinity of Boston. Boston common was at that time used as a place of pasturage for cows; and Mrs. Hancock, in her dilemma, requested the life-guards and the servants of her family to take pitchers, mugs, and bowls, and to milk all the cows on the common. If any persons interfered, they were to be sent to her for explanation. This novel proceeding made a laughable exhibition to the public, but it was a success, and offended no one.

Eleven o'clock was the hour for breakfast. At the appointed time, the officers were seen entering the farthest end of the Common, in front of the Governor's house. Mrs. Hancock often in after life described that scene; and, though naturally very calm and tranquil in manner, when speaking of that day she always showed great animation, seeming to feel again the fire and excitement of the scene. She said the sun shone brightly on the gold lace that elaborately adorned the French officers; and, in their march to the house, the brilliant display exceeded any thing she ever saw before or afterwards of military parade. The Admiral soon after returned the compliment by giving a grand dinner on board his ship to the Governor and his wife. Mrs. Hancock occupied the seat of honor, and at her right hand was a large rosette of ribbon, attached by a strong rope to something under the table. This mysterious apparatus caused her no small curiosity. At the moment when the toasts were to be given, the Admiral's aid, who sat next her, requested that she would draw up the ribbons. She obeyed, and in doing so she fired the signal gun, which in an instant was answered by every vessel in the fleet. This was a distinguished honor paid her, in return for the attention shown to the Admiral and his officers.

At the annual commencement of Harvard College, it was the custom for the Governor and the "Boston Cadets" (his escort) to be present at the college exercises. It was Mr. Hancock's pleasure that this military company should take their breakfast with him that morning; and as the services at Cambridge commenced at nine, a very early breakfast had to be given, in order that all might be in readiness for their place and duties at the appointed time. The Governor would have this plan carried out for several years, in spite of the great inconvenience it caused to his wife. She was compelled, in order to be present at the breakfast table, to summon her hairdresser at four o'clock in the morning; and the day was always one of extreme fatigue to her.

Many of the colored people were in the habit of marching in procession annually, on a certain day, before the Governor's house. When they stopped in front of it, he would address them from the balcony. In the summer he was in the habit of riding through the country. If he came to an unfinished church, he would inquire why it was left so, and, if money was needed to complete the building, he would encourage the people to proceed, saying: "I will pay for the glazing if you will go to work and have it finished." This he did many times.

He kept the yearly fast in spring on *fish*, but for his dinner had always the first salmon of the season, for which he paid a guinea. He had a fine dinner-set of pewter ordered from England. It was the duty of his household to see that this pewter was kept at the highest point of brightness, and used every day, to the exclusion of the valuable India china set, also owned by him. He preferred to use the pewter, because, as he said, the contents of the plates and dishes were not so apt to slide off; also, that the use of them caused no clatter in contact with knives and forks. He had a large quantity of silver, much of it bearing the tower-stamp of England. He had four dozen silver forks matched with the same number of silver spoons; also several silver tankards of different sizes. One, holding a gallon or more, he devoted exclusively to hot punch; this he called "Solomon Townsend," in honor of a friend. He had also a large silver porter-cup, holding two quarts or more, with two massive handles; intended, probably, to be passed from guest to guest, that each might quaff in turn from the same cup. Much of the silver not only bore the "towerstamp," but had also his own coat of arms engraved on it. I remember a silver wash-bowl, silver salvers, asparagus-tongs, four heavy silver chafing-dishes, four silver butter-boats, with various other articles; also six heavy silver candlesticks, and a silver snuffers and snuff-dish. The last is in my possession. It has the Hancock arms engraved on it.

The Governor had a passion for the portraits of his distinguished guests, which were painted to his order for his hall of paintings. Hancock ordered from England a whole piece of crimson silk velvet of richest quality, from which he had a coat and vest made. His wife refused a dress off the piece, as too heavy for her light figure. The Governor wore diamonds on great occasions. A silver dollar—engraved on one side with the united arms of Mrs. Hancock's parents, on the other with her maiden name and the date 1764—the coin bearing the date 1689, and the stamp of James II.,—is a prized relic in the family, with a tortoise-shell whiskercomb, imported from England, belonging to Hancock's dressing-case. Mrs. Hancock's wedding-fan was from Paris, and made of white kid, painted with appropriate designs. "Fan-mounting" was then done in this country by ladies of respectable families. One who was Mrs. Hancock's fan-mounter, and others who were her dressmaker and hairdresser, have their descendants among the leaders of Boston society at the present day. The city was searched at that time in vain for gold or silver bells with coral for "the baby," though a rattle of the description was found. The christening suit, from England, was of embroidered India muslin, with stomacher and trimming of thread lace. Mrs. Hancock sent at the same time for a hat of lavender-colored silk trimmed with flowers, and a mantilla of muslin lined with lavender silk. She gave six dollars a yard for a piece of muslin, in India, before it was cut from the loom. One of the breakfast-cloths used at the great breakfast given to the French fleet, was lately exhibited at a party given by Mrs. Cutts, in Boston, a great-niece of Mrs. Hancock, who presented her with the cloth. It had been used once since the breakfast; at a dinner given by Mrs. Cutts to Daniel Webster. Another relic was a silver cake-basket, given by Mrs. Hancock, with the request that it should make its appearance at the wedding receptions of her nieces and nephews. Six heavy silver candlesticks, a large salver, chopping-dish, and other articles of plate, bearing the Hancock coat of arms, belong to her great-nephews, Clapp, in Portland, Maine.

Hancock had an epicurean taste, and all the delicacies of the season might be found upon his table. After his death his wife kept up his custom in these matters. Once she said: "The Governor's hobby was his dinner-table, and I suppose it is mine." From early morning till eleven at night, her house was open for the reception of friends and strangers, as it had been while her husband was living. She was for years one of the "wonders of the age;" and, as the widow of Governor Hancock, she was visited till the close of her life by distinguished persons from foreign countries as well as her own. So long had she studied the tastes of her husband, that she excelled in the preparation of rich and delicate viands. With recollections of Hancock House are associated venison dinners and mince pies, which vanished when that house was taken down, and cannot now be had in the same state of perfection as in those palmy days.

Governor Hancock was the son of a clergyman, but adopted by his uncle, who left him a very large fortune for the period in which he lived. At twenty-one he went to England, was presented at Court, and kissed the hand of King George. He was a man of warm sympathies as well as strong will. His manners were gracious, in the old style of dignified complaisance. One morning, going to town in his phæton, at an early hour, he saw a poor woman, with a large bundle, trudging along the road. He ordered the horses stopped, and asked where the woman was going. Being informed she was a washerwoman, on her way to the town, he had her and her bundle placed in the open carriage, and took her to her stopping-place. Such acts made him king in the hearts of the people. His temper, indeed, was sometimes so violent as to lead some to question his benevolence; for when suffering from a fit of the gout he would almost outrage common sense. An instance illustrative may also serve to show what strict obedience he required of his servants. Shut up in his sick-room, he could not always be sure that his orders were carried out to his full requisition. He had repeatedly forbidden the use of the china table-service, directing that the pewter should at all times be used. The unreasonableness of this direction consisted in the difficulty of keeping a pewter set in constant fitness for use. On one occasion he called Cato, his favorite colored servant, to his room, and asked if the china set had been used that day. Being answered in the affirmative, he said: "I thought so. Now go down stairs and bring up a pile of china dishes." The servant soon returned with the dishes in his hands. The Governor said, "Now, open the window and throw them out." Cato did as he was told; but took good care to open a window over a bank of soft turf, and to give them a gentle slide as he let them drop, so that none of them were injured. The Governor said, "I don't hear them *break!* Go down, Cato, and bring them up again." The dishes were a second time produced. "Now," said he, "open the window over the paved coachyard, and throw them out." This order being obeyed, the dishes were destroyed.

Sullivan describes Hancock, in June, 1782, as wearing "a red velvet cap, within which was one of fine linen; the last turned up two or three inches over the lower edge of the velvet. He wore a blue damask gown lined with velvet, a white stock, a white satin embroidered waistcoat, black satin small-clothes, white silk stockings, and red morocco slippers." At this visit the Governor took from the cooler on the hearth a full tankard of punch, drank first himself, then offered it to those present.

Governor Hancock was one day driving out with his wife, when they met Samuel Adams walking with the sheriff beside him. Hancock asked, "What is the meaning of this?" Adams replied, "I am going to jail, as I cannot satisfy the sheriff's demands." The Governor said he would see to that and settle the demand, and bade the sheriff leave his prisoner. Many times was his purse opened for Mr. Adams's benefit, under similar circumstances.

The Governor had a very large marquée made, which he wished to see displayed for once at least on the ground occupied by the present State House. His wish, however, could not be gratified. The time for its erection was to be on the day of the annual general review of all the military companies, in October. He requested his wife to have a collation provided on that occasion for all the officers. He was at that time prostrated with his last fatal attack of the gout. He did not appear to comprehend that he was so near the close of his earthly career. Mrs. Hancock was informed by the physician that his death might occur at any hour. She could not, therefore, make the necessary preparations for such a public display. At her refusal to comply with this long-cherished wish of his heart, her husband was much displeased, and she often said she could not feel satisfied that she had his full forgiveness for not carrying out his plans on that occasion. He became increasingly ill, and at ten o'clock on that very day it was announced that he was dying. The companies were ordered to leave the Common; and hushed were the drum and fife, with all their military inspiration, while the Commander-in-Chief of the State was passing into the immediate presence of the Great Judge of all men. This was in October, 1793.

Governor Hancock left orders that he should be buried without public honors, and forbade the firing of a gun over his grave. The State government chose to have the management of the whole affair, and told Mrs. Hancock that the funeral and its expenses belonged to the State. She submitted reluctantly to the arrangement; but she finally had to pay the bill of the obsequies, which amounted to eighteen hundred dollars. A will, unsigned, was found after his death, in which he gave the bulk of his property to the State.

Mrs. Hancock was acknowledged to possess superb beauty. She was also thoroughly high-bred, had a courtly manner, and a high-toned spirit that showed itself in her conversation. She was always dressed with care, and a dignified propriety, rather than a wish to display, was evident. She was heard to say she would never forgive a young girl who did not dress to please, nor one who seemed pleased with her dress. She died

February, 1830, in her eighty-second year, going but little into society for some time previous.

Besides the Quincy family, the most distinguished in Boston society were those of Otis, Winthrop, Apthorp, Amory, Emery, &c. The Bradfords—of whom Alden Bradford was for many years Secretary of State in Massachusetts—belonged to the same class.

A lady noted in society in New England was Catherine, the daughter of John Littlefield, born on Block Island, in 1753. Her girlhood was chiefly passed in the house of Governor Greene, a few miles from Providence, commanding a view of Narraganset Bay. Mrs. Greene was her aunt. Catherine was a belle—gay, joyous, and full of frolicsome humor; her form was light and graceful, and she possessed extraordinary quickness of apprehension and activity of mind. Her conversation was enriched with knowledge gained, almost by intuition, from every source. She had a lively imagination and great fluency of speech, with a ready tact that gave her irresistible fascination. This bright, volatile, coquettish young creature took captive the heart of her kinsman, Nathaniel Greene, and lost her own in return. They were married in 1774. Little did the bride dream that her husband's broad-brimmed hat covered brows which would one day be wreathed with living laurels won by genius and patriotism. When General Greene took his part in the great drama of the Revolution, his wife gave him aid and encouragement. The papers of the day notice her presence at head-quarters; but her home was at Coventry, a Rhode Island village,—a princely mansion, on the banks of one of those small streams that form so beautiful a feature in Rhode Island scenery. She gave up this house for hospital uses when the army before Boston was inoculated for the small-pox.

General Greene's letters show how much he prized the society of his wife. While in winter quarters with him, she was very intimate with Mrs. Washington. Following her husband south, they established their home at Mulberry Grove, a plantation presented to Greene by the State of Georgia. Her lively letters give a picture of the times. After the General's death she removed to Cumberland Island, where she lived much in society, exercising extensive hospitality. It was Mrs. Greene who introduced to the world the invention of the cotton-gin, by her patronage of Eli Whitney.

The incident of her quitting her own house when Aaron Burr claimed her hospitality, after his duel with Hamilton, leaving the house for his use, and only returning to it after his departure, illustrates her generous and impulsive character. In her later years she retained her singular power of fascination, and would hold a company in breathless attention with her winning tones and brilliant sketches of character or tales of adventure. She had, in truth, a faculty of charming all who approached her.

Mary Wooster was the widow of General David

Wooster, killed in Connecticut in the war of the Revolution. She was the daughter of Dr. Clapp, at one time President of Yale College, and was married at sixteen years of age. Gifted with beauty and noble intellectual powers, well educated, and with a mind stored with a great variety of knowledge, she was very prominent in society and much sought by admiring friends. In conversation she was uncommonly brilliant. Her piety was exemplary, from youth to advanced years; and when she was bereaved of husband and children, and lost her fortune, she found in religion a consolation trials could not impair.

Sarah Thompson—the Countess Rumford—who died at Concord, New Hampshire, in December, 1852, is mentioned by Curwen as a woman who exercised much social influence. She was the grand-daughter of Rev. Timothy Walker, the first clergyman in Concord, and the only daughter of Benjamin Thompson—born in 1774. Her father left the United States suspected of loyalism, and entered into the employ of the Elector of Bavaria at Munich, where he received the title of Count of the Holy Roman Empire, with a pension for life of nearly two thousand dollars a year. To this title he added Rumford, the name of his residence at Concord. His daughter joined him in London, in 1796, and shared his home and fortune till his death in France, in 1814. She was in Munich when it was about to be bombarded by the Austrians; but her father, being Commander-in-Chief of the Bavarian forces, succeeded in preventing it.

He was held in much honor among the savans of Europe; and the daughter was received with caressing attentions among the most select circles in Paris. When left an orphan, she inherited the title as well as the estates of her father. She went to England and settled on an estate at Brompton belonging to her, receiving the most marked attentions from many eminent persons among the literati. In 1845 she returned to her native State. She never married, but passed the remainder of her life in a quiet circle of society, aloof from the stir of city life, with an adopted daughter for her companion. The grounds around her residence were tastefully ornamented with trees and shrubbery. She had considerable property, saved from her father's estates, with a pension of nearly a thousand dollars a year from the Bavarian government for the services rendered by her father. This she bestowed chiefly in charity, and, dying at seventy-eight, left fifteen thousand dollars for an asylum at Concord for widows and female orphans.

V.

The society of Philadelphia, about the middle of the last century, appears to have been divided into two classes of families; the first, some of whom had come with Penn, adhering to the Quaker tenets, or bound by hereditary custom, if not religious faith, to deny the world and abjure the pageants of life. Such were the Morrises, the Logans, the Shippens, the Lloyds, the Pembertons, the Rivingtons, and many other families of antiquity in their sect. At a later period came in another class, chiefly from England; they had cultivated the liberal accomplishments; among them were men of extensive learning, both merchants and professional men; and they were noted for a high degree of social refinement. Such were the Hamiltons, the Ashetons, the Lawrences, the Chews, the Conynghams, the Allens, the Inglises, the Bonds, the Plumsteds, and others. This class was strengthened, as wealth and civilization spread, by the return of proprietary descendants to the Established Church. Then was added the element of patriotism, in Revolutionary times, forming another distinct class, of such as Bradford, Biddle, Butler, Reed, Boudinot, Mifflin, McKean, &c., comprising many of the preceding, and drawing to themselves, by their own actions, public consideration and respect.

The family of Willing was one of the most prominent among the English families of the second class above mentioned. Their social connections were extensive and powerful; and on this account, with the weight of personal influence and high character, they enjoyed an enviable distinction. The name originated in Germany, but obtained no eminence till it was borne by residents of Philadelphia. The first known of the family was Joseph Willing, of Gloucestershire, who married Ava Lowre, an heiress. His son Thomas married Anne Harrison, and brought his son Charles to America in 1728. Charles entered into commercial life, and became the founder of the family in this country. His house stood in Third Street, its grounds occupying an entire square, and shaded by primeval oaks. His wife was Anne Shippen, grand-daughter of Edward Shippen, the first mayor of Philadelphia, and their son was Thomas Willing, born in 1731.

The women of Philadelphia, in the latter part of the century, were distinguished for their attractions. The Duke de Lauzun speaks enthusiastically of their grace, beauty, and intelligence; and the gay Marquis de Chastellux is warm in his admiration of the ladies who gave life to society after the close of the war. Philadelphia became the centre of fashionable gayety, as she had been the heart of the nation; and it was found that the ravages of war had swept away none of the elegance and refinement, or the social spirit, by which her coteries had been distinguished. One lady, pre-eminent by universal acknowledgment, who exercised indisputable sway over the manners and pleasures of the metropolis, and reigned a queen to whom all vowed allegiance, was Anne, the daughter of Thomas Willing. She received in the home of her father, who was a man of liberal education, the best instruction which could be given, and grew up a maiden of wonderful loveliness. She passed much time in the family of Washington. At the age of sixteen, on the 26th of October, 1780, she was married to William Bingham, by Rev. William White, afterwards the first Episcopal bishop in Pennsylvania. Bingham was United States senator from Pennsylvania, and owned large estates. He was congratulated from high quarters for having won so fair a bride; John Jay wrote from Spain to felicitate him on his nuptials "with one of the most lovely of her sex." A few years after the marriage, Mr. and Mrs. Bingham went abroad, and spent some time in France. Mrs. Bingham was presented at the Court of Louis XVI., and attracted much attention among the nobles and aristocracy. Miss Adams wrote, after mentioning a dinner at which she met the Binghams, in October, 1784, "Mrs. Bingham gains my love and admiration more and more every time I see her. She is possessed of greater ease and politeness in her behavior than any person I have met." At a dinner at La Fayette's, some months later, she again wrote: "Mrs. Bingham was, as ever, engaging;

her dress was of black velvet, with pink satin sleeves and stomacher, a pink satin petticoat, and over it a skirt of white crape spotted all over with gray fur; the sides of the gown open in front, and the bottom of the coat trimmed with paste. It was superb; and the gracefulness of the person made it appear to peculiar advantage." Mrs. Adams wrote: "Mrs. Bingham has been twice to see me. I think she is more amiable and beautiful than ever."

After spending some time at the Hague, Mrs. Bingham accompanied her husband to England, where "her elegance and beauty attracted more admiration than, perhaps, was willingly expressed in the old Court of George the Third." The reputation of American women for beauty was great; yet Mrs. Adams wrote: "I have not seen a lady in England who can bear a comparison with Mrs. Bingham."

Miss Adams wrote from London, February, 1786:—

"Mamma went to court to present Mrs. Bingham, and papa presented Mr. Chew. Mamma says, if admiration could make this lady happy, she must be so; for she never saw one so much stared at. 'There she goes,' cries one; 'what an elegant woman!' Some gentlemen told mamma she had presented the finest woman they had ever seen. I suppose she is not free from vanity, and if not, must have been gratified."

"Lady Talbot is not a Mrs. Bingham, who, taken altogether, is the finest woman I ever saw. The intelligence of her countenance, or rather, I ought to say, its animation, the elegance of her form, and the affability of her manners, convert you into admiration; and one has only to lament too much dissipation and frivolity of amusements, which have weaned her from her native country, and given her a passion and thirst after all the luxuries of Europe."

Mrs. Adams afterwards mentions "the dazzling Mrs. Bingham and her beauteous sisters" in Philadelphia. The Adams family was intimate with the Binghams during their stay in London. Miss Adams says of Mrs Bingham:—

"She is coming quite into fashion here, and is very much admired. The hairdresser who dresses us on court-days inquired of mamma whether she knew the lady so much talked of here from America—Mrs. Bingham. He had heard of her from a lady who had seen her at Lord Duncan's. At last, speaking of Miss Hamilton, he said, with a twirl of his comb, 'Well, it does not signify, but the American ladies do beat the English all to nothing.'"

"I think, from the observation I have made upon those ladies from Philadelphia with whom I have been acquainted, that they are more easy in their manners, and discover a greater desire to render themselves acceptable, than the women of Boston, where education appears to be better—and they seem to be sensible of their consequence in society. I have seen some good specimens of their brilliancy; first, in Mrs. Bingham, and now in Mrs. Stewart."

During her stay of five years abroad, Mrs. Bingham found everywhere the same caressing reception in the highest circles. Her immense wealth enabled her to live in a style of luxury and display, without which beauty, elegance, or worth, would stand, especially in England, little chance of recognition. Returning to her own country, she seemed resolved to show that she had not lost the wish to find herself at home there. Mr. Bingham had studied the domestic architecture of London and Paris to advantage, and being desirous of building a house in Philadelphia, he selected as a model the Duke of Manchester's residence. It was, indeed, a home where taste, wealth, and hospitality might appropriately dwell; a palace of splendor; known as "The Mansion House," and a credit to the city. It stood in Third Street above Spruce, forty feet from the street, and approached by a circular graveled carriage-way, opened by gates of iron tracery, and shut in by a low wall. The grounds were diversified by walks, parterres, and shade trees, and were adorned by statuary. They covered three acres, and adjoined the houses occupied by Mrs. Bingham's father and two of her aunts. In this princely abode Mrs. Bingham, who had been distinguished among the ladies in the Presidential court, became the centre of a court of her own. In her neighborhood were the residences of numerous family connections, of commanding social influence. The southeast was then the fashionable part of the town; and whenever Mrs. Bingham wished to have a large yet select party, she had only to send invitations to her own circle of relatives and connections, to have her spacious rooms filled with a brilliant assemblage. The house had a broad stair-way of fine marble, the pavement of tesselated marble; the first of the kind known in America. On the left hand were parlors; on the right, the study; and opposite was the library, separated by a lateral hall. The drawing-room and card-rooms were on the floor above; the windows looking on an extensive conservatory adjoining the lower parlors. There were various and extensive domestic offices surrounding the dwelling. The furniture and carpets were of French manufacture, and the halls were hung with paintings chiefly selected in Italy.*

The Binghams had a country-seat—"Landsdowne"—on the west bank of the Schuylkill, where the summers were passed. General Washington was a frequent visitor, both here and in their town house. The same elegant variety, richness, and excellent taste in entertainment, marked their hospitality in both places.

One of the customs brought from Paris by Mrs. Bingham, and introduced by her into society in Philadelphia, was that of the servants' announcing the names of guests, on their arrival at a party, in different places, from the hall to the drawing-room. A republican gentleman who was a stranger to the innovation,—one who was afterwards President of the nation,—one evening, hearing his name called out repeatedly while he stopped to divest himself of his outer garment, cried out, "Coming!" "Coming!" and in a louder tone, as he heard his name at the drawing-room door, "Coming! as soon as I can get my great-coat off!"

All that was illustrious in statesmanship or brilliant in society was now congregated in Philadelphia. It was the residence of the diplomatic representatives of European Courts and eminent persons from every quarter of the world. Its first circles were composed of those who would have ranked highly in any country, and who possessed every accomplishment of refined culture. The

---

* See "THE REPUBLICAN COURT."

external luxury and splendor of the society were in striking contrast to the unadorned simplicity which had marked the sway of Mrs. Washington. Mrs. Bingham "led the ton." in this brilliant world, and was unquestionably at the head of American society; not only by virtue of her husband's political position and her father's honorable career in the country's service, but in her own personal right. Her style illustrated all that was imposing and superb in the social life; and her acknowledged judgment and taste in dress and in the arrangements of her house, her influence over all with whom she came into contact, the splendors with which she was ever surrounded, and the aristocratic character of her parties, gave her a celebrity which became historical in the annals of higher social life in America.

Her beauty was of a striking and dazzling order; her figure was tall, and her carriage light, airy, and the perfection of grace. Her manners had resistless fascination—easy, sprightly, frank, and winning, and inspiring with interest all who conversed with her. She was indeed a most gifted and favored being, ever smiled upon and flattered, courted and served with the alacrity of genuine regard; happy in every change; awakening no envy or jealousy, in spite of her personal and social advantages; never the object of unkind feeling or malignant aspersion; giving offense to none, in spite of her great ambition to maintain superiority; pleasing all by her manner, even while refusing favors, and, while really exclusive, leaving even on the excluded the impression of being obliged. This singular charm of tact may account for the great traditionary reputation of her personal influence, as fresh in recollection now, and almost as much wondered at, as when she lived. She gave entertainments often, and they were very expensive and elaborate, while marked by good taste and elegance of style. She had a happy faculty and discretion in selecting and grouping her guests, so as to harmonize the circle and guard against disagreement. Her dress was a model for imitation, such was its exquisite adaptation and propriety, and its subdued tone combined with costliness.

Thomas Jefferson was one of Mrs. Bingham's admirers. He wrote her from Paris, describing the contrast between foreign and domestic fashionable life:—

"At eleven o'clock, it is day *chez madame*. The curtains are drawn. Propped on bolsters and pillows, and her head scratched into a little order, the bulletins of the sick are read and the billets of the well. She writes to some of her acquaintances, and receives the visits of others. If the morning is not very thronged, she is able to get out and hobble round the cage of the Palais Royale; but she must hobble quickly, for the *coiffeur's* turn is come, and a tremendous turn it is. Happy if he does not make her arrive when dinner is half over. The turpitude of digestion a little passed, she flutters half an hour through the streets, by way of paying visits, and then to the spectacles. These finished, another half hour is devoted to dodging in and out of the doors of her very sincere friends, and away to supper. After supper, cards; after cards, bed; to rise at noon next day, and to tread like a mill-horse the same trodden circle over again. Thus the days of life are consumed, one by one, without an object beyond the present moment; ever flying from the ennui of that, yet carrying it with us." — "In America, on the other hand, the society of your husband, the fond cares for the children, the arrangements of the house, the improvements of the grounds, fill every moment with a healthy and useful activity. Every exertion is encouraging, because to present amusement it joins the promotion of some future good. The intervals of leisure are filled by the society of real friends, whose affections are not thinned to cobweb by being spread over a thousand objects."

Chastellux mentions a ball at Chevalier de la Luzerne's, at which "the Count de Damas had Mrs. Bingham for his partner, and the Viscount de Nouaïlles, Miss Shippen. Both testified respect for the manners of the country by not quitting their handsome partners the whole evening."

The Viscount de Nouaïlles, brother-in-law to La Fayette, in the summer of 1795, came to America in company with Mr. Bingham, whose guest he was, though he occupied a third-story room in a block of buildings at the extreme west end of Bingham's garden. He gave a dinner to D'Orleans and other gentlemen of rank, using Bingham's plate and kitchen, and being waited upon by his servants. The same story was told of him as of Louis Philippe, who is said to have lived in Philadelphia, and occupied a room over a barber's shop, where he once gave a dinner, apologizing for seating half his guests on one side of a bed; he had himself "occupied less comfortable places without the consolation of such agreeable company." The young prince, at that time twenty-three years old, was introduced into Mr. Bingham's family, and is said to have proposed for one of the daughters, but the Senator declined the alliance. "Should you ever," he said, "be restored to your hereditary position, you will be too great a match for my daughter; if not, she is too great a match for you."

Mr. and Mrs. Bingham were guests at the dinner given by General Washington, when he bade farewell to the President elect and the heads of the departments. Among the other guests were Mr. and Mrs. Liston and the Marquis and Marchioness d'Yrujo, Mr. and Mrs. Cushing, Mr. Adams, Mr. Hamilton, Mr. Jefferson, Bishop White, &c.

The first masquerade ball in Philadelphia was said to have been given at Mr. Bingham's. Mrs. Bingham did not appear to be fond of theatricals, like Mrs. Adams; she and her set rarely went to the theater, and on that account Manager Wignell refused, on any terms, to let her a private box. She offered to furnish and decorate the box at her own expense, but would keep the key, allowing no one to enter without her permission. The manager feared to offend the fierce spirit of liberty and equality in the masses by such a concession.

Sir John Oldmixon, celebrated in England as "the Bath beau,"—rivaling Nash or Brummell,—was then flourishing. It was said he was a gardener in 1796, and carried his own cabbages to market. His wife, formerly Miss George, was an actress; sang at the theater, and returned at night in the vehicle which carried the vegetables. Actors then "held their own" in society, and a grand-daughter of Franklin is said to have married one—Mr. Harwood.

7

During the winter of 1795-6, when Judge Samuel Chase was in Philadelphia, a curious story is told of a great dinner given to him by Mr. Bingham. The Judge was placed on Mrs. Bingham's right hand, and coolly adjusted his spectacles to view the superb repast, which, unfortunately for him, had been prepared by a French cook. Having searched in vain for a familiar dish, he turned to the lady, and remarked: "A very pretty dinner, Madam; but there is not a thing on your table I can eat." With her habitual presence of mind and urbanity, Mrs. Bingham inquired if she could procure any thing more suitable to his taste. "A beefsteak, or a piece of roast beef, Madam," was the reply, "will please me better than any thing else." A servant was called and a word whispered in his ear, whereupon he vanished. Very soon he reappeared, bearing a dish of roast beef, which Chase attacked with vigor and appetite, washing it down with a couple of bottles of brown stout, in lieu of French wines. Having concluded his labors, he turned to his hostess, and with a satisfied air exclaimed: "There, Madam, I have made a sensible and excellent dinner, but no thanks to your French cook."

This gifted and brilliant woman was early removed from the sphere she adorned. Returning from a party of pleasure soon after the birth of her only son, exposure to cold in a sleigh brought on an illness, which was soon discovered to be of a dangerous character. A milder climate was recommended; and a vessel was fitted up with care to convey her to the Bermudas. On her departure, carried on a palanquin from her superb mansion to this vessel, her friends gathered around her to bid farewell, and hundreds thronged to see her. The hope of restoration was vain; after months of gradual decline, Mrs. Bingham died in the Bermuda Islands, May 11th, 1801, in the thirty-seventh year of her age. Mr. Bingham went to England, where he died at Bath three years later. His eldest daughter, Anne, married Alexander Baring, afterwards Lord Ashburton. Maria married the Count de Tilly; afterwards Henry Baring, and the Marquis de Bluisel.

In the winter of 1795-6, Robert Morris, the great financier, was in the splendor of his prosperity. He had laid the foundation of a palatial residence on the south side of Chestnut Street, just above Seventh, intending to have the building occupy the whole space. His home was ever the abode of generous and cordial hospitality, and was rendered delightful by his simple and affable manners. Mrs. Adams says, in Philadelphia, "I should spend a very dissipated winter if I were to accept one-half the invitations I receive, particularly to the routs and tea and cards." A passion for gambling prevailed at the time, and it was not uncommon to lose three or four hundred dollars at a sitting.

Chastellux thus describes a dinner in the then American fashion: "There are two courses, one comprehend ing the *entrées*, the roast meat and warm side-dishes; the other, sweet pastry and confectionery. The cloth is then taken off, and apples and nuts are produced; healths are drunk; and coffee is the signal to rise. It is an absurd and barbarous practice to call out to each individual that you drink his health! it causes confusion. Also, the asking to take wine with one; the ridiculous custom borrowed from England and laid aside by her."

At the balls given in Philadelphia Mrs. Morris was always led in first to supper; the visitor remarks, "as the richest woman in the city; all ranks here being equal, and men following their natural bent by giving the preference to riches."

VI.

Some writers of the day comment on the addiction of American women to extravagance in dress at this period. Count de Rochambeau observed, at the close of the war, that "the wives of merchants and bankers were clad to the tip of the French fashions, of which they were remarkably fond;" and the Duc de Liancourt says: "Ribbons please young Quakeresses as well as others, and are the great enemies of the sect."

The women in 1800 wore hoops, high-heeled shoes of black stuff, with silk or thread stockings, and had their hair tortured four hours at a sitting to get the curls properly crisped. The hoops were succeeded by "bishops" stuffed with horse-hair. In the early days, ladies who kept their coaches often went to church in check aprons; and Watson mentions a lady in Philadelphia who went to a ball in full dress, on horseback.

Brissot wrote: "If an idle man could come into existence in Philadelphia, on having constantly before his eyes the three amiable sisters—Wealth, Science, and Virtue, the children of Industry and Temperance—he would soon find himself in love with them, and endeavor to obtain them from their parents." The Duc de Liancourt observes: "The Americans have an excessive avidity of becoming rich," and thinks it a mistake to suppose pure republican manners prevalent. Perhaps as a consequence of enervating luxury, the Abbé Robin remarks: "At twenty the American women have no longer the freshness of youth; at thirty-five or forty they are wrinkled and decrepit. The men are almost as premature." And Chevalier Felix de Beaujour: "The beauty of American women fades in a moment. At the age of twenty-five the form changes; and at thirty all the charms have disappeared. As long as they are unmarried they enjoy great liberty; but as soon as they have entered the conjugal state they bury themselves in the bosom of their families, and appear no longer to live but for their husbands." "The manners have there established in society distinctions more marked than anywhere else; distinctions rendered the more odious for being founded on riches, without any regard to talents, or even to public functions. There the rich blockhead is more considered than the first magistrate; and the influence of gold is counterbalanced by no illusion or reality."

Towards the close of the century, it was noticed that the forms of society underwent some change, as the leveling process of France began to be felt. Powder became unfashionable; a looser dress was adopted for the legs; the fashion of wearing the hair tied gave place to short locks. Dark or black cloth was substituted for colored coats, and buckles disappeared. But the style of living was not less expensive. Parties were more crowded, and more form and display were seen, with less freedom of sociability than ever.

The Wistar parties, for gentlemen, were commenced by Dr. Caspar Wistar, in 1799. He was accustomed to call the members of the Philosophical Society once a week to his house during the winter. The parties were continued till his death, in 1818, and were kept up by members afterwards at their several houses.

The fête of the Mischianza had been the most celebrated that ever took place in Philadelphia. It was given by the British officers to Sir William Howe, just before he relinquished the command to Sir Henry Clinton, May 18, 1778. It commenced with a grand regatta, followed by a tilt and tournament, wherein the knights of the Burning Mountain and the Blended Rose vindicated the charms of the ladies in whose honor they appeared; a ball and fireworks closing the evening.*

The next entertainment in order of pre-eminence was given on the birthday of the Dauphin, by the French Minister, after the close of the war. Weeks of preparation preceded it, and hundreds came to see the building erected for dancing, fronting sixty feet, the roof supported by lofty pillars, painted and festooned. There were banners and pictures for internal decorations; and a garden surrounded the building, with walks, seats, groves, and fountains. Nothing else was talked of in the city for ten days. At an early hour a corps of

---

* For the particulars of this fête, see "Women of the American Revolution."

hairdressers took possession of the room assigned to the city watchmen. Some ladies had their hair dressed between four and six in the morning. The company assembled at seven in the evening, ten thousand spectators thronging the streets.

"At eight o'clock," says Dr. Rush, "our family entered the apartment, received through a wide gate by the Minister, and conducted by one of his family to the dancing-room. The numerous lights distributed through the garden, the splendor of the room, the size of the company, which already consisted of about seven hundred persons, the brilliancy and variety of their dresses, and the band of music, had, together, an effect which resembled enchantment. Here were to be seen heroes, patriots, and members of Congress, in close conversation with each other; Washington and Dickinson held several dialogues together; Rutledge and Walton from the South, here conversed with Lincoln and Duane from the East and the North; and Mifflin and Reed accosted each other with all the kindness of ancient friends. The dancing commenced at half-past eight; at nine, fire-works were exhibited; at twelve, supper was served in three large tents in the grounds; before three the company had dispersed."

A lady distinguished in Philadelphia society was Elizabeth, youngest daughter of Dr. Thomas Graeme, a physician of note, and for a time colonial collector of the port. His wife was the daughter of Sir William Keith, the Governor of Pennsylvania. His house, "The Carpenter Mansion," was rendered attractive and celebrated by the talents and accomplishments of Elizabeth, who was the center of literary coteries accustomed to meet there. She was sent to Europe for her health, and was introduced into the best society abroad. She attracted much attention by her mental accomplishments, and was particularly noticed by the King of England. On her return to Philadelphia she presided in her father's house, which became the head-quarters of literature, refined taste, and hospitality. Her husband, Hugh Henry Ferguson, a Scotch gentleman ten years her junior, espoused the royal cause in the war; his wife was a patriot, and their political difference led to a separation. Her charity and labors for the soldiers obtained the respect of both parties, and she always enjoyed the highest social position.

Sarah, the only daughter of Benjamin Franklin, was born in Philadelphia, in September, 1744, married Richard Bache in 1767, and was prominent in the best society. Her house was the rendezvous for the committee superintending the making of shirts for the army. In 1792 she accompanied her husband to England; and two years afterwards they were settled on their farm near the Delaware, where they exercised unbounded hospitality for thirteen years. She had an impulsive and generous disposition, with cheerful, strong good sense, and a ready flow of wit. She was a zealous republican, and chid a school-teacher for treating her children with peculiar distinction as "young ladies of rank." "There is no rank in this country," she said, "but rank mutton."

Miss Vining was a famous belle in Philadelphia. In 1783 she wrote to Governor Dickinson, complaining that the town had lost its gayety with the departure of Congress. Her rare beauty commanded admiration, while her intellectual endowments and sparkling wit entertained the literati. The French officers so praised her in their letters, that her name became familiar in Paris; and Queen Marie Antoinette expressed to Jefferson a wish to see her at the Tuileries. She had a large correspondence among the great men of the Revolution. When she retired from her place in society, she took up her residence in Wilmington, Delaware, where she received distinguished visitors, foreigners of rank soliciting introductions to her. Among the guests she entertained were the Duc de Liancourt and the Duc d'Orleans (Louis Philippe). It is said that General Miranda, passing through Wilmington at night, too late for a call, left his card for her at the post-office. Her last days were passed in seclusion, not exempt from poverty.

One of the most admired belles of Philadelphia, at a period when loyalists were prominent among the higher classes, was Margaret, the youngest daughter of Edward Shippen, Chief Justice of Pennsylvania. Shippen was grandson to the first city mayor, in 1701, who had a "great and famous orchard, in which reposed herds of tranquil deer;" lawns, and a summer-house in the midst of the garden, having tulips, pinks, carnations, roses, &c. He was said to be "the biggest man, with the biggest house, and the biggest carriage in Philadelphia." The Marquis de Chastellux describes a tea-drinking at the house of the Chief Justice, on the first occasion that he saw music introduced as an amusement: "Miss Rutledge, after Madame de Marbois, played on the harpsichord; Miss Shippen sang. The Vicomte de Nouailles took down a violin mounted with harp-strings, and made the young ladies dance." At the age of eighteen, in so princely a home, belonging to a family distinguished among the aristocracy of the day, beautiful, brilliant, and spirited, it is no wonder that Margaret was the toast of the British officers and the favorite of society, called "one of the brightest of the belles of the Mischianza." The volatile and fascinating young creature, accustomed to the pride of life and the homage paid to loveliness in high station, was captivated by the splendor of Benedict Arnold's equipments and his military ostentation. She became his second wife. Major André was one of her visitors and correspondents. No evidence, however, exists to sustain the accusation of the third Vice-President of the United States, that Mrs. Arnold "instigated one of the most startling crimes in history." Though ambitious, she was not a Lady Macbeth; and there is no proof even of her acquaintance with the dark design of her husband. Aaron Burr would have it that "the chief miscreant of the American Revolution could say, 'Margaret, my wife, she gave me of the tree of treason, and I did eat.'" But she was not yet nineteen when her husband opened the correspondence with Sir Henry Clinton; nor could she have counterfeited the anguish described as following the discovery of his treason. She found her way back to the shelter of her father's house; but in a few months she was ordered by the Executive Council of Pennsylvania to leave the

State, and not return during the war. She followed Arnold to New Brunswick, where she resided at St. Johns, sad and stricken indeed, but lovely and fascinating enough to be sought after and admired. Her residence was finally in London, where she died in 1804.

Rebecca Franks, a young lady distinguished for beauty, intelligence, and wit, occupied a brilliant position in the society of Philadelphia in the days of the Revolution. She was the youngest of three daughters of David Franks, a wealthy Jewish merchant. The eldest married Oliver de Lancey, who accepted a commission in the British army after the outbreak of the war; the second, Andrew Hamilton, owner of "Woodlands," the finest rural residence in Philadelphia. Rebecca was more celebrated for wit and repartee than any lady of the day. Her pointed shafts spared neither friend nor foe, though generally aimed to chastise presumption and folly. She was universally courted for the charms of her conversation; General Lee called her "a lady who has had every human and divine advantage." She was one of the princesses of the "Mischianza." Few were able to enter the lists in satire with this scornful belle. In a letter from New York, she described social life in that city:—

"You ask a description of Miss Cornelia Van Horne. Her person is too large for a beauty, in my opinion, and yet I am not partial to little women. Her sister Kitty is the belle of the family. By the bye, few ladies here know how to entertain company in their own houses, unless they introduce the card-table. Except the Van Hornes, who are remarkable for their good sense and ease,

I don't know a woman or girl who can chat above half an hour, and that on the form of a cap, the color of a ribbon, or the set of a hoop, stay, or *jupon*. I will do our ladies, that is, the Philadelphians, the justice to say, that they have more cleverness in the turn of an eye than those of New York have in their whole composition. With what ease have I seen a Chew, a Penn, an Oswald, or an Allen, and a thousand others, entertain a large circle of both sexes; the conversation, without the aid of cards, never flagging, nor seeming in the least strained or stupid. Here in New York, you enter a room with a formal set curtsey, and after the howdos, things are finished; all is a dead calm till the cards are introduced, when you see pleasure dancing in the eyes of all the matrons, and they seem to gain new life. The maidens, if they have favorite swains, frequently decline playing, for the pleasure of making love; for, to all appearance, it is the ladies, not the gentlemen, who now-a-days show a preference. It is here, I fancy, always leap-year. Indeed, scandal says, that in the cases of most who have been married, the first advances came from the lady's side, or she got a male friend to introduce the intended victim and pass her off. I suspect there would be more marriages were another mode adopted; they have made the men so saucy, that I sincerely believe the lowest ensign thinks he has but to ask and have; that a red coat and smart epaulette are sufficient to secure a female heart."

Soon after the war, Miss Franks was married to Lieutenant-General Sir Henry Johnston, who had been knighted for his gallantry in one of the outbreaks of rebellion in Ireland. In 1810 she was living at Bath in great style, exercising a liberal hospitality, with all the graces and virtues that adorn social life. General Scott visited her some years later, with a letter of introduction from her great-niece. He remembered hearing of her as "the belle of Philadelphia, handsome, witty, and an heiress; also high in toryism and eccentricity." He recollected that when Mrs. Washington gave a ball to the French Minister, in honor of the recent alliance between Louis XVI. and the United States, which had led America to unite the cockades of the two countries—white and black—Miss Franks had caused this token of alliance to be tied to the neck of a dog, and by bribing a servant got the animal, thus decorated, turned into the ball-room. In 1816, the vivacious lady, from ill health, had become prematurely old; "a near approach to a ghost, but with eyes still bright, and other remains of her former self." On receiving the letter of introduction, Lady Johnston sent her amiable husband—a fine old soldier—to fetch the stranger. Scott was fortunately acquainted with her eccentricities. She had been rolled out on the lawn in an easy-chair to receive him; and he was transfixed by her eager gaze. "Is this the young rebel?" were her first words. "Yes, it is," she added, quickly; "the young rebel; and you have taken the liberty to beat his Majesty's troops!" Scott pleasantly parried the impeachment; but she followed it up with specific references. At last the American soldier found himself seated beside her, a hand clasped in both hers, which were cold and clammy as death. Suddenly she exclaimed: "I have gloried in my rebel countrymen!" Then, lifting both her hands towards heaven, she added: "Would to heaven I too had been a patriot!" Sir Henry here interposed with a gentle remonstrance. Turning on him with the earnestness of truth, she said: "I do not—I have never regretted my marriage! No woman was ever blessed with a kinder—a better husband; but I ought to have been a patriot before marriage!" In relating this incident, Scott used to say that Lady Johnston's eyes were the only ones free from tears.

The wife of one, and the mother-in-law of another signer of the Declaration of Independence, Mrs. Annis Stockton, of Princeton, New Jersey, adorned high position by elevated character and superior endowments. She was the descendant of Elias Boudinot, a French Protestant, who fled after the revocation of the edict of Nantes. Elias Boudinot of New Jersey was her brother. She was born about 1733. After her marriage to Richard Stockton, she lived at his seat near Princeton, and shared with him the perils and privations incident to war. Her husband's letters to her from England, romantically addressed to his "dearest Emilia," portray the most charming of characters. She had refined literary taste and cultivation, and was the author of a volume of poems. Washington praised her pastoral on the capture of Cornwallis, and complimented her talents in several letters. Her social influence was acknowledged by an extensive circle of friends. She was called "The Duchess" for her elegance and dignity. Her daughter Julia became the wife of Dr. Benjamin Rush. Mrs. Stockton died in 1801.

Rufus King, in 1786, married Miss Mary Alsop, the only child of John Alsop, an opulent merchant of New York, and a member of the first Continental Congress. She was noted for beauty; having an oval face, with regular features, blue eyes, and a clear brunette complexion; black hair and fine teeth. Her movements were graceful, her manner was gracious and winning; her voice was music. She possessed quick faculties of mind, and was carefully educated. Though reared in the lap of indulgence she had an unspoiled nature, and had little fondness for display, notwithstanding that she was the object of general admiration.

When the British occupied New York, in 1778, Mary went with her father to Middletown, Connecticut, where her girlhood was passed. The family returned to New York after peace. Mary was but sixteen at the time of her marriage. Her grandson, Rufus King, married a lady who since, as Mrs. Peters, has become a celebrity in Cincinnati; well known for her active charities and zeal in every good work. She was Miss Worthington. In 1867 she accompanied some friends to Europe.

———

A region of country near the Hudson, where the old aristocratic families are held in reverence, is familiar with the name of Blandina Bruyn, the daughter of Petrus Edmundus Elmendorf, born at Kingston, then called Esopus, in 1753. Her mother, Mary Elmendorf, was known through a large part of New York, New Jersey, and Pennsylvania, having studied medicine that she might practise among poor families. She took great pains with the education of her daughter, who learned to speak and write fluently English, Dutch, and French.

Blandina was engaged to Jacobus S. Bruyn, who afterwards became a colonel in the American army; they were married in 1782, and fixed their residence in Kingston, where Mrs. Bruyn was a leader in society, liberally entertaining many visitors. Her charity and piety are traditional in the place. She died in 1832.*

---

* The country-seat of Colonel Morris, which became afterwards the head-quarters of General Washington—about ten miles from New York—was the residence of the singular woman known as Madame Jumel, the wife of Aaron Burr. She lived on Washington Heights, and died in 1865, in her ninety-second year. She was known in the court circles of France, though she never had any position in American society. She was intimate with Patrick Henry, Thomas Jefferson, General Knox, La Fayette, and others among the leaders in the Revolutionary struggle. She met Burr when he was a captain in the army, and at Lady Stirling's parties; and it is said that scores of men of high position and talents worshiped at her shrine. Many were her escapades and adventures, and marvelous tales were told of her.

She married Stephen Jumel, who amassed in the wine trade a fortune that gave him rank among merchant princes. Their residence was for a time in Paris; but after Jumel lost his fortune, his wife, in 1822, returned alone to New York, and lived on her own estate. Jumel was killed by a fall in his seventieth year.

Colonel Burr was then practising law with great success, though seventy-eight years of age. Madame Jumel called on him for legal advice about her estate; the acquaintance ripened, and she invited the great lawyer to dinner. He was charmed with her, and is reported to have said, on handing her to the table, "Madame, I give you my hand; my heart has long been yours." At length he proposed, and was rejected; but persevered in his suit. Having advanced so far as to obtain an undecided "No," he said one day in a jocular manner that he should bring out a clergyman to Fort Washington, at a certain time, and then would expect a more favorable answer. He came at the time appointed, accompanied by Dr Bogart, and took advantage of the lady's embarrassment and dread of a new scandal. So they were married, the ceremony being witnessed only by the members of the family and the servants, and followed by an excellent supper. Some bottles from Jumel's wine-cellar that had not

Catharine Schuyler was the only daughter of John Van Rensselaer, the great land-holder, called the Patroon of Greenbush. She married Philip Schuyler. The family residence was near Albany, and was built by Mrs. Schuyler while her husband was in England, about 1760. It was a large house, ornamented in the Dutch style, and was a place of resort for British officers and travelers of note during the French war. Fourteen French gentlemen, paroled prisoners, were here entertained at one time. In 1801, Mrs. Schuyler and some of her family, visiting Montreal and Quebec, were gratefully welcomed by the children of some of those prisoners. After the surrender of Burgoyne, he and his suite were received and entertained by General and Mrs. Schuyler, though he had destroyed their elegant country-seat near Saratoga. Madame de Riedesel described

been opened for half a century were produced on the occasion, and the party was exceeding merry.

At Burr's advice, his wife sold out her shares in some Connecticut property, and gave the proceeds to him for investment. Texas was then beginning to attract the tide of emigration, and Burr embarked the money in an enterprise for settling a colony of Germans on a tract of land there. The speculation proved a failure, and the title to the lands defective. Burr had not mentioned the Texas scheme to his wife, and he refused to account for the funds invested. A coolness and estrangement followed. Burr continued to speculate and lose his wife's money; her patience was exhausted, and she filed a complaint against him, to deprive him of control in her affairs. He suffered the proceedings to go by default; but they went no further than to restore to the lady sole authority over her property. After a few months of alternate reconciliation and estrangement, the marriage was in effect—though never in law—dissolved.

After the separation, the wife never bore Burr's name, but lived almost solitary in her home on the Heights. Her grandchildren inherited her property.

their reception as that of intimate friends rather than enemies. So much delicacy and generosity drew from Burgoyne the observation to his host, "You are too kind to me, who have done so much injury to you." The noble-hearted victor replied: "Such is the fate of war; let us not dwell on the subject." Even from the ruins of his beautiful villa the General had written to his wife to make preparations for entertaining their late foes. The best apartments and an excellent supper were provided, and the honors done with a grace that moved the British general to tears.

Like many other women of her family, Mrs. Schuyler was remarkable for vigorous intellect and judgment. Many instances of her heroic spirit are recorded in another work. Her social influence was widely recognized, and was transmitted to her accomplished daughters. The second of these, Elizabeth, married Alexander Hamilton in December, 1780. She was described as "a charming woman, who joined to the graces all the candor and simplicity of the American wife." When Hamilton was mortally wounded, he said: "Let Mrs. Hamilton be immediately sent for; let the event be gradually broken to her, but give her hopes." Thus the love of his admirable wife was the great man's strongest feeling in the hour of death. When he saw her frantic grief, he remonstrated with her gently: "Remember, my Elizabeth, you are a Christian." His residence was at the corner of Wall and Broad Streets, opposite Federal

Hall. His country-seat on the island was called "The Grange."

There was a story of Mrs. Hamilton's having met Burr in 1822, at a dinner on board a steamboat, and swooning from the shock; but it was untrue. Parton says she met the slayer of her husband on a small steamboat between New York and Manhattanville, but that nothing unusual occurred. Mrs. Hamilton is said to have founded an orphan asylum in New York. She was one of the few ladies for whom Talleyrand professed deep respect and admiration.

During the hostilities between France and England, after the French Revolution, a French man-of-war, with the First Consul Napoleon's brother, Jerome Bonaparte, on board, was chased by two English frigates into the harbor of New York. The future king of Westphalia was thus constrained to visit the United States. He was received in different cities with extraordinary marks of attention. Hamilton made a great dinner for him in New York, while he lived at "The Grange." The company waited long, after assembling, for the host, who did not appear, to the chagrin of Mrs. Hamilton and the disappointment of the distinguished guest. After creating much uneasiness by the delay, Hamilton at length arrived and finished a hasty toilet; and the tact with which he made his graceful apologies to the company removed all embarrassment. On that occasion he had a lively chat in French with Miss Patterson, of

Baltimore. Bonaparte lost his heart to this beautiful young lady.

It is a subject for wonder that Napoleon should have been blind to the capabilities of the American wife of Jerome Bonaparte. With her airy manner, her beauty, and her wit, so fair and piquante, she would have made an excellent princess. Jerome, who had been sent to sea, assumed the airs of a prince in Baltimore. Elizabeth Patterson was the daughter of a rich and respected merchant, of a family belonging to the aristocracy. In birth and education she was the equal of Jerome; in intellect and character, his superior. With her father's consent, the marriage was celebrated December 25th, 1803, by Bishop Carrol, Roman Catholic Bishop of Baltimore. A few months passed in wedding festivities and social gayeties.

The First Consul was declared Emperor before Jerome received his answer to the announcement of his marriage with the fair American. A French law existed prohibiting the marriage of any French subject under twenty-five without the consent of his guardians; and, availing himself of this, the Emperor refused to recognize his brother's marriage, and summoned him home, forbidding the French vessels to give Madame Bonaparte a passage, and threatening her with arrest if she dared accompany her husband to his own country. A pension of sixty thousand francs was offered her, on condition of her not assuming the name of Bonaparte. Jerome took her to Lisbon, where he left her, while he went to Turin to meet his imperial brother. With a meanness of soul no royalty could cover, he offered to give up wife and child, repudiating his marriage, and submitting to the will of Napoleon, who gave him to wife a German princess, and made him king of Westphalia. Madame Bonaparte was left unprotected and without provision in a foreign country, not yet eighteen, and with a new-born infant. Abandoned by her husband, subjected to the bitterest outrage, the legality of her marriage denied, stripped of means, and flung upon the world, she yet managed to sustain her difficult position with a calm spirit and scornful courage. She was in Paris in 1816, and much in society; the most distinguished among the literati belonging to her circle. In the autumn of 1819, she wrote to Lady Morgan, with whom she was intimate, that she had "heroically resolved to support the ennui of her fate in America," but was compelled to go abroad for the means of education for her son.

"You know," she says, " we have been nearly ruined in America by commercial speculations; and even I have suffered, as my tenants are no longer able to pay me the same rents, and the banks have been obliged to diminish the amount of yearly interest." Speaking of her son, she says: " His father never has and never will contribute a single farthing towards his maintenance. We have no correspondence since the demand I made two years ago, which was merely that he would pay some part of his necessary expenditure. This he positively refused; therefore I consider myself authorized to educate him in my own way."

Jerome Bonaparte, in later years, lived on familiar terms in London with Lady Morgan's circle. Vain, selfish, inconsiderate, and extravagant, he owned no obligation but his own whims. In 1849 Madame Bonaparte wrote from Baltimore to Lady Morgan: "There is nothing here worthy of attention save the money-market. Society, conversation, friendship, belong to older countries, and are not yet cultivated in any part of the United States which I have visited. You ought to thank your stars for your European birth; you may believe me when I assure you it is only distance from republics which lends enchantment to the view of them. A residence of a few months in the Etats Unis would cure the most ferocious republican of the mania of republics." Nevertheless, the evening of her life passes serenely in Baltimore. Beyond fourscore, she enjoys excellent health, which she attributes, in part, and no doubt justly, to early hours. Her habits are active, and she is able to enjoy the visits of her friends and strangers.

Mrs. Wilson was celebrated in New Jersey, both in the days of her girlhood and widowhood. She was the daughter of Colonel Charles Stewart, and was born in 1758, at Sidney, the residence of Judge Johnston, her maternal grandfather. The old mansion was one of the most stately and aristocratic of colonial residences in that section of New Jersey. Its square, massive walls and heavy portals, made for defence against the Indians, formed a stronghold for the wealthy proprietor, his relatives and dependents for miles around. "The big stone house" was in fact extensively noted as a place of refuge from danger. For thirty years before the Revolution, Judge Johnston was chief magistrate of that section of the colony, holding court every week in his spacious hall. The house was situated on an elevated terrace, overhung by parklike woods, at the confluence of the Capulory and a branch of the Raritan. Colonel Stewart had a place adjoining this estate. His hospitality was really unlimited; besides that his house was the resort of choice spirits in intellect and public influence, the stranger and the wanderer "were almost compelled to come in."

Miss Stewart always presided at his bountiful table. In 1776 she married Robert Wilson, a young Irishman of the Barony of Innishowan, and went with him to Philadelphia. Widowed after three years of married life, she returned to her residence at Hackettstown, where her situation was favorable for observation and knowledge of important military movements. She here entertained the leading spirits of the Revolution. Washington, La Fayette, Generals Greene, Gates, Maxwell, and others, were her frequent guests. On one occasion, she had ordered dinner provided for thirty or forty, when news was privately brought to her that General and Mrs. Washington were coming, escorted by a troop of horse. She was soon ready to welcome them. The party stayed till the afternoon of next day, and crowds came to see the chief. To gratify the people, Mrs. Wilson had a fine horse brought up, and invited the General to go out and inspect it. On another occasion, when there was a similar crowd, a tory lady obtained permission to stand in the hall while the General passed through, and was so much affected by the majesty of his deportment that she discarded her loyalism.

In her journeys to and from the camp, Mrs. Washington stopped to visit Mrs. Wilson. During the Presidency of Washington, when Mrs. Wilson came to Philadelphia with her daughter and entered society, she was distinguished by particular attentions from his family.

Her father's house was robbed by bandit tories in 1783.* Till his death in 1800, Mrs. Wilson continued at the head of his family, and in the exercise of her proverbial hospitality. General Maxwell of New Jersey was a constant visitor. She was often heard to express regret that full justice had not been done to this valued friend by some impartial biographer. "As a soldier and a patriot, he had few superiors," she was wont to say; "and in integrity, strength of mind, and kindness of heart, but few equals." She saw him first at a review of his regiment, the second raised in New Jersey. He distinguished himself in many battles, and testimony is

---

* See "Women of the American Revolution." General Maxwell was the grand-uncle of the author of this work.

8

borne to his high character and services, in numerous letters and journals of the day. Before the close of the war he resigned his commission, in displeasure at the appointment over him of an inferior officer. His death took place at the house of Co'onel Stewart.

For fifteen years after her father's death, Mrs. Wilson devoted her time to the settlement of his large estates, and the care of two orphan nephews, one of whom was the distinguished missionary and author, Rev. Charles Stewart. In 1808 she removed to Cooperstown, New York; but her last years were spent at "The Lakelands," the beautiful residence of her daughter, near that town. Hers was a lovely close of life, universally respected and honored; it might better be called a ripening for immortality.

VII.

Oloff Stevenson Van Cortlandt, the ancestor of a distinguished family, died in this country about 1683, leaving seven children. Two years later, his eldest son obtained from Governor Dougan a patent for large tracts of land purchased from the Indians in Westchester, Putnam, and Duchess Counties. The old-fashioned stone mansion that stood on the banks of the Croton—known as the Cortlandt Manor House—was the residence of the family for many years preceding the Revolution, and it was here that Cornelia, second daughter of Pierre Van Cortlandt and Joanna Livingston, was born, in 1752. Her father, a zealous patriot, was Lieutenant-Governor of New York under George Clinton, from 1777 to 1795. Her husband was Gerard G. Beekman; and their home, after marriage, was in New York, till the storm of war drove them back to Croton. When the Peekskill Manor House, a large brick building two miles north of Peekskill, was completed, the Beekmans removed thither, remaining during the war. It was a picturesque spot, but too convenient, as a place of encampment for the army, not to be exposed to peril and aggression. Of these Mrs. Beekman had her full share from the tories; on one occasion, when she was constrained to fly, finding the house despoiled of every thing on her return. Her social qualities and unbounded hospitality made her famous throughout the country. The leading American officers were entertained, and one room was called "Washington's"—the house having been his and General Patterson's head-quarters. The charity and kindness of Mrs. Beekman were as widely known as her hospitality; and the poor of the country blessed her for many acts of self-sacrificing generosity. The trials and privations she endured for her patriotism, and the depredations with which her property was visited, are described in another work.*

The lands in the manor of Philipsburgh, having been vested in the State of New York by the attainder of the owners, were sold in parcels; and Mr. Beekman purchased the tract in the vicinity of Tarrytown in which stood the old Manor House, to which he removed his family in 1785. "Castle Philipse" was the ancient residence of the lords of Philipsburgh, and strongly fortified, in the early days of the colony, for defense against the Indians. The embrasures, or port-holes, now form the cellar windows. With additions made by Rodolphus Philipse, this fort was a convenient dwelling; looking on the old Dutch church built in 1699 by Frederick Philipse and Catharina Van Cortlandt his wife. Tradition says, while superintending its erection, she rode from New York on horseback, on moonlight nights,

---

* "Women of the American Revolution."

mounted on a pillion behind her brother, Jacobus Van Cortlandt. This church, which was struck by lightning, and rebuilt with modern improvements, is described in "The Legend of Sleepy Hollow" with the wide, woody dell, and the bridge over the shaded stream, where Ichabod Crane met with his adventure. Mrs. Beekman often expressed her indignation that Irving had given the name of "Sleepy Hollow" to a spot so near her own residence, when the ravine on the other side of the hill was the actual locality of the legend. The Pocanteco, or Mill River, wanders here, replenished by crystal rills, through a region of romantic beauty, by dark woodlands, over grassy meadows, and beneath rugged heights. The Manor House was fronted by trees surrounding a silver sheet of water; and near it was the old mill, with its moss-covered roof, where many bushels of grain were ground free of toll for the poor. The windows commanded a most picturesque view of the landscape through which the stream wound, to lose itself in the bosom of the Hudson. Here passed the later years of Mrs. Beekman's life, in the midst of a circle of friends, to whose improvement and happiness she contributed. She was well pleased to welcome La Fayette on his last visit, and talk with him of days gone by. She survived her husband many years, and died in the midst of loving kindred, in her ninety-fifth year. Her funeral was attended by an immense concourse, in carriages, on horseback, and on foot. The hearse was drawn by two white horses with sable trappings, while the tolling of the old church bell broke the silence. She was known as an accomplished lady "of the old school." With steadfast principles, she had a lofty sense of honor; with force of will and stern resolution, a heart alive to all kindly feelings. In her prime she was noted for beauty of person, refinement, and dignified courtesy; while her conversation was brilliant and interesting. Amid her stores of anecdote were thrilling tales of the olden time. Her mental faculties were unimpaired to the last; though her sight failed. Calmly she awaited death, with the clear faith of a Christian, and, while counting the failing beats of her pulse with one hand, signed her name with the other, shortly before she breathed her last. Of her brothers and sisters, General Pierre Van Cortlandt and Mrs. Van Rensselaer alone survived her. Her daughter was Mrs. De Peyster, and her son was Dr. Beekman of Tarrytown.

Mrs. Gates, the wife of General Gates, was his intelligent and efficient helpmeet, managing his house and estate in his absence. She was Miss Phillips, the daughter of a British officer. She and General Gates lived for years in Virginia, but afterwards at their country-seat—"Rose Hill"—near New York, where they exercised almost unlimited hospitality. "My Mary" was always quoted with deference by the General, and had a frank welcome for his friends.

CATHARINE M VAN CORTLANDT FIELD

MRS. FIELD, the grand-daughter of Cornelia Beekman, has the blood of the most distinguished families in America in her veins. The De Peysters, Livingstons, Beekmans, Van Cortlandts, and Van Rensselaers, among whose branches the intermarriages would puzzle a genealogist, were all more or less closely connected with her ancestors. It is curious to trace back such a descent. Taking that of De Peyster—one of the French Protestant families driven from their native land by the persecution of Charles IX.—we find the first American resident to be Johannes de Peyster, a native of Haarlem, and a merchant of wealth and respectable standing. He was descended from a long line, and filled various positions in the church and magistracy; being Deputy Mayor of New Amsterdam in 1677. Portions of massive and elegant plate, and gems of art in the way of pictures, brought by him from Holland, are preserved by his descendants. He was assessed among the wealthiest inhabitants of the city, and his name is chronicled in connection with movements of importance in the colony. The office of Schepen was held by him; and after the cession of the Dutch colony to England, he was promoted to the highest offices in the municipality. Two of his sons and a son-in-law were successively Mayors of New York. Of the sons, Abraham was a prominent politician, of great wealth, and one of the largest owners of real estate in the colony. His wife was Caterina De Peyster, who was married to him in Holland in 1684. He was one of Leisler's adherents in the revolution of

1689; was Judge, and then Chief Justice of the Supreme Court, and died in 1728. His son, Colonel Abraham De Peyster, at different times advanced large sums for Government use. He was a friend of Bellamont and William Tell the patriot. His eldest son, Abraham, succeeded him in the office of Treasurer of the Province of New York about 1721, and his eldest daughter, Catharine, was married to Philip Van Cortlandt, whose son was the well-known Lieutenant-Governor Pierre Van Cortlandt, of Croton. His daughter, Elizabeth, was the wife of Hon. John Hamilton, the Governor of New Jersey. His seventh son, Pierre Guillaume De Peyster, married Catharine Schuyler, the sister of Peter Schuyler, who was famous for his extraordinary influence among the Five Nations of Indians. The second son of this Pierre Guillaume was the distinguished Colonel Arent Schuyler De Peyster, of the British army, whose services secured the overthrow of French influence in the great Northwest, thus giving the empire of the lakes to the Anglo-Saxon race. Abraham, who held the office of Treasurer forty years, had a descendant in the British army, who met with marvellous accidents. He was blown up, and buried for more than an hour, by the explosion of a mine at the siege of Valenciennes; swallowed up twice by the explosion of another mine in front of the French works near Menin, and so completely covered that only the fringe of his sash protruded from the ground, leading, after a long search, to the recovery of his body. A few days afterwards he fell in action at Lincelles, in 1793.

The Colonel Arent Schuyler De Peyster alluded to was remarkable as a soldier and diplomatist. The British government owed to him its vast Northwest territory. He wielded a vigorous pen, and had a poetical controversy with Burns through the Dumfries Journal. One of Burns's fugitive pieces, addressed to him in 1796, began—

> "My honored Colonel, deep I feel
> Your interest in the poet's weal.
> Ah, how sma' heart ha' I to speel
> The steep Parnassus,
> Surrounded thus by bolus pill
> And potion glasses."

This really "wonderful man" was buried with honors in Dumfries. His nephew, namesake, protégé, and intended heir, one of the first American circumnavigators, sailed twice round the world, doubling the Cape of Good Hope fifteen times, and discovering the De Peyster Islands.

Frederick, the son of James De Peyster and Sarah Reade, was born in 1758, and married Helen Hake, the daughter of the claimant of the title of Lord Hake, and the grand-daughter of Robert Gilbert Livingston. His second wife was Ann, daughter of Gerard G. Beekman, and grand-daughter of Pierre Van Cortlandt, of Croton. He had one son and seven daughters, of whom the youngest was Catherine Matilda Van Cortlandt De Peyster, the lady of whom we make brief mention, as one of the few Americans who can look back upon the wonderful deeds of distinguished ancestors, and refer to a thick volume of genealogy.

Miss De Peyster was carefully educated, and from childhood associated with the numerous connections of her family who have their residences on the Hudson and in New York. In 1838, she married Mr. Benjamin Hazard Field, a descendant of Sir John Field, the astronomer. He is the owner of the tract of land in Westchester County which has been kept in the family over two hundred and fifty years; but his residence has been chiefly in New York, where Mrs. Field has hospitably entertained numerous friends from time to time, and devoted herself to the care of her two children. In 1863, her "silver wedding" was celebrated by a very large party and the offering of splendid presents. A large mirror over the mantel was encircled by a plateau of green moss, suitable to the Christmas season, with the letters, "Silver Wedding," formed by rose-buds, through the center of the half circle. Rich bouquets and baskets of flowers were ranged on either side, and on each side the corresponding mirror in the hall; the reflection having a fine effect when the folding-doors were thrown open. Poetry, as well as flowers, adorned the festive occasion. The Bishop of Western New York, Rev. Arthur Cleveland Coxe, gave to Mrs. Field some impromptu verses, referring to another gay party which they had mutually enjoyed when he was a youth, not yet devoted to the sacred calling. Even an early effusion from such a mind is worth preserving.

TO MRS. B. H. FIELD.

"I take your word—it must be so,
   This is your silver wedding-day!
I thought we still were young—but lo!
   My hair is turning silver-gray.

"And, now you mention it, the time
   Comes back to mind, and that gay board,
When first I prophesied, in rhyme,
   Ben should be soon your wedded lord.

"Merry we spoke and merry laughed;
   And bright your crimson blushes glowed,
As foaming bumpers then we quaffed,
   And wished you life's most flowery road.

"Full soon the oracle came true.
   But scarce can I believe mine ears,
When, now, once more it comes to view,
   Well kept for five-and-twenty years.

"So lasts and lives the generous wine;
   And so, well kept, the vintage flows
Afresh, when years are sped, and fine
   And mellow too its flavor grows!

"I did not pledge so long a lease
   Of love and joy, your destined fate;
Though married bliss and home-born peace
   I knew full well would bless your mate.

"For years 'tis God alone can give:
   And solemn must the questions be,
How long together ye shall live?
   Who shall your *golden* wedding see?

"How long shall yet the merry ring
 Of friends that saw your gladsome start
Unbroken last? What year shall bring
 To one, or all, the broken heart?

"With Heaven still let the secret rest!
 Happy, if with assurance calm
We wait, each one—to be a guest
 At the *great wedding of the Lamb.*'

VIII.

The revocation of the edict of Nantes, in the days of Louis XIV., drove from their homes thousands of the best among the French population. Many of those who sought refuge in America settled in the Carolinas, where their industry created homes for their families. Among these were the Hugers, the Petigrus, the Desaussures, the Gourdins, and others eminent in society. In the Revolution all adhered to the cause of the patriots.

Charleston, in South Carolina, was in advance of any other Southern city as the seat of social elegance and refined and generous hospitality. The private residents were so liberal in entertaining strangers that inn-keepers complained of their business suffering. The ladies wore the rich and tasteful costumes of the middle of the century; and their milliners and tailors kept up communication with Paris, as the preference was given to French fashions. From four o'clock in the afternoon business was given up, and the people thought only of amusement. There were two gaming houses, which were always full. The women were not so handsome as in Philadelphia, but were interesting and agreeable. At a public concert and ball given when Washington was in Charleston, they wore bandeaux of white ribbon interwoven in the head-dress, with heads of Washington painted on them, and the motto, in gilt letters, "Long live the President."

Among the Charleston ladies most prominent in society, some loyalist women formed the material of the large parties given by the leading officers of the British army. Local tradition remembers among them, as belles of the city during its occupation by the royal troops, the Misses Harvey; three sisters, of rich, exuberant beauty, and wild, passionate temper. "Moll Harvey," as she was familiarly called, was a splendid woman, with dark, Cleopatra-like eyes, and tresses long, massive, and glossy black. "A more exquisite figure never floated through the mazes of a dance." Her intellect was subtle, and she was keen and quick at repartee, free of fancy, and of a bold and reckless spirit. It is said that one of her flirtations was with Prince William, afterwards William IV., then a lieutenant in the navy. The prince became madly in love with her, and the rumor went that he proposed a secret marriage; but her proud spirit would be content only with public espousals. Another royalist lady was Miss Mary Roupell, a proud beauty, and haughty as a queen. Paulina Phelps was an heiress, and of highly respectable family; she made a conquest of Major Archibald Campbell—"Mad Archy," as he was termed.

The fashionable Mrs. Rivington was the widow of a wealthy planter, and lived in Broad Street. Her husband had been one of the royal counsellors for the province. She was a fiery tory, and led the ton among them all, ruling with absolute sway as long as the British had possession of Charleston, and turning her back on the Rutledges, Gadsdens, and other Whig families. She was indeed an important acquisition to the garrison. She was wealthy, fair, and forty, though not fat; her suppers were excellent. Thus Cornelia Rivington had numerous admirers, but rejected all matrimonial overtures. Having suffered as a wife, she took revenge as a widow, and the stout majors of foot who besieged her heart were compelled to sigh in vain. She gave levees for conversation and evening parties; and at her "mornings" her rooms were open from eleven to one.

Mrs. Richard Singleton was sprung of the best Virginia stock, and was devoted to the American cause. Her husband had lost his life in the last struggle with the French, when the Indians ravaged the frontier. Her house was in Church Street near Tradd, and it was a favorite point of meeting with the patriots. "Hither, in the dark days that found their husbands, sons, or brothers in exile, or in camp, or in the prison-ship, came the Rutledges, the Laurens, the Izards, and most of the distinguished families of the low country of South Carolina, to consult as to the future, to review their condition, to consider their resources; and, if no more, to 'weep their sad bosoms empty.'" Among these Whig ladies were the wife of General Gadsden, a dame of stately pride; Mrs. Savage and Mrs. Parsons, described by the witling as "tragedy queens," &c.; and the names of Edwards, Horry, Ferguson, Pinckney, and Elliott, were represented with dignity and patriotism. They all attended Mrs. Singleton's "evenings." Grave studies occupied their time; their work was to go continually from the city to the interior, gathering reports of the signs of the times, and conveying intelligence, and sometimes ammunition, to friends in the army, or devising schemes for the deliverance of the city. Thus the social assemblages sometimes led to large results. Notwithstanding political troubles, Charleston was gay at that time; there were *fêtes champêtres*, and brilliant evening parties; parties and picnics for Haddrill's, Sullivan's, James's, and Morris Islands; drives into St. Andrews, Goose Creek, and Accabee, &c. Tradition remembers a grand ball given in a mansion in Ladsden's Court, then occupied by Biddulph, the paymaster of the British forces. The whole court was lighted up, and every room was filled with the select of the garrison and the distinguished of the city, without regard to politics, so far as ladies were concerned. Mrs. Brewton, a patriotic woman, celebrated for her talent for repartee, was there. A young officer of the Guards offering to take letters for her to Mrs. Motte, her sister-in-law, she replied: "Thank you, Lieutenant, I should like much to write, but I really have no wish to have my letters read at the head of Marion's brigade." It was believed that the same officer's capture, which really occurred on his expedition, was owing to the secret intelligence conveyed by Mrs. Brewton; and she was expelled from the city.

The story went, that "Mad Archy" invited the handsome heiress, Miss Paulina Phelps, to take a drive to Goose Creek. The rector of the parish, Mr. Ellington, lived there, and was seen on the piazza as they drove up. Campbell flung the reins to a servant, sprang out, and lifted out Paulina, who seemed in extreme agitation, for she had no sooner reached the piazza than she sank into a chair, and faintly asked for a glass of water. Campbell was in great haste to be married; he had laid a wager; the lady said nothing, but seemed terribly frightened; the parson was in rare embarrassment. At last "Mad Archy" drew out a pistol. "You must marry us directly, or I'll blow your brains out!"* he exclaimed. There was no choice. They were shown into the parlor; the books were prepared, and the ceremony was performed; the lady afterwards protesting that she was surprised and terrified into acquiescence.

Another ball given by Colonel Cruden, who then had the spacious mansion of General Pinckney, on East Bay, was long remembered as the greatest display of the season. The illuminations were brilliant, the gardens being absolutely draped with light. At the end of every avenue the lights were multiplied from pyramidal lusters of steel bayonets, burnished muskets, and sabers grouped in stars and crescents. The guests were numerous, and invited from both parties. Rousing bowls of punch furnished refreshment, and from one splendid-

---

* Mr. W. G. Simms.

ly enameled vase on a table, which held several gallons, it was served in large cups of filagreed china. An incident that occurred gave occasion for sundry witticisms; Miss Mary Roupell was leaning against a window-seat, when the sash fell heavily upon her wrist. She swooned with the pain. A Mr. Stock, in his anxiety to revive her, seized the mammoth bowl of punch, and threw its contents over her face. Major Barry wrote the following epigram on the occasion:—

>"When fair Roupell lay fainting in her pain,
>'Oh, what,' cry all, 'will bring her to again?'
>'What!—what!' says Stock, 'but punch—a draught divine!
>'Twill ease her pain: it always conquered mine!'"

Rebecca Motte, celebrated for her heroic conduct in giving Lee the bow and arrows to fire her dwelling when it was occupied by the British, was the daughter of Robert Brewton, and was married in 1758. Her two eldest daughters married, in succession, General Thomas Pinckney; the third was the wife of Colonel William Alston, of Charleston. Her descendants are among the most distinguished families in South Carolina. They cherish her name with pride and affection, regarding her fame as a rich inheritance. She died in 1815, at her plantation on the Santee.

Mrs. Gibbes, the wife of Robert Gibbes, lived in a beautiful house near Stono River, on St. John's Island, two hours sail from Charleston. The extensive lawn, the river walks, the live oaks and orange-trees, and flower-gardens, were pleasant adjuncts; and "Peaceful

Retreat" was the seat of elegant hospitality. Every luxury art could furnish was added to the beauties of natural scenery, and a cultivated taste presided over all. The fame of this noble country-place induced some of the British to resolve to transfer themselves into such desirable quarters, and one night they landed with the intention of forming their establishment. Mrs. Gibbes hastily dressed herself and the children, her husband being a cripple from gout, and prepared to receive the enemy. When the soldiers advanced, the door was thrown open, discovering the invalid surrounded by his helpless family. During the stay of the intruders, Mrs. Gibbes continued to preside at her table, with a dignified courtesy that kept the rudest in reverence. When the American authorities sent two galleys to dislodge the British, she removed her family in haste to a plantation three miles distant. The heroic conduct of her eldest daughter, who went back to save a child, and carried him in her arms through the fire of the soldiery, has been the theme of song and story.* Mrs. Gibbes had a house in Charleston, but during the latter years of her life resided at Wilton, the country-seat of Mrs Barnard Elliott.

The name of Mrs. Barnard Elliott is familiar in South Carolina. Her maiden name was Susannah Smith; she was the daughter of Benjamin Smith, Speaker of the Provincial Assembly. In June, 1776,

---

* See "Women of the American Revolution" for a memoir, with details of the incident.

she presented two standards of richly embroidered colors to Colonel Moultrie's regiment of infantry, with an appropriate speech, and received thanks. One of these was planted by Jasper on the works before Savannah, three years afterwards; the gallant soldier received his death-wound, and sent a message to Mrs. Elliott that he had lost his life supporting her colors.

Susannah was an orphan heiress, and brought up by her aunt, Rebecca Motte, of patriotic memory. The niece also gave her sympathies and efforts to her country's cause. General Greene acknowledged her services. She was a beauty, and a universal favorite both before and after her marriage. Many anecdotes of her heroic spirit and patriotism are related, which are given in another work.

A beauty and leader in social circles, who had a picturesque life, was Sabina, the wife of William Elliott. Their family residence—"Accabee," seven miles from Charleston—was noted during the war as a place of refuge. Its garden and lawn extended to Ashley River; the grounds were shaded by magnificent live oaks, decorated with the floating silvery moss peculiar to the Southern lowlands. There, too, were the graceful fringe-tree, and the magnolia grandiflora, with other ornamental trees in front and on either side the mansion. The rear portico looked on an avenue of flowering locusts nearly a mile long. In the spacious hall, a circular flight of stairs led to Mrs. Elliott's study. This charming country-seat was her residence in the winter and early spring; her summers were passed at Johnson's Fort, on John's Island.

The eldest daughter of Mrs. Elliott became the wife of Daniel Huger; the youngest, Ann, married Colonel Lewis Morris, eldest son of Lewis Morris, of Morrisania, one of the signers of the Declaration of Independence. Ann Elliott was born at Accabee. She was an ardent patriot, and was called by the British "the beautiful rebel." While the British had possession of Charleston, she wore a bonnet decorated with thirteen small plumes. Kosciusko was her admirer and correspondent. The second son of a noble English family became so enamored of her that he offered to join the American army; but, though he besought friends to intercede, she refused him and his gifts with scorn. She saved the life of Colonel Morris when her house was visited by the Black Dragoons in search of him.

Colonel and Mrs. Morris owned a cotton plantation on the Edisto River, four miles from Charleston, called the "The Round O." They had also a residence upon Sullivan's Island. Mrs. Morris was one of the belles distinguished at the levees of the first President, and at the "Republican Court." During the latter part of her life she lived at Morrisania. She died in New York, in 1848, at the age of eighty-six.

Jane Elliott married Colonel Washington, whom she first saw as a wounded prisoner, while engaged in the supervision of the hospital. She was the only child of Charles Elliott, of St. Paul's parish. Gifted with beauty and wealth, her frank and winning, yet dignified manners, and noble character, gained general admiration. Political friend and foe alike paid homage to her charms. Major Barry addressed a poem "To Jane Elliott, playing the guitar," commencing thus:—

> "Sweet harmonist! whom nature triply arms
> With virtue, beauty, music's powerful charms;
> Say, why combined, when each resistless power
> Might mark its conquest to the fleeting hour?"

Her marriage to Washington took place in 1782. Her residence was the family seat, "Sandy Hill," in South Carolina. She died at sixty-six, in 1830.

Anna Elliott was the daughter of the brave patriot Thomas Ferguson. She labored for her country, and was an angel of mercy to the poor and afflicted. Her power of fascination, even over enemies, was remarkable. Many favors were granted at her request by British officers, while they held Charleston. Tradition preserved her reply to a royal officer in her garden, when he asked the name of a flower: "The rebel flower," she answered. "Why so called?" he asked. "Because it always flourishes most when trampled on."

When Ferguson was banished, his daughter, whose nature was all impulse and feeling, came to Charleston, and obtained leave to accompany him. She went on board the ship, and strove to cheer and encourage her father; but her feelings overcame her, and she fainted in the cabin.

The mother of John C. Calhoun was Martha Caldwell, whose parents emigrated to Virginia about 1749. They were descended from French Huguenots. Martha, with Patrick Calhoun, her husband, lived in Abbeville, South Carolina. Her sister, Elizabeth Caldwell, was a sufferer, with her mother, in the perils and persecutions of the Revolution. She married Robert Gillam, and lived to a great age, residing with her son, General James Gillam. She and other members of the Caldwell family were very prominent in society. John C. Calhoun, in 1811, married Floride Calhoun, the daughter of John Ewing Calhoun, his cousin, a former United States senator from South Carolina. She brought him an accession of fortune.

Esther Wake was the sister of Lady Tryon, the wife of Governor Tryon, of North Carolina. These two lovely and accomplished women exercised great influence, not only in society, but in matters of State. The Governor's dinners were princely; the fascinations of the ladies irresistible; and they helped to sustain the Executive authority. It was owing to their endeavors that a grant was obtained from the Assembly for building a splendid palace; and when the name of Tryon County was discarded, on account of the loyalism of those who bore it, the resolution to alter that of Wake was rejected by acclamation. Thus the county in which Raleigh is situated is consecrated in popular remembrance by association with the memory of beauty and virtue.

Margaret Gaston, the mother of Judge Gaston, of North Carolina, was born in England, about 1755, and educated in a French convent. While on a visit in North Carolina, she met Dr. Alexander Gaston, and was married to him at the age of twenty. He was barbarously killed by the tories, in 1781. The widow had thenceforth but one object in life—the education of her son. Her piety and lovely character gave her the highest appreciation in North Carolina.

Mrs. Wilie Jones was the daughter of Colonel Mountfort, and was conspicuous in society, being said to be "loved enthusiastically by every being who knew her." Born to ample fortune, she dispensed it with munificence, and an elegant hospitality rarely seen in a new country. She was charitable, and had a "native nobility of soul." The famous reply to Tarleton, when he sneeringly expressed a wish to see the rebel colonel, Washington, that he ought to have looked behind him at the battle of the Cowpens, has been attributed both to her and her sister, Mrs. Ashe. Mrs. Jones died in 1828. Mrs. Long (Miss McKinney) was the wife of Colonel Nicholas Long, commissary-general of the North Carolina forces. She possessed great energy and high mental endowments, and was greatly admired by the officers on both sides.

Mrs. Ralph Izard, in her youth, was noted as a beauty in the gayest circles of New York society. She was the daughter of Peter De Lancey, of Westchester, grand-daughter to Etienne De Lancey, a Huguenot nobleman, who came to America in 1686. Many women of this distinguished family married eminent men. Susan, daughter of Colonel Stephen De Lancey, married Lieutenant-Colonel William Johnson, and afterwards Lieutenant-General Sir Hudson Lowe, and was the beautiful Lady Lowe praised by Bonaparte. Charlotte married Sir David Dundas; another of the family, Sir William Draper. In later years, one of them became the wife of J. Fennimore Cooper. Alice married Ralph Izard, of Charleston, a gentleman of accomplishments and liberal fortune, in 1767. He took his bride to Europe, and lived in Paris some time; his family remaining abroad till peace was concluded. The old family residence, "The Elms," in South Carolina, was noted for their liberal hospitality. During the illness of her husband, Mrs. Izard managed his large estate and wrote his business letters, besides taking care of three families of children.*

* A fair relative of General Washington had a very remarkable experience. Born of wealthy parents, in Virginia, she was a widow at seventeen, living with her father, who had lost fortune and emigrated to Florida. His home was a log cabin with two rooms, in the unbroken solitude of a primeval forest. Colonel Gadsden was a neighbor, and often spoke of his friend—the Prince Achille Murat—exiled, with a price set on his head, living like a hermit on his plantation. He was introduced at length, and became enamored of the beautiful Kate. After some months she was married to the son of the Neapolitan monarch, the consent of his exiled family having been obtained. Madame Murat took the management of the plantation. In the Florida war Murat had the friendship of an Indian chief, who was accustomed to come at night, build a fire in his

dwelling, and stay till morning. "You and your squaw safe," he would say, when they trembled at the terrible deeds they witnessed. Twenty-five years after the marriage Murat died; but the princess continued to live on her Florida property, among her slaves; attending to the hospitals during the war, and selling her jewels to feed the destitute. Afterwards she visited England and France, and was received by the Emperor and Eugenie; returning to the gardens and fields of her beloved Southern home.

IX.

About 1779, Governor Caswell, of North Carolina, appointed Isaac Shelby lieutenant-colonel (Anthony Bledsoe being colonel) of the military company of Sullivan County. When Shelby returned from Kentucky, he became the affianced husband of Miss Susan Hart, a celebrated belle among the western settlements at that time. He took command, soon after, of the gallant volunteers who encountered the forces of Ferguson at King's Mountain, October 7, 1780, and, coming home crowned with the victor's wreath, found that his betrothed had gone with her brother to Kentucky, leaving for him no invitation to follow her. A lively little damsel was Sarah, the daughter of Colonel Bledsoe, and as the young officer spent much time at her father's, she often rallied him on his dejection at this cruel desertion. Shelby would reply by expressing resentment at the treatment he had received at the hands of the fair coquette, and protesting that he would not follow her, nor ask her of her father; he would wait for little Sarah Bledsoe, a far prettier bird than the one that had flown away. The flippant maiden, then some thirteen years old, would laughingly return his banter by saying, "he had better wait, indeed! and see if he could win Miss

Bledsoe, who could not win Miss Hart!" The arch damsel was not wholly in jest; for a youthful kinsman of the officer—David Shelby, a lad of seventeen or eighteen, who had fought by Isaac's side at King's Mountain—had already captivated her merry fancy. She remained true to this early love. The gallant colonel, who had threatened infidelity to his, did actually, notwithstanding his protestations, go to Kentucky the following year, seek out Miss Susan Hart, and marry her. She made him a faithful and excellent wife.

"Little Sarah" Bledsoe married David Shelby in 1784, and had her home in the midst of the wilderness of Cumberland valley. Shelby established himself as the first merchant in Nashville, in 1790. He afterwards removed to Sumner County; maintaining a high and honorable position, and giving valuable aid in building up the new State, in which his wife took her part. Her history, indeed, would embrace that of Tennessee. The names of Bledsoe, Shelby, Sevier, Robertson, Buchanan, Rains, and Wilson, are conspicuous in the country's annals; and amid the toil and heroic deeds that have made them celebrated, no woman did her share more nobly than Mrs. Shelby. She lived to see the helpless colony increase to a goodly State; residing, for the last twenty years of her life, with her son, Dr. Shelby, at his beautiful country-seat, "Faderland," near Nashville. Here she received and conversed with all interested in the early history of that region, and daily exhibited the beauty of an earnest "walk by faith." She died in 1852, aged eighty-six.

The wife of the first Governor of Tennessee—the lady of "Plum Grove"—is worthy of a record. Catherine Sherrill came with her father's family, in one of the pioneer parties, from the banks of Yadkin, North Carolina, across the rugged mountains, to seek new homes in the valley of the Watauga. Mr. Sherrill's residence was on the Nola Chucka, and known as "Daisy Fields." The station was attacked by the Indians in 1776; and among the flying women who were pursued by them was Miss Catherine Sherrill, whose family had removed for safety to the fort only the day before. The young lady was distinguished for courage and fleetness; it was said she could outrun and outleap any other woman; "could walk more erect, and ride more gracefully and skilfully than any other in all the mountains round about." On this occasion she did "run her best." Her figure was tall and straight, and her appearance was such as to attract the special notice and pursuit of the savages. They intercepted the direct path to the fort, and she was compelled to make a circuit, with a view of scaling the walls or palisades. At her first attempt, some one within the defenses tried to assist her; but his foot slipped, or the object on which he stood gave way, and both fell to the ground on opposite sides of the inclosure. The Indians were close at hand, and determined to capture the maiden. She said: "Their bullets and arrows came like hail: it was now leap the wall or die, for I would not live a captive!" She sprang, and in a moment was over, and within the defenses, "by the side of one in uniform." It was Captain John Sevier, and this was her first sight of her future husband. Sevier was then married; but his wife died in 1779, and in the following year he married Miss Sherrill. Their happy union lasted forty years. Sevier had selected an estate on the Watauga and Nola Chucka, and it received the name of "Plum Grove." Mrs. Sevier devoted herself to the duties of her station as mistress of a large household. Then the women did not disdain the employments of spinning, weaving, and making up most of the clothes worn by backwoods people; and all young girls were taught how to do such things. Mrs. Sevier's first work after marriage was to make the suits worn by her husband and his three sons at the battle of King's Mountain; and she often said, "Had his ten children been sons, and old enough to serve in that expedition, I could have fitted them out." She became the mother of eight children.

Colonel Sevier's life was one of incessant action and contest. He took a principal part in the Indian wars of East Tennessee, in the settlement of the country, and the organization of the State government. The Indian prisoners captured by him—at one time thirty in number—were taken care of in his own house. Mrs. Sevier's influence over them was salutary. When tories threatened invasion, she would not leave her home to seek refuge in a block-house. "The wife of John Sevier knows no fear," she was accustomed to say. The respect she manifested for her husband, and her own womanly dignity, had a favorable influence in promoting both his zeal and usefulness in the public service. She relieved him of all home cares. At one time the tories, infuriated against him, came to take him prisoner, determined to hang him; and when Mrs. Sevier refused to inform them where he was, threatened to shoot her if she persisted in her silence. "Shoot! shoot!" she exclaimed, in defiance; "I am not afraid to die. But remember, while there is a Sevier upon the earth, my blood will not be unavenged!" She proved her ability to defend her property on more than one occasion. She was liberal and charitable to the poor, and always welcomed the sick and wounded to the care and nursing she gave the soldiers. Many of the Colonel's Indian expeditions were fitted out and supplied by her exertions with money and provisions.

In 1784, occurred the scenes of the "State of Frankland," a name given by the people of East Tennessee to a separate and independent government, organized in consequence of dissatisfaction with the condition of affairs under North Carolina. John Sevier was the first and last governor of the new State. The establishment of this little republic was regarded as no less than a declaration of revolt by the Governor of North Carolina, and those concerned in it were sternly commanded to return to their allegiance and duty. In the conflict of authorities, and the civil and personal contests that grew out of this state of things in the revolted territory, the prudent and judicious conduct of Mrs. Sevier added to her husband's reputation and popularity. Their house was a place of general resort; being known to be open freely to all friends of the rights of self-defense and independence. All who came for counsel or aid were deeply impressed by Mrs. Sevier's dignity and noble bearing. Measures of adjustment were at last adopted. This gave some offense, and Governor Sevier was entrapped and carried off by enemies into North Carolina. His wife, with a courage and daring few women could have shown, promptly raised up friends who rescued him. When, after those scenes were past, he was called, again and again, by the unanimous voice, to preside as governor over the State of Tennessee, and when he was elected to the Congress of the United States, then did her great heart swell with thankfulness, as she acknowledged that she had not endured peril, toil, and sacrifice in vain. During the twelve years that he was Governor of Tennessee, she made his home delightful; a place of repose for the weary, an asylum for the afflicted; known far and wide as "the hospitable mansion of the people's favorite." This admirable woman was self-educated. She said: "I picked up a good deal from observation of men and their acts, for that was a business with us in the early settlements." She was the instructor of her children. Her own time was always filled up with employment of some kind; she plied her knitting-work while in conversation, and always wore a bunch of bright keys at her side.

After the death of Governor Sevier, in 1815, his widow removed to Overton County, in Middle Tennessee, where most of her children lived. Her retired residence was in a romantic and secluded spot—about ten or fifteen acres—on a high bench or spur of one of the mountains, a few miles from Obed River. A bold stream flung its waters down the mountain, and a dense wood shaded the spring near the house. Mrs. Sevier was known for years as the lady of "The Dale," seldom coming down from her eyrie; for the aged eagle had lost her mate, and she breathed the air nearest heaven, among the lofty oaks on the heights. Yet she was always cheerful, and, in her pointed and expressive language, would often relate anecdotes of the early settlers. With some pride she preserved an imported carpet, which had been presented to "the first governor's wife." It was, indeed, the first article of the kind ever laid on a "puncheon," or split log floor, west of the Alleghanies. It was usually spread out when company was expected; and when they had gone, Susy and Jeff, the servants, dusted, folded, and boxed it up. Cleanliness and order reigned in the abode, and "godliness with contentment." The lady herself was always neat and tidy; she wore a white cap with black trimmings, and sat erect as a statue, with her feet on the hearth-rug, her work-stand beside her, and her Bible upon it, or on her lap. The governor's hat hung on the wall. She quitted this mountain hermitage only when her last son removed to Alabama; dying in 1836, in Russelville, at the age of eighty-two.

Ruth, the second daughter of Governor Sevier by his second marriage, was born at "Plum Grove," in that part of North Carolina now known as East Tennessee; those settlements then forming the extreme borders of the country inhabited by civilized Americans. During the Indian wars in which Governor Sevier commanded the troops, and was acknowledged as "the friend and protector of the exposed settlements," Ruth evinced a strong interest in the history and character of those warlike tribes. She learned the Cherokee language, and won favor with the savages, who called her "Chucka's Rutha." Her form was of rare symmetry; she had "a face and a figure for a painter," and never stood, sat, or walked, but with a native ease and grace that won admiration. A young captive, adopted by the Indians, and named Shawtunk, saw and loved her, and won her affections. They were married, and Ruth not only taught her husband the elements of education, but accompanied him to military posts as his secretary; making out his reports, and performing the duties of which she could relieve him. In Natchez and other towns she became a brilliant belle in social circles; "the cynosure of neighboring eyes" for her beauty and unlimited influence. She was married a second time to a wealthy planter of Mississippi. Their residence was a beautiful and highly improved country-seat—"Burlington "— within view of Port Gibson, in Mississippi. Here were entertained a continual succession of visitors, with hospitality more splendid than had yet been seen in the western country. The stately abode was made charming by the cheerful temper and genial kindness of its mistress. She was a model housewife, and had all things in perfect order, while showing attention to her numerous guests. Her death occurred in 1824, while she was on a visit to Maysville, Kentucky.

One of the pioneers of Kentucky—the pride of her State, and celebrated as an ornament to the country— was Anna, the widow of Hon. Henry Innis. Her early days were passed in the wild woods, and yet in the society of such men as Clark, Wayne, Shelby, Scott, Boone, Henderson, Logan, Breckenridge, and all the great and heroic spirits of the West. She became the chronicler of her own times, interweaving traditions of the past with her narrative. With a cheerful disposition and a powerful intellect, she was blessed in store and in the children given her. Her daughter was the first wife of Hon. J. J. Crittenden. She died at Cedar Hill, near Frankfort, in 1851.

Another eminent daughter of Kentucky was the mother of General Leslie Combs. Her maiden name was Sarah Richardson. She was of a Quaker family in Maryland, connected with the Thomases and Snowdens. When her son Leslie started as a volunteer to join the

Kentucky troops ordered to the northern frontier under General Winchester, in 1812, she reminded him of his father's history and her own trials and dangers in the early settlements; and bade him "die rather than fail in duty." Her residence was six miles from Boonesborough.

Charlotte Reeves, the wife of General James Robertson, was born in North Carolina, 1751. She crossed the mountains and shared the dangers and sufferings of the early settlers of Tennessee. Her husband was the special protector of the infant colony, and was obliged to make long and arduous journeys every winter to attend the Legislature in North Carolina. Mrs. Robertson took charge of the family and maintained their place in society. Her adventures have been elsewhere recorded.* In 1805 Nashville is said to have had but one brick house; but Mrs. Robertson witnessed its growth to a large town.

The name of Simon Kenton, in the annals of the early pioneers, stands second only to that of the renowned woodsman, Daniel Boone. A county of Kentucky was named after him, and the incidents of his life were more thrilling than any romance. Elizabeth, his second wife, had a celebrity different from that of the other pioneer women of the West. She was the youngest daughter of Stephen Jarboe, a Frenchman, who removed to Kentucky about 1796. His daughter was

* "Pioneer Women of the West."

then seventeen, and, possessing rare attractions of person and manners, had numerous admirers. She was tall and graceful, with blue eyes and dark hair. Kenton, the hero of Indian encounters, saw and loved and laid siege to her. They were married at Kenton's Station in 1798. They removed to Cincinnati, and thence to the Mad River country. Their adventures, privations, and perils are chronicled elsewhere.* In their pleasant home they did as much as any one else in Kentucky to stamp the character of the State for liberal hospitality. Kenton was extensively known, and, possessing large land-claims in Kentucky, was reputed wealthy. His house was the resort of every shelterless emigrant, soldier, or land-hunter; even the wandering Indian stopped there for the supply of his wants. The continual influx of visitors, and the provisions necessary to supply their wants and those of a large family, entailed privations which Mrs. Kenton bore with cheerfulness for ten years. In 1810 General Kenton removed to Urbana, where he lived eight years. The dishonesty of agents and various misfortunes involved him in trouble and lawsuits. He was reduced from opulence to poverty, and was hunted like a felon, arrested and imprisoned. These wrongs and sufferings embittered the life of Mrs. Kenton. In 1818, they took up their residence on some wild land in what is now Logan County, and lived simply, remote from those who had thronged around them in days of pros-

* "Pioneer Women of the West."

perity. General Kenton died in 1836. His wife removed to Indiana, and died at the house of her son-in-law in 1842.

Mrs. Talbot, of Michigan, the daughter of Commodore Truxton, was a celebrated beauty, and in advanced years retained the dignified manners of the old time. She lived on her farm near Pontiac, in an ancient log-house embowered in eglantine; within, however, were evidences of refined taste, which invested with dignity the homeliest materials.

Louisa St. Clair was the daughter of the Governor of the Northwest Territory. He removed in 1790 from his plantation, "Pott's Grove," in Pennsylvania, to Marietta, Ohio. Louisa was distinguished among the ladies of that period for grace and beauty; and possessed indomitable energy and a strong intellect in a strong frame. She was a splendid equestrian—fearless, blooming, and graceful—and managed the most spirited horse with perfect ease, dashing at full gallop through the open woodlands of the West, and leaping over the logs in her way. In skating she was equally expert; her speed and dexterity were unrivaled; and her elegant person and neat dress were shown in rapid gyrations over the broad frozen surface of the Muskingum, close to the garrison. In short, she was the ideal of a soldier's daughter, and a model huntress, like Diana, loading and firing with the accuracy of a backwoodsman. With all these masculine accomplishments, and that of being a tireless walker, her refined manners rendered her the ornament of drawing-room circles. Her beauty was the more bewitching from her high intellectual culture; for she had received the best education Philadelphia could afford. The athletic exercise of the country strengthened both her mental and physical powers, and her rare spirit was suited to pioneer times and manners. After the Indian war, she returned to her early home in the romantic glens of Ligonier valley. The French emigrants who came from Paris to Marietta, and were entertained at the Governor's, wondered, as they descended the Ohio in "Kentucky arks" or flat-boats, at the broad rivers and vast forests of the West; and hardly less at the fearless spirit of the daughters of the land.

Sarah Sibley was Miss Sproat, the daughter of a Revolutionary officer. She was born at Providence, Rhode Island, in 1782, and was married at twenty to Solomon Sibley, a distinguished lawyer from Massachusetts, who finally fixed his home in Detroit. The fort there was garrisoned, and had Southern officers; the inhabitants of the town were mostly French; some descended of noble families, and priding themselves on superior refinement; these formed a most agreeable society. The families of British merchants living on the opposite side of the river often joined in their gayeties. For six months in the year they were shut off from intercourse with the outer world by the snows and want of facilities for travel; depending on their own limited circle for amusement. Mrs. Sibley went in August, 1804, to visit her parents, in Marietta, Ohio;

encamping in the woods on her journey, and keeping the wolves off by fires at night. Her horse died on the way, and many inconveniences had to be endured before she reached her destination.

Detroit was destroyed by fire in June, 1805; and Mr. Sibley was obliged to fit up another dwelling, which he and his family occupied thirty years. Mrs. Sibley bore a heroic part in the scenes of the war of 1812, and, some years after the peace, again visited her relatives in Ohio. During the whole of her married life she was the centre of an admiring circle. Her height was commanding, and her face and form were beautiful; she possessed rare intellectual powers, well trained, and most pleasing manners. With a truly noble character, rich in feminine graces, she was the object of profound and marked respect. Her husband was for many years Judge of the Supreme Court of the Territory of Michigan. He lived not only to be the last relic of the ancient Bar of Michigan proper—dating back to 1798—but the last remaining link, in that State, of the profession in the present day to that of the Northwest Territory. Judge Sibley was associated with General Cass in negotiating a treaty with the Indians by which the Indian title to Michigan was extinguished. He was successively a delegate from the Territory to Congress, District Attorney of the United States, and Judge of the Supreme Court of the State of Michigan.

The wife of Hon. John Walworth, one of the earliest settlers of Lake County, Ohio, shared the toils and privations of the pioneers, and shone conspicuous in hospitality, benevolence, and social influence. To her winning and attractive manners, her sprightliness and vivacity, must be attributed the resort to her house of the polished and highly respectable in the community. Twice she traveled on horseback to the farthest part of Connecticut and back, to visit friends. She was a belle at the first ball given at Cleveland, July 4, 1801, in Major Carter's log cabin. There were a dozen ladies and fifteen or twenty gentlemen; and the dancers kept time on the puncheon floor to Major Jones's violin, refreshed occasionally by sling made with whisky and maple-sugar. The dances were lively and hilarious; the "scamperdown double-shuffle," "western swing," "half moon," &c., &c.

Rebecca Heald was the daughter of Colonel Wells, of Kentucky, and the wife of the commander of Fort Dearborn, Chicago—a place associated with the scenes of the massacre on the 15th August, 1812. Near the junction of Chicago River with Lake Michigan, directly opposite the fort, from which it was separated by the river and a few rods of sloping green turf, stood the dwelling and trading establishment of Mr. John Kinzie. On the 7th April, 1812, while he was playing the violin and his children were dancing, his wife having gone up the river to see a sick neighbor, another neighbor rushed in, screaming, "The Indians! They are at Lee's place, killing and scalping!" The family hurried into two old pirogues, moored near, and paddled across the river to the fort. Early in August, Captain Heald received orders to evacuate the fort, and started to obey; Mr. Kinzie volunteering to accompany the troops, and leaving his family in the care of friendly Indians, who promised to convey them in a boat round the head of Lake Michigan to a point on St. Joseph's River. The boat had scarcely reached the mouth of the river, when a second message from the chief of St. Joseph's band came to detain them. This chief had already warned Kinzie that mischief was intended by the Pottowattamies, who had promised to escort the detachment. Mrs. Kinzie was a woman of uncommon strength and presence of mind, with rare energy; but her heart died within her as she folded her arms around her infant children, and saw her husband and eldest son marching to almost certain destruction. Mrs. Heald was placed in the boat with Mrs. Kinzie and her children, and covered with a buffalo robe, silence being enjoined. The boat returned to Kinzie's house, and the family were conveyed from the Pottowattamie encampment, closely guarded by their Indian friends. The fort was then fired. After new dangers and escapes, the family of Kinzie was carried to St. Joseph's, and afterwards to Detroit.

Mrs. Helm was the step-daughter of Mr. Kinzie; her mother, the widow of Colonel McKillip, having married him in 1803, and removed with him to Chicago, then a mere trading-post among the Pottowattamies. She married Lieutenant Helm. She was a witness to the terrible attack and massacre. Her life was saved by an old Indian, who dragged her into the lake, and when the firing subsided led her up the sand-banks into a wigwam.*

Mrs. Kinzie was the daughter-in-law of John Kinzie, the earliest resident of Chicago, whose trading establishment, as mentioned, stood near the junction of the river with the lake. At that time the peninsula of Michigan was a wilderness peopled with savages, with only one or two families of settlers besides the garrison. Many members of the Kinzie family were associated with the early history of this region.

Mrs. Kinzie took several excursions on horseback through the primeval forests of Illinois, before the pioneer settlers had yet penetrated its northern portion. She was accustomed, on these journeys, to camp out at night, without lodging or roof, save the canopy of heaven. Her home was fixed in Chicago, where she was looked up to with high respect as a social leader and a woman of superior endowments.

The residents of Ann Arbor, Michigan, will remember as a remarkable woman Mrs. Elizabeth Allen, who passed her later days in that village. She was Miss Tate, born among the mountains of Virginia, and was so great a belle, she was said to have had sixteen offers be-

---

* For a full account, see "Pioneer Women of the West."

fore she was eighteen. One overforward suitor, riding home among the mountains from the burial of his wife, overtook Miss Tate's horse, and, riding alongside, ventured to express a wish that she would consent to fill the place of the dear departed. The young lady blushed with indignation, and sternly forbade him to name the subject again "under a year." When the year had expired he proposed, and was rejected. She had a proud and happy bridal in the Old Dominion, and went cheerfully into the backwoods of the West with her husband, always remembering her brilliant girlhood, and often talking of it. Her gentle dignity and force of character gave her unusual influence, and her habits were those of a matron of the olden time.

Miss Frances Trask figured as a belle of the early days of Washtenaw County, Michigan, residing in Dixboro'. She had brilliant natural gifts, well cultivated. Her accomplishments were unusual, and gave her acknowledged superiority, which was maintained by her excellent qualities of character. She had great force, energy, and decision; a piquant wit, and a happy audacity that charmed even while she startled the prudence of her friends. Greatly admired in society, she was devotedly charitable, and abundant in ministrations to the sick. Like other maidens in that wild region, she excelled in athletic exercises; was accustomed to fire at a mark, and could cut off a chicken's head at an incredible number of rods; could ride with any racer, and was the sprightly leader at picnics and pleasure parties.

X.

Mrs. Polk was born in Tennessee, and was the daughter of Captain Joel Childress. She was a pupil at a Moravian Institute, and pursued her studies for two years under the care of instructors among this singular people. Perhaps the quiet, gentle, benevolent traits of character with which she became familiar in such association contributed to mould her own, or at least to encourage the growth of those womanly and Christian virtues for which in after life she was distinguished, and which adorned the eminent position she occupied.

Soon after her education was completed, Miss Childress left North Carolina, her father having taken up his residence in Murfreesborough, Tennessee. Here, in the bloom of nineteen, she was married to Mr. James K. Polk, who had been lately elected to the Tennessee Legislature. In 1825 he was elected a member of Congress. During fourteen sessions he continued a National representative, spending the winters at Washington; and in all but one Mrs. Polk was with him. Being often appointed the chairman of important committees, Mr. Polk's house was frequented by persons of political distinction; while the estimable qualities of his wife drew around her the best in the social circles of the metropolis. Among their visitors were many illustrious persons, whose services to their country have become historical, besides those entitled to distinction on the score of intellectual and social accomplishments. All were charmed with Mrs. Polk; and her womanly grace and dignity, her mild and amiable temper, her reserved yet winning and fascinating manners, crowned with humble and fervent piety, impressed all who were acquainted with her, and exercised a widely beneficial influence. She was always consistent in her walk, and governed her life by religious precepts rather than by regard to the opinion of the world. She was eminently charitable, and it is said that no applicant worthy of assistance, or engaged in any work of true benevolence, ever failed to receive aid at her hands. To many objects deserving support, her donations were munificent. These good deeds were always performed in a manner so simple and unostentatious that others either did not discover, or knew little of them. They were not for the voice of public praise.

Some complimentary verses on her leaving Washington were addressed to Mrs. Polk, in February, 1839, by the eminent jurist, Hon. Joseph D. Story, and showed his friendly regard. In that year Mr. Polk was called to fill the office of Governor of Tennessee. Mrs. Polk's devotion to his interests at all times, her spirit of conciliation and kindness, and the attractive graces of her deportment, had an important influence, not only on friends, but on members of the Legislature opposed to the governor. Although never desirous of the distinction of a female politician, she had taken great pains to make herself well acquainted with public affairs. One who knew her intimately, said there were few days in the year in which she did not spend a certain time reading the leading journals containing the grave productions of superior minds. The matter which only healthy, strong, and reflective minds could comprehend or digest, was always preferred by her to the light, frivolous literature of the day. Yet she rarely conversed on the subject of politics, and never was vehement in argument, or heated in advocating the side her judgment approved.

When James K. Polk was inaugurated President of the United States, in March, 1845, the home of his family was in the city of Washington. Mrs. Polk remained with him during the four years of his administration, with the exception of the summer of 1847, which she passed among friends in Tennessee. In this eminent station, where so much lies in the power of a true-hearted woman, she won from all parties not only approval, but unqualified admiration. Wide as were the differences of opinion relative to the President, visitors, friends, opponents, were unanimous in their praises of the grace and dignity with which Mrs. Polk presided over her department. A lady's letter to South Carolina says: "She is one of our sex of whom I feel justly proud, on account of her efficient good sense, admirable tact, experienced judgment, quiet decision, and irreproachable conduct, during her husband's whole administration; and I am sure that, without distinction of party, she has secured the unqualified approbation and good-will of every person who has visited her at the White House."—" She possesses, in a remarkable degree, kindness of feeling, equanimity of temper, good-humor, and conversational power, with affability of manner, and firm though unobtrusive determination of purpose. She is peculiarly fitted by nature, education, and extensive intercourse with the best society, to adorn her elevated station. In various positions she has always been self-possessed and equal to the occasion; being easy without familiarity, and dignified without restraint."

Mrs. Polk partook of the prejudices of many members of the Presbyterian Church, and would not permit dancing or cards in the house of which she was the mistress. At church a stranger would not be struck with any difference in her dress from others in the congregation; but, the same writer remarks, " at her grand levees, in full dress, she is a most imposing, magnificent-looking woman, and receives her numerous guests with grace, eloquence, and charming affability."—" She disarms envy by her unaffected good sense and good feeling, and fully appreciates the folly of upstart assumptions of aristocratic superiority."—" I have every reason to believe that when her husband resigns his office, she will carry with her into retirement the unqualified respect and esteem of the whole American people."

Many testify to Mrs. Polk's faculty of making herself popular with all classes; it might emphatically be said of her: "None named her but to praise." Besides her attractive personal appearance, the kindly warmth of her manner bespoke heartfelt sympathy. A visitor at the White House, at a levee given on New Year's day, thus describes the scene and Mrs. Polk: "The foreign courts were well represented in the imposing splendor of official costumes and uniforms shining with gold. The audience-room was nearly filled. Many ladies, beautifully attired, stood near the wife of the President; but among them all I should have selected her as fitly representing, in person and manner, the dignity and grace of the American female character. Modest, yet commanding in appearance, I felt she was worthy of all the admiration which has been lavished on her. She was richly and becomingly dressed, and easy and affable in deportment; looking, indeed, worthy of the high station which Providence had assigned her."

Mrs. Maury, in her "Englishwoman in America," mentions Mrs. Polk among the three ladies who have shared in the honors of the presidency whom she has seen. "Truly," she says, "among the queens whom I have seen, not one could compare with the regal grace of Mrs. Madison, the feminine, distinguished personnel of Mrs. Polk, and the intelligent and ladylike demeanor of Mrs. Adams. The first of these ladies is still, at the age of eighty-six, eminently beautiful, with a complexion as fresh and fair, and a skin as smooth, as that of an English girl. Mrs. Polk is a very handsome woman. Her hair is black, and her dark eyes and complexion give her a touch of the Spanish donna. These American ladies are highly cultivated, and perfectly accomplished and practiced in the most delicate and refined usages of distinguished society. It is not possible to observe the affectionate and deferential manner of Mrs. Polk towards the august lady who is now the 'mother of the republic,' without feeling for each the warmest admiration. Mrs. Polk is very well read, and has much talent for conversation; she is highly popular; her reception of all parties is that of a kind hostess and an accomplished gentlewoman. She has excellent taste in dress, and both in the morning and the evening preserves the subdued though elegant costume which characterizes the lady. She is ready at reply, and preserves her position admirably. At a levee a gentleman remarked: 'Madam, you have a very genteel assemblage to-night.'—'Sir,' replied Mrs. Polk, with perfect good-humor, but very significantly, 'I have never seen it otherwise.'

"One morning I found her reading. 'I have many books presented to me by the writers,' said she, 'and I try to read them all; at present that is not possible; but this evening the author of this book dines with the President, and I could not be so unkind as to appear wholly ignorant and unmindful of his gift.' I wore a brooch in which was contained the hair of my husband and children, very tastefully displayed. Mrs. Polk carried it to the window, read the names of the 'eleven,' compared their hair, and asked many questions about them. Saving her gracious majesty, I could have put my arms around her neck and kissed her."

An eloquent poem was addressed to Mrs. Polk by the accomplished novelist, Mrs. Ann S. Stephens, from which we give a brief extract:—

> "There, standing in our nation's home,
>   My memory ever pictures thee
> As some bright dame of ancient Rome,
>   Modest, yet all a queen should be.
> I love to keep thee in my mind,
>   Thus mated with the pure of old,
> When love, with lofty deeds combined,
>   Made women great and warriors bold.
>
> "When first I saw thee standing there,
>   And felt the pressure of thy hand,
> I scarcely thought if thou wert fair,
>   Or of the highest in the land;
> I knew thee gentle—pure as great,
>   All that was lovely, meek, and good;
> And so I half forget thy state
>   In love of thy bright womanhood."

Some complaint being made about the discontinuance of dancing at the White House, Mrs. Polk replied to the dissatisfied ladies, "Why, I would not dance in the *President's* house, would you?" intimating that a more private drawing-room was a more suitable place.

With her strict religious views, and regular attendance at church, Mrs. Polk was free from austerity or bigotry, and always exercised the largest charity in her judgment of others. Her life was directed by a genuine Christian faith, out of which grew a warm interest in the welfare of those she knew; a simple spirit of charity, and a deep, abiding solicitude for the advancement of the holy cause to which her whole being had been early consecrated. Influenced thus by the purest and highest motives, her conduct was at all times exemplary, and it is no wonder she was universally regarded as "a perfect woman nobly planned," whose name was always associated with what is lovely, pure, and of good report—with what is gracious and holy.

Towards the expiration of the term of Mr. Polk's administration, when the President elect, General Taylor, came to Washington, he was invited, with Vice-President Fillmore, to dine at the White House, and all the courtesies usually extended to the new chief magistrate were shown by Mr. Polk, notwithstanding the confusion attending his breaking up housekeeping and removal, and the close of a session of Congress. Mr. and Mrs. Polk left the White House the evening before the new President entered on his office. On the Wednesday evening previous, the house had been thrown open and brilliantly lighted up for the largest levee of the season; General Taylor and his family and suite—a company of forty persons, belonging to both political parties—having been entertained at dinner.

The life of Mrs. Polk was unvisited by any deep sorrow till she was bereaved of the husband to whom she had been so affectionately devoted. He had purchased, for a permanent residence, an elegant mansion, surrounded by extensive grounds, in the city of Nashville, Tennessee. This has ever since been the home of his widow. Under a temple in the grounds, within view from the side windows, is the tomb of President Polk— a plain monument, with an inscription recording the principal events of his history and the posts of distinction in which he served his country. This place is visited by many citizens and travelers, the grounds being kept open to the public. A room in the house, occupied by the President as a study, has been kept sacredly in the same condition in which he left it; his papers laid about, his pen as if just fallen from his hand, and every thing as if in use by the occupant. The deep sorrow of Mrs. Polk shrouded the house as well as her heart in mourning; but Time, the great softener of grief, has alleviated the first anguish of her loss, and the faith of a fervent Christian looks to re-union beyond the grave. When a large number of members of the General Assembly of the Presbyterian Church called upon her, as a mark of respect for one who had shared the honors of the nation's chief magistrate, and for the consistent Christian example she had maintained, both in her high position and in her secluded retirement, she invited to dinner many of those who called, and won their unfeigned admiration by her refined and graceful deportment, and the deep religious spirit evinced in her conversation. It was known that while presiding at the White House she was always ready to receive ministers of the gospel, when obliged to excuse herself from other visitors.

Rumors prevailed at the time that Mrs. Polk intended

to reside, at least for a time, in Washington, and that she had visited England after her husband's death; but they were without foundation. Nashville is her chosen home, and, having no children, she sought solace in the society of her niece and adopted daughter.

The Legislature of Tennessee was in the habit of calling in a body on Mrs. Polk, on the first of January in every year. This was the highest compliment ever paid by the State authorities to any lady. On one occasion, they expressed a wish to pay their respects on the 22d of February, in honor of the anniversary of Washington's birthday. Mrs. Polk received and entertained them with great cordiality. The people of Tennessee always manifested gratification at this mark of respect paid by their representatives to the distinguished wife of one of Tennessee's greatest statesmen.

On another occasion, various military companies, escorted by the Union Guards, came to pay their respects, approaching the grounds by the main entrance, and filing through them in front of the house. Such genuine manifestations of esteem and sympathy could not but be pleasing to Mrs. Polk. But she was always careful not to show any marked preference at such times for the Democratic party, of which her husband had been so many years the pride and support. She had so earnestly shared his sentiments, that it was natural she should ever feel a lively interest in the success of the Democracy and a wish for the ascendency of its principles: yet, holding inviolate her lady-like reserve and her sense of what was due to her position, she could not distinguish between parties in receiving public marks of respect.

The wife of Judge Huntington, of Indiana, was Susan, the daughter of Dr. Christopher A. Rudd, a physician of eminence in Springfield, Kentucky. He was of the Carroll family of Maryland, and his ancestors came with Lord Baltimore. He married Anna Benoist Palmer, descended from an old Huguenot family settled in Charleston, South Carolina.

Susan was born in Springfield, in 1821. She was placed early in a Catholic convent for her education, and acquired many brilliant accomplishments. She excelled in music, was a good linguist, and possessed such a knowledge of general literature as to develop and cultivate a rare taste. When only sixteen she was married to Clark Fitzhugh, of Louisville, Kentucky, a nephew of General George Rogers Clark, of Kentucky. They resided in Louisville till her husband's death. Mrs. Fitzhugh was surrounded by a circle of admiring friends, and was esteemed one of the brightest ornaments of Western society. Pure in heart, affectionate and kind in her nature, and disposed to exercise every office of sincere friendship and tender charity, accomplished in her manners, and brilliant in mental attainments, as well as beautiful in person, she soon became the favorite of her circle. Only a little more than a year, however, did this union last. One daughter was left to the widow; this daughter became the wife of Allan Polk, of Arkansas, a nephew of President Polk.

In 1842, Mrs. Fitzhugh went to Washington with her cousin, Mrs. Florida White. Here she became a courted belle in the fashionable world. Her beauty was in its blooming perfection. Her form was tall and exquisitely proportioned. She possessed a commanding dignity of mien, with faultless grace in every movement. Her complexion was fair; her eyes were dark blue, with long brown lashes; and her dark brown hair fell in heavy waves almost to her feet. Her features had the regularity of a Greek outline, and their classic beauty was rendered more charming by the refined intelligence that illumined her whole countenance. Her voice was musical, and she had fascinating eloquence in conversation. The elegance of high-breeding in her was harmonious with her feminine gentleness, and her playful humor gave her still more powerful attraction. Among her gentlemen admirers were the most distinguished men in the Capital. It was during this visit that she met the Hon. E. M. Huntington, then Commissioner of the General Land Office at Washington. She was married to him in November of the same year. President Tyler, who was a special friend of Mr. Huntington, offered him the position of Judge of the United States Court in Indiana. He fixed his home at Terre Haute; but he and his wife traveled extensively, and wherever they went, Mrs. Huntington was the centre and star of attraction. The judge was a man of learning and literary accomplishments, and served on the bench, associated with the Hon. John McLean, of Ohio, long enough to render his name celebrated. He died at St. Paul, Minnesota, in 1862.

The health of Mrs. Huntington had failed in 1853, when she accompanied her husband to Louisiana, and afterwards to San Antonio, Texas. Here they remained during the winter. The disease, however, gained upon her, notwithstanding the change of climate and the attention of her physicians. In December, 1854, she faded like a flower, dying at the early age of thirty-two. She was the mother of five children.

This lovely woman had a ruling influence in social circles, but one more valuable in the hearts of those nearest to her. Her life was an exemplification of the sweetest womanly virtues, elevated by unaffected piety. Beloved in her home and by numerous friends, her Christian faith allied her to higher natures in a purer world.

Ellen Adair, the daughter of Governor Adair, of Kentucky, who married Colonel White, of Florida, was usually called "Mrs. Florida White," in allusion to the State represented in Congress by her husband. She was a fashionable belle in Washington for several years, and was celebrated for her magnificent person and her accomplishments throughout the Gulf States. She spent some time in Europe. In her widowhood, while on a visit in New Orleans, she met Mr. Beattie, a native of Ireland, whom she accepted for her second husband. Her residence afterwards was in Florida.

Her sister, Mrs. Benjamin F. Pleasants, was much admired in Washington society, and took an interest in public affairs. These were two of the seven daughters of Governor Adair, all of whom were women of mark for beauty and talents.

Pamela Williams was born in Williamston, Massachusetts, about 1785. At the age of eighteen she married General Jacob Brown, whom she met at the house of her brother, Judge Williams, of Utica, New York, and went with him to reside at Brownsville, in Jefferson County. She was his constant companion in Washington, where her associations were with many elevated in station and brilliant ornaments of social life. The Madisons, Hamiltons, Schuylers, Calhouns, &c., were among her most intimate friends. Her rare qualities of mind and heart, her unassuming dignity, graceful ease, and finished culture, were highly appreciated in the best circles of the national capital. Her house was the centre of a polished coterie, where were welcomed not only the statesman and the scholar, the gifted and distinguished, but the less fortunate, who stood more in need of sympathy and encouragement.

When the General's death left his widow in sorrow, she received from General La Fayette a tender letter of condolence:—

"Paris, March 30, 1828.

"My Dear Madam:

"Amidst the heavy blows I have to bear this side of the Atlantic, by the loss of a young and beloved grand-daughter, and of an old friend and relation, the melancholy account from Washington has filled my heart with inexpressible grief. Previous information had given me the hope of improvement in the state of the excellent General's health, and has rendered the lamentable event still more painful to me.

"You know, dear madam, the intimate and most confidential friendship that has been formed between us. Our personal acquaintance was recent, although our characters had long been known to each other; but no old intimacy could be more affectionate, no mutual reliance better established.

"While I deeply regret him on my account, be assured, my dear madam, that I most affectionately sympathize in your affliction, and the feelings of your family. My son and M. L. Vasseur beg to be remembered; and I am, most cordially,

"Your affectionate and mourning friend,
"LA FAYETTE."

The wife of Henry Clay of Kentucky was the daughter of Thomas Hart of Lexington, one of the leading men of the State.

Mrs. Joshua Francis Fisher, the daughter of Henry Middleton, at one time United States minister to Russia, is noted at the present day in Philadelphia for musical accomplishments, social influence, and liberal hospitality. She was a native of South Carolina. Several persons of mark have belonged to the Middleton family, which is one of the oldest in the State.

In later years, Miss SALLIE WARD was extensively known as a fashionable belle in the West. The high position of her family, her extraordinary personal beauty and fascinations, and her connection with noted persons, placed her, even in youth, among the conspicuously observed. Her ancestors came of one of the most respectable of the ancient Huguenot families who fled from French persecution, bringing to the Southern States the best blood infused into the veins of the young nation. Her grandfather, Major Mattheus Flournoy, served with distinction in the war of the Revolution. He purchased a country-seat in Scott County, Kentucky, where the subject of this sketch was born. Her father, Hon. Robert J. Ward, possessed the intellectual qualities that make men great, with those moral ones which secure lasting friendship. At twenty-eight he was elected Speaker of the Kentucky Assembly, his ability and eloquence giving promise of a splendid public career. So great became his popularity that he might have obtained any office in the people's gift, had he remained in public life; in comparative retirement, his generous character and virtues gave him influence during life, and endeared his memory to numerous friends.

Mrs. Ward was one of the most remarkable women of the day, prominent for intellectual gifts and personal loveliness. No one in Kentucky has entertained so much company, or with such "success" in charming her guests and rendering her home famous as the centre of social enjoyment. She still holds an admired place in society.

The daughter of such parents might be expected to have every advantage of education and moral training; and thus it happened that the young and lovely girl, reared in the lap of luxury, idolized by her family, enjoying every pleasure wealth could bestow, and received in society with the most flattering homage, escaped being spoiled by adulation, and grew up as amiable and as well developed in mind as if stern discipline and severe trial had moulded her character in early years. She had rare natural gifts; a remarkable memory and quick perceptions enabled her to acquire foreign languages with readiness, and to retain what she had learned; and especially for music she possessed talent which the most careful and scientific cultivation improved into surpassing skill.

Every class in Louisville, Kentucky, where she lived, seemed to take pride in the loveliness of this young girl. It was a curious kind of popularity, more like that of a French princess in her hereditary province, in whom her people claimed a sort of ownership, than the simple admiration of republicans for a fair being highly favored of fortune. If a child had a pet kitten or a bird of remarkable beauty, it was fondly named "Sallie Ward." If a farmer rejoiced in the possession of a young lamb or heifer which he wanted to praise to the utmost degree of comparison, he would recommend it as "a perfect 'Sallie Ward.'" She was the ideal of all that was pure, beautiful, and sacred to young people who saw her only at a distance in her father's carriage, or walking, attended, or at church. Once, when a mother was teaching her bright little girl, six years of age, to say her prayers, and to meditate on the grandeur and power of the Almighty Creator, she told her how God made the glorious sun, the stars, and all the beautiful flowers,—the child interrupted her with, "And, mamma, He made Sallie Ward!"

"The Louisville Legion" was a source of great pride to the city. It is now identified with the memory of gallant services in the war with Mexico. The call upon the Governor of Kentucky for a regiment of infantry for service was responded to by the entire body of the "Legion," which was mustered into service in May, 1846, and embarked at Portland for New Orleans. The company of the "Louisville Guards" was quartered on board the steamboat "Scott," which came up to the foot of the falls to give the men a last look at their homes.

The morning of the departure of the brave Kentucky troops was bright and exhilarating, though many hearts were wrung with anguish at the parting. The troops marched to the residence of Mr. Ward, followed by friends who crowded to look their farewell. There was scarcely a dry eye in the vast throng as the youthful daughter of Mr. Ward appeared with a beautiful silken flag bearing the stars and stripes. This she presented; and as the soldiers received it, and its rich folds were flung to the breeze, a burst of inspiring music filled every heart with new hopes. The noble fellows marched away to the music amidst loud cheerings and faltered blessings. One of the principal officers of that celebrated "Legion" was General William Preston, who distinguished himself in the Southern army.

Miss Ward, accompanied by friends, drove to Portland to present the star-spangled banner also to the "Louisville Guards." She often described the scene with emotion. "As those brave fellows marched by the open carriage in which I sat, each one lifting his hat to me, it was the proudest moment of my life. I esteemed the honor of being selected to present the flag to those noble sons of Kentucky far greater than all the flattery and homage of a ball-room."

After the return of the troops, covered with honor, from the army, Miss Ward was one afternoon seated on her horse for a ride, when the two companies to whom she had presented the flags marched up and halted before her father's house. Unfurling the regimental banners, which they had carried through the entire campaign, they gave her a joyous greeting, "such as only brave men can give a woman. And, with my *whole soul*," she said, "I bade them welcome. I gazed with pride upon those flags, borne with honor and success through so many battles by the brave men before me."

A letter-writer, describing an evening at the White Sulphur Springs, thus mentions Mrs. Johnston, another daughter of Mr. Ward:—

"The cynosure of all eyes, the nucleus around which all gathered, was the newly arrived bride from Louisville, Kentucky, the daughter of Mr. Ward of that city, who is among the guests. We do not believe Tom Moore found any thing fairer when he went angel-hunting under the shade of the sumachs, than the picture-like face of this child-bride. Although her exquisite loveliness of feature, bright with the flush of early youth, is such as to throw the pretensions of others into the shade, yet her disposition seems so gentle, her naïveté so captivating, that it would be impossible to cherish one jealous feeling against her. To our mind, the chief charm of this young creature is the shy, sweet tenderness in her face. Her diamonds and point d'Alençon would have rejoiced the courtly pencil of Vandyke."

The White Sulphur Springs, in the mountainous region of Virginia, and surrounded by magnificent scenery, had long been the favorite resort of Fashion from the Southern and Southwestern States. Many were the belles who flourished here, season after season, and many were the fancy balls, that rivaled those of Saratoga and Newport.

At a fancy ball given by Mrs. Robert J. Ward, her daughter Sallie was described as the centre of attraction. As Nourmahal, she wore a pink satin skirt, covered with silver lama, the bodice embroidered with silver and studded with diamonds; the oriental white sleeves adorned with silver and gold; the satin trousers spangled with gold. Her hair was braided with pearls and covered with a Greek cap; her pink slippers were embroidered with silver, and splendid jewels profusely decorated the whole costume. The second dress—Nourmahal at the feast of Roses—was of white illusion dotted with silver, with a veil of silvery sheen and wreath of white roses, and white silk boots with silver anklets. She bore the charmed lute.

During her subsequent sojourn and travel in Europe she had opportunities for enjoying the master-pieces of art in all its forms, and her taste became critical, while her own powers were more developed. All who have known her bear testimony to her high intellectual culture and varied accomplishments, as well as to her faultless grace, and her excellence in the relations woman is called to bear, of daughter, wife, and mother. A distinguished man remarked, that she "had the mind of a man, with the gentleness and refinement of a true woman."

Not only in her native State, in the South, and in the courtly circles of London, but in other portions of the United States, was this gifted lady admired and courted as a leader of fashion. Her beauty was said to be absolutely dazzling. Her bright spirit, her "imperial elegance," combined with unaffected simplicity, her impulsive gayety united to gentleness, her charming wit and sprightliness in conversation, rendered her a favorite in every society. She was tall, with a form exquisitely symmetrical, combining majesty with bewitching grace. Her hands and feet were aristocratically small; her fair complexion, large blue eyes, and delicately penciled eyebrows, with a wealth of auburn hair, were distinctive of a blonde. Her voice is melodious, low, and sweet, and admirably modulated; "an excellent thing in woman," and rare in America. No justice to a woman's beauty can be done in a written description. But that she possesses a heart and mind of superior order, a soul above conventional distinctions, is evident to all who know her. She never seemed to prize the reputation of the fashionable belle, nor wished to be remembered merely as the idol of frivolous admiration; she would rather turn from such adulation. The true and tried friendship of those she judges worthy of esteem, the disinterested kindness of noble hearts—these she "grapples to her soul with hooks of steel;" these she appreciates and values. A gentleman from New York, who had refused a letter of introduction to her, saying he was sure he would not like her, chanced to meet her at a friend's house, was introduced without hearing her name, and entered into animated conversation with her, not knowing, for hours, that the lady who had so charmed him was formerly the Miss Ward so celebrated. He became one of her most devoted friends, and often said he "never knew a woman who had been so little understood."

The refined taste which showed itself in this lady's love of music, painting, and sculpture, always appeared in her style of dress. This was rich, but never ostentatious nor incongruous. A French gentleman who was presented to her expressed his surprise at her faultless costume, saying, with enthusiasm, "If the rest of her character corresponds with her taste in dress, she must be perfect," and observing that he had rarely seen such in American ladies.

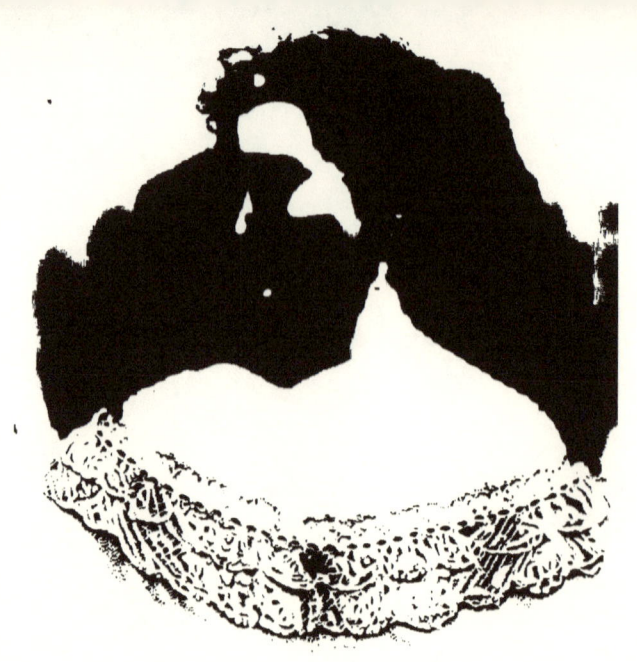

MRS. SALLIE WARD HUNT.

The generous charity of Mrs. Hunt has ever been warm and free. The poor were always her friends. The little daughters of her dressmakers and workingpeople, who were named after her, were always noticed kindly, and she seemed more pleased with the compliment from them than from wealthy parents of little "Sallie Wards" covered with lace and jewels.

Before her marriage, Miss Ward had been accustomed to spend the winters in New Orleans. After she was married to Dr. Hunt, and before the civil war, her residence was in New Orleans for seven years. Her home was a palace in splendor. The furniture for some of her rooms was made after the model of that used in the apartments of the Duchess of Orleans, in Paris; covered with white satin embroidered with chenille in wreaths and bouquets, with gilded framing richly carved; and divans and sofas covered with light blue satin, embroidered with white lilies, in rose-wood frames. The style in which Dr. Hunt lived corresponded with this magnificence. Several carriages were kept, with a retinue of servants. The dinner-parties were splendid, and always accompanied by music from the orchestra of the French Opera. The dining-room opened on a marble court, in the centre of which was a beautiful marble fountain, with jets arranged so as to play in figures. One of these was turned on every day just before dinner was announced; and the freshness and music of falling waters were an agreeable adjunct in that warm climate to the enjoyment of the meal. Surrounded with luxury by a husband whose wealth was devoted to her gratification, Mrs. Hunt was the centre of a choice circle of friends, dispensing hospitality in a style suited to her liberal feelings, and happy in promoting the enjoyment of those around her. The house was adorned with the finest statuary and paintings. Her superb entertainments were the delight of distinguished guests, as marked by refined taste.

At a fancy dress and masquerade party given by Miss Lillie Ward, in compliment to one of the belles of Cincinnati, Mrs. Hunt's light blue moire antique dress was remarkable for its decorations of magnificent point lace and diamonds of wonderful size and brilliancy. The necklace was composed of thirty-two "solitaires" of immense value. She wore a superb point lace shawl. The fair young hostess appeared as a Polish princess at the Russian Court, in a dress of heavy white silk, the skirt trimmed with ermine, and four rows of wide scarlet satin bands embroidered with gold. The corsage was high, and striped across the front with scarlet satin bands and gold lace. A hussar jacket of scarlet satin, embroidered with gold and trimmed with ermine, hung from her left shoulder, fastened with a gold cord and tassel. A jaunty cap of scarlet satin, with band of ermine and the emblematic Polish feather, fastened with opal and diamonds, completed the costume.

A general, distinguished in the late war, who met Mrs. Hunt at a party in Louisville, wrote an eloquent description of her. "For each epoch of life," he said,

"the style of her beauty was the appropriate model."
"What I noted chiefly was, the fullness of soul, the expression of refined intellect, that beamed from her eyes and was revealed in every lineament and movement. Her every word expressed a thought, while her language and manner were unaffected and simple as a child's."
"Her benevolent spirit finds exercise in diffusing delight."

In her domestic life at her present home, Mrs. Hunt displays the noble gifts and graces of her true nature. Death has bereaved her of her devoted husband;—but, surrounded by affectionate relatives—and engrossed by the employment of teaching her only child, a bright and noble boy, forming and developing his character for the greatest usefulness in life, and giving time and efforts to aid religious works under the auspices of her church—she has crowned a lovely youth with the meek virtues of Christian womanhood. It is rarely that the flower reared in the perilous glare of the world's homage thus preserves its bloom and fragrance to brighten the shady walks of life. Perhaps, in the United States, there has been no woman so much flattered and courted; and the fact that the pure simplicity of her character has not been impaired, argues a truly elevated mind. She seems to desire, above all worldly things, to be loved by her family and friends; and amply is her wish gratified, while the society in which she lives owns the gentlest and sweetest of womanly influences.

XI.

In preparing a limited sketch of Mrs. Madison, one labors under many difficulties. The subject must interest every American; yet the outline cannot be filled up with such details of life and character as would make a picture worthy of the noble original. Those of her own family who knew and loved her must be sensible of this disability. Her life, too, was so closely interwoven with that of Mr. Madison, by their mutual devotion to each other's interests and happiness, and their perfect unison of opinion and feeling in outside affairs, that a memoir of the lady must be incomplete without continual reference to her husband. Her kind and genial disposition, her delicate tact and good sense, were brought into exercise chiefly in the "aid and comfort" rendered to him; as also were those graces of mind and person which made the home of the Secretary of State, of the President, and, lastly, of the retired patriot and statesman, so charming a retreat, and so attractive alike to political friends and opponents.

The true character of Mrs. Madison can only be delineated properly by a faithful description of the whole tenor of her life, and of her consistent conduct during her eventful experience. I must deprecate, therefore, in the commencement of this brief notice, the criticism of her friends, who have a right to expect a portraiture satisfactory to their recollections. Such would require a volume of itself. This imperfect sketch may, however, suggest an extended memoir by some able pen, before the materials are lost.

John Payne, the grandfather of Mrs. Madison, was an English gentleman of wealth and liberal education. He came to reside in this country, and settled in Goochland County, Virginia. His wife was Anna Fleming, grand-daughter of Sir Thomas Fleming, who landed at Jamestown in 1616, and afterwards settled in the county of New Kent. Their son, John Payne, removed to North Carolina, where was situated the plantation his father had given him. He married Mary, the daughter of William Coles, a native of Enniscorthy, in Ireland. Not long after his marriage he returned to Virginia, and purchased an estate in Hanover County. He served as captain in the American army during the Revolutionary war. He had six children, of whom the oldest and youngest were sons. The eldest daughter is the subject of this sketch. Of her three sisters, Lucy, in 1792, married George Steptoe Washington (a nephew of General Washington), who owned a splendid estate in Jefferson County, Virginia; and afterwards, in 1811, Thomas Todd, of Kentucky, one of the Justices of the Supreme Court of the United States.

Anna Payne married Hon. Richard Cutts, member of Congress from the District of Maine, in 1804; and

Mary Payne, in 1800, was wedded to General G. J. Jackson, a prominent member of Congress from Virginia.

Dorothy Payne was born May 20, 1772, while her parents were on a visit to North Carolina, and received her name in honor of a beloved relative, Mrs. Henry, of Virginia. Both her parents became strict members of the Society of Friends, and were among the first of their sect in Virginia who had conscientious scruples as to the right of holding slaves as property. In 1786, their plantation in Virginia was sold, and with their negroes they removed to Philadelphia, where they gave all the slaves their freedom. One of the women, "Mother Amy," the nurse of the little Dorothy, would not consent to leave her kind master and mistress. She remained in their household, and was always faithful to their service. Being thrifty and saving, she laid up her wages, and at her death bequeathed five hundred dollars to Mrs. Payne.

In early youth Dorothy was remarkable for personal beauty and for grace of manners, joined to a modesty and gentleness that disarmed envy. She was bright and lively, endowed with a power of fascination felt by all who approached her, and withal was kind-hearted and full of sympathy. As her parents were in moderate circumstances, she owed neither to wealth nor hereditary possession the attention she received. In 1791, she was married to John Todd, of Philadelphia, a wealthy young lawyer, who also belonged to the Society of Friends. The youthful pair lived in simplicity and seclusion, but were not long united. Mr. Payne died a few months after the marriage, and in 1793, during the prevalence of the yellow fever in Philadelphia, Mr. Todd fell a victim to the disease, leaving Dorothy a widow with two children, one of whom survived its father but a short time. The other son, John Payne Todd, lived to be nearly sixty years of age.

Mrs. Todd returned to the home of her widowed mother in Philadelphia. Young and lovely as she was, her natural frank gayety prevailed over the depression of sorrow, and she soon became a great favorite in society. She was surrounded by suitors for her fair hand. One among them—James Madison, then a member of Congress from Virginia—was successful in laying siege to her heart. In truth, it is said she never before knew what love was till he became her affianced husband.

Towards the close of 1794, the youthful widow, accompanied by her son, her sister Anna, and other friends, among them her accepted lover, left Philadelphia for Herewood, the country-seat of her sister, Mrs. Washington. The gay party spent a week in making the journey, and shortly after their arrival Mrs. Todd was married to Mr. Madison; the Rev. Dr. Belmaine, of the Episcopal Church, who resided in Winchester, performing the nuptial ceremony. The event was celebrated with the festivities usual on such occasions, and the bridal pair proceeded to Montpelier, in Orange

County, Virginia, where they took up their residence with the father of Mr. Madison.

The hospitality of the Virginia planter, now a tradition, was then in its golden prime. Mr. Madison's house overflowed with guests, and various social pleasures made the hours and days pass rapidly. Mrs. Madison's mother and sister were invited to share in the enjoyments of her new home, and she, on her part, became devotedly attached to the mother of her husband. Harmony and mutual affection, with the enlivening society of friends and the luxuries a liberal fortune could command, made the place a little paradise. Mr. Madison continued in Congress—then holding its sessions in Philadelphia—until 1797. During these years of home and social pleasures, his beautiful wife had gradually changed the sober dress and grave manners of the Quakeress for an attire and deportment better suited to the part she was destined to take as a leader in society. She retained, however, the fundamental principles of the faith in which she had been educated; and no contact with the world could divest her of that softness of manner and gentle dignity, that sympathizing kindness of heart and universal charity, which she inherited from her parents as a part of her nature.

Mr. Madison was appointed Secretary of State by President Jefferson, in 1801, and removed his residence shortly after to Washington. The new National capital was at that time little better than a wilderness. The house to which Mrs. Madison was brought stood on a barren waste, in which were scattered rough masses of stone half hidden by the foliage of oak trees, like ruins over which moss and ivy clustered. The silence and solitude of the premises were almost appalling. The society of the place consisted of families unaccustomed to the new aspect of things, and not harmonized by similarity of habits, nor by established modes of living. They formed, in truth, a motley throng, in need of mutual aid and adaptation to bring them into the degree of unison necessary to make their association in any way agreeable. Here Mrs. Madison's ready sympathies and exquisite tact came into full requisition. She did much to unite the discordant elements, and make her neighbors, as Mr. Jefferson said, "like one family." The spirit of union and kindly feeling began to pervade society, and grew as the social intercourse, unshackled by etiquette or empty ceremony, became more genial and extended. In the absence of Mr. Jefferson's daughters, Mrs. Madison presided in the Executive mansion, and her influence was the true fostering genius to which the happy change was due. The house of the Secretary of State, next to the President's, was the resort of the greatest number of guests. Foreign ministers and visitors, senators, representatives, and persons of various political opinions, there met and conversed freely, while party spirit lost its bitterness in that pleasant atmosphere. How much of this softening of asperities was owing to the peculiar charm of the manner of the fair hostess, to her gracious affability, her cordial ease and frankness, and her faculty of banishing the evil cloud from the horizon, probably none knew, for the sweetest moral influences are felt rather than discerned by outward sense. The table of the Secretary was continually surrounded by guests, and was spread with the profusion of Virginian hospitality, sometimes at the expense, it must be confessed, of the refined elegance of European taste The wife of a foreign minister once ridiculed the enormous size and the number of the dishes with which the table was loaded, and remarked that it was more like a harvest-home supper than the entertainment of a Secretary of State.* On hearing of this observation, Mrs. Madison replied, that she thought abundance preferable to elegance; that customs were created by circumstances, and tastes by customs; and that, as the profusion so repugnant to foreign ideas of propriety arose from the happy circumstance of the superabundance and prosperity granted by a bountiful Providence to our favored land, she did not hesitate to sacrifice the delicacy of European taste to the less elegant but more liberal fashion of Virginia. That profusely spread table, indeed, supplied the daily food of many poor families.

Mr. Madison held the office of Secretary of State for eight years. During this time the same hospitable and kindly relations were sustained with the citizens,

---

* I have availed myself of a sketch of Mrs. Madison in the "National Portrait Gallery," written by Mrs. S. H. Smith, an old and esteemed friend of the family. I am indebted for other materials to Mr. Richard D. Cutts, of Washington, the nephew of Mrs. Madison.

and reciprocal civilities strengthened mutual good-will. While her husband was absorbed in public business, Mrs. Madison discharged the duties devolving upon her, as his helpmeet and the mistress of his home, in social entertainments and as a visitor to others. Never was woman better fitted by nature and attainments for the difficult and delicate task. In her conspicuous position, exposed to jealousy and misconstruction, she managed to conciliate the good-will of all without offending the self-love of any one. Every visitor left her, it is said, under the impression that he or she had been received with favor, and had secured some portion of the esteem of the charming lady. One of her peculiarities was, that she rarely or never forgot a name, a face, or any occurrence worth remembering. Her quickness of recognition, and ready recurrence to the peculiar interest of an individual, doubtless went far to enlist the feelings of those with whom she conversed; yet her sympathies were genuine, and she never feigned a regard she could not feel.

While in the exercise of hospitality and in dispensing charity, her profusion was unchecked, Mrs. Madison's house was plainly furnished, and her dress was far from extravagant. In this respect her example is an admirable one for the ladies of the present day.

As the time approached for the election of another President—Mr. Madison being a candidate—political intrigues were rife in Washington. The times were trying beyond precedent, and the war of conflicting parties was severe. Here was a field for more than diplomatic tact;

for the play of woman's true wisdom, and her gentlest ministrations in reconciling differences. Mrs. Madison proved herself "equal to the situation." She met political assailants with mildness, and by "the soft answer" turned away the rancor of hostile party feeling. Many a political foe did she convert into a friend and follower of Madison. The bitterness of opposition was neutralized by her amiable civilities, which she took care should never be influenced by party politics. "Her snuff-box," says a friend, "had magic influence; who could partake of the offered dainty and retain enmity?" Thus the most violent partisans in her presence stood smiling and courteous, and the kindly feelings her generous politeness awakened in the end triumphed over animosities. No human heart can resist the gentle approach of "melting charity," and the excellent effect of Mrs. Madison's tactics—if so they may be called—was soon evident. Her husband was elected to the Presidency of the United States, and was inaugurated in March, 1809.

At the first reception given, Mr. Jefferson was surrounded by a crowd of admiring friends, anxious to express their regret for his impending departure. As the fairer portion of the throng pressed forward, a gentleman said, "The ladies will follow you."—"That is right," replied the ex-President, "since I am too old to follow them;" and added, "I remember, in France, when Dr. Franklin's friends were taking leave of him, the ladies almost smothered him with embraces. On his introducing me to them as his successor, I told them that, among the rest of his privileges, I wished he would transfer this enviable one to me. But he answered, 'No, no; you are too young a man.'"

One of the ladies whispered, "Why does he forget that that distinction no longer exists?"

A splendid ball celebrated the inauguration of Madison, and Jefferson came early to receive his successor. The band struck up at the entrance of each party. Mrs. Madison was led to a seat at the upper end of the room. She "looked and moved a queen." She wore a robe of buff-colored velvet, with rich pearls on her neck and arms, and a Paris turban with a bird-of-paradise plume. Jefferson, who was all life and exhilaration, replied to a remark on the paleness and apparent exhaustion of the new President: "Can you wonder at it! My shoulders have just been freed from a heavy burden; his just laden with it." When the manager brought Mrs. Madison the first number in the dance, she said, smiling: "I never dance; what shall I do with it?"—"Give it to the lady next you," was the answer. "No; that would look like partiality."—"Then I will," said the manager, and presented it to her sister.

The Presidential mansion now became more than ever the center of a gay and brilliant society. Large dinner parties were given every week, and a drawing-room was opened, where the beauty and fashion of the nation had a suitable field for display. The stiff formality and rigid ceremonials which had marked the rule of Mrs. Washington, were exchanged for ease, freedom, and lively conversation, all unnecessary etiquette being banished. Mrs. Madison's own manner was distinguished by sweet dignity and an amiable courtliness that adorned her high station, without the least admixture of pride or pretension; it was gracious and winning without familiarity, and modest without too much reserve.

Mrs. Adams wrote to her daughter, June, 1809: "With respect to Mrs. Madison's influence, it ought to be such as Solomon describes his virtuous woman's to be,—one who should do him good and not evil all the days of her life,—so that the heart of her husband may safely trust in her. I believe I may say with safety that her predecessors left her no evil example."

The bright aspect of affairs was soon changed. War raged over the country, and brought desolation in its train, as it threatened the National capital in 1814. The terror was wide spread; the inhabitants fled to neighboring towns for refuge as the advancing cannon was heard booming in the distance, and dismay came upon all who remained. The President had gone to hold a council of war, and no entreaties could prevail on Mrs. Madison to leave the city of Washington in his absence. In vain the friends who implored her to escape had the carriage brought to the door; she refused to enter it. At this juncture, her feelings may best be seen by her letter to her sister:—

"TUESDAY, AUGUST 23, 1814.

"DEAR SISTER:—

"My husband left me yesterday morning to join General Winder. He inquired anxiously whether I had courage and firmness to re-

main in the Presidential house till his return, and on my assurance that I had no fear but for him and the success of our army, he left me, beseeching me to take care of myself and of the cabinet papers, public and private. I have since received two dispatches from him, written with a pencil. The last is alarming, because he desires I should be ready at a moment's warning to enter my carriage and leave the city; that the enemy seemed stronger than had been reported, and that it might happen that they would reach the city with intention to destroy it. * * * *
I am accordingly ready. I have pressed as many cabinet papers into trunks as to fill one carriage. Our private property must be sacrificed, as it is impossible to procure wagons for its transportation. I am determined not to go myself until I see Mr. Madison safe, and he can accompany me, as I hear of much hostility towards him. * * * Disaffection stalks around us. * * *
My friends are all gone; even Colonel C., with his hundred men, who were stationed as a guard in this inclosure. French John (a faithful domestic), with his usual activity and resolution, offers to spike the cannon at the gate, and to lay a train of powder which would blow up the British should they enter the house. To the last proposition I positively object, without being able, however, to make him understand why all advantages in war may not be taken.

"*Wednesday morning, twelve o'clock.* Since sunrise I have been turning my spy-glass in every direction, and watching with unwearied anxiety, hoping to discern the approach of my dear husband and his friends; but alas! I can descry only groups of military wandering in all directions, as if there was a lack of arms or spirit to fight for their own firesides!

"*Three o'clock.* Will you believe it, my sister, we have had a battle or skirmish near Bladensburgh, and I am still here within sound of the cannon! Mr. Madison comes not. May God protect him! Two messengers, covered with dust, come to bid me fly; but I wait for him. * * * At this late hour a wagon has been procured; I have had it filled with the plate and most valuable portable articles belonging to the house. Whether it will reach its destination, the Bank of Maryland, or fall into the hands of British soldiery, events must determine.

"Our kind friend, Mr. Carroll, has come to hasten my departure, and is in a very bad humor with me, because I insist on waiting until the large picture of General Washington is secured, and it requires to be unscrewed from the wall. This process was found too tedious for these perilous moments; I have ordered the frame to be broken and the canvas taken out. It is done, and the precious portrait is placed in the hands of two gentlemen of New York for safe-keeping. And now, dear sister, I must leave this house, or the retreating army will make me a prisoner in it, by filling up the road I am directed to take. When I shall again write to you, or where I shall be to-morrow, I cannot tell."

Such was the truly gallant conduct of this admirable woman on a most trying occasion, and such her tender anxieties for the husband from whom she would never permit herself to be separated for more than a day or two, during their forty-two years of married life.

When Mrs. Madison did the honors of the Presidential house, on the news of peace, in 1815, she was in the meridian of her life and queenly beauty. She was described on that occasion as radiant with joy, and dispensing hospitalities and exchanging congratulations with unrivaled grace. Washington Irving mentioned her " as a fine, portly, buxom dame, who has a smile and a pleasant word for everybody." Her sisters, Mrs. Cutts and Mrs. Washington, he playfully compared to " the merry wives of Windsor."

During the remainder of Madison's administration he lived in a private house, but continued to receive and entertain company with undiminished hospitality. At the close of his second term, March, 1817, he quitted Washington, and returned to his mountain home—Montpelier—where he passed the remaining years of his life, with annual visits to Charlottesville, to serve as a member of the Board of Visitors of the University. One visit he paid to Richmond, in 1829, to preside over the Convention called to revise the Constitution of Virginia. Mrs. Madison always accompanied him on these excursions; and when they went to Charlottesville they were the guests of Mr. Jefferson, as long as he lived.

The following letter from Judge William Johnson, of the United States Supreme Court, to Mrs. Madison, may show the estimation in which she was held, and the general feeling at her departure from Washington:—

"WASHINGTON, 1817.

"I am this moment on the eve of leaving Washington, and shall leave it without a parting interview with one whom I must be indulged in the liberty of comprising among the most respected and most cherished of my friends.

"But you, madam, cannot mistake the feelings which dictate to me this mode of making you an humble tender of a most affectionate adieu.

"You are now about to enter upon the enjoyment of the most enviable state which can fall to the lot of mankind—to carry with you to your retirement the blessings of all who ever knew you. Think not, madam, that I address to you the language of flattery. It is what no one but yourself would hesitate at conceding. And be assured that all who have ever enjoyed the honor of your acquaintance, will long remember that polite condescension which never failed to encourage the diffident, that suavity of manner which tempted the morose or thoughtful to be cheerful, or that benevolence of aspect which suffered no one to turn from you without an emotion of gratitude.

"Permit, madam, one who has shared his due proportion of your attentions to make you a sincere tender of the most heartfelt gratitude and respect, and to wish that you may long enjoy every blessing that Heaven dispenses to the meritorious.

"Do me the favor to tender to Mr. Madison also a respectful adieu, and a cordial and sincerely friendly one to your son.

"Very respectfully,

"WILLIAM JOHNSON, JR."

Montpelier was a beautiful place, less than a day's journey from Monticello, whence the Blue Ridge could be traced a hundred and fifty miles. Thus Jefferson and Madison were neighbors in the Virginian acceptation of the term. The tranquillity and dignity of domestic retirement were very agreeable to Mr. and Mrs. Madison. Their house was large and commodious, arranged more with a view to comfort than ornament, and stood at the foot of a lofty and densely wooded hill, commanding a view of scenery remarkable for its picturesque beauty. There was a fine garden and grounds, and an extensive lawn shaded by forest trees. The place was called "Montpelier" on account of the salubrity of the situation. One wing of the building was appropriated entirely to the use of the venerable mother of Madison; it had offices and a garden attached to it. The aged matron was attended by her old family servants, and surrounded by children and grandchildren. Thus under one roof were exhibited the customs of the end and the beginning of a century. By opening a door, you passed from the refined elegancies and the gayeties of modern life, into all that was venerable and dignified in by-gone days; from airy apartments and windows opening to the ground and hung with light silken drapery—from French furniture, light fancy chairs, gay carpets, &c., to solid and heavy, carved and polished mahogany furniture, darkened by age; to the thick, rich curtains and comfortable adjustments of our great-grandmothers' time. It was a great favor to gay visitors to be permitted to pay their respects to the President's mother. She usually sat upon a couch, beside which stood a small table, nearly covered with large, dark, well-worn quarto and folio volumes. "The venerable matron closed one of them, and took up her knitting. 'Look at my fingers,' she said; 'you will perceive I have not been idle.' Delicate fingers they were, and polished by knitting. 'I owe every thing to *her*,' she added, pointing to her daughter-in-law, Mrs. Madison. 'She is *my* mother now, and tenderly cares for all my wants.' Never was Mrs. Madison so lovely in her splendid drawing-rooms, surrounded by courtly and brilliant circles, the center of attraction—never so estimable, as in her loving attendance on this venerable woman." She took delight in the society of the young, and participated in their pleasures, to which she always contributed by her presence. A more affectionate and devoted wife never existed; and tenderly did she soothe and comfort her husband in his long imprisonment with illness.

An extract from one of her letters to Mrs. Richard Cutts is illustrative of life at Montpelier at the period when it was written:—

"MONTPELIER, July 5, 1820.

"I have just received yours, my dear sister, and rejoice that you are all well. * * * * * *

"Yesterday we had ninety persons to dine with us at one table, fixed on the lawn, under a large arbor. The dinner was profuse and handsome, and the company very orderly. Many of your old acquaintances were here—among them the two Barbours. We had no ladies except Mother Madison, Mrs. Macon, and Nelly Willis. The day was cool and all pleasant. Half a dozen only staid all night, and are now about to depart. President Monroe's letter this morning announces the French Minister; we expect him this evening, or perhaps sooner, though he may not come until to morrow; but I am less worried here with a hundred visitors than with twenty-five in Washington, this summer especially. I wish you had just such a country home as this, as I truly believe it is the happiest and most independent life, and would be best for your children. * * * * * * *

"Your devoted sister,
"D. P. MADISON."

Within a few months after Mrs. Madison had been bereaved of her husband, her health utterly failed; and during the winter of 1836–37, she suffered greatly from a painful affection of the eyes; being compelled to keep her bed, with closely drawn curtains, for the greater part of the time. As the spring advanced she began to recover; and, as her physician earnestly recommended change of air and scene, she went to spend part of the summer at the White Sulphur Springs, in Virginia. At the end of August she returned to Montpelier, much improved in health. On many accounts she dreaded the solitude of a winter residence at this mountain home. Her brother John and his family, who had been living for many years in her immediate neighborhood, in that autumn removed to Kentucky, leaving one of his daughters—Anna Payne—in the charge of Mrs. Madison. It was, therefore, not surprising to her friends that she decided on another visit to Washington. She owned a house situated in the most pleasant part of the city, near to the children of her sister Anna and to many of her most valued friends. These, and indeed the whole society of Washington, including many who were strangers to her, warmly welcomed her return in 1837.

Finding a residence here more congenial to her feelings, she remained in Washington, with occasional visits to Montpelier. If she could not enjoy social gayeties as she formerly did, her benevolence and sympathy for those in distress were as lively as ever. Many times did she interpose with aid in cases of suffering or injustice, and her charities were limited only by her means. These became much straitened in the later years of her life; and the loss of fortune was felt most severely by her in the deprivation of her ability to extend liberal assistance to the needy, and to entertain the friends to whom her sincere and tender heart clung with undeviating affection.

It was a sad day for her when her pecuniary embarrassments compelled Mrs. Madison to consent to the sale of Montpelier. In 1842, accompanied by her niece, Miss Payne, and her nephew, Richard D. Cutts, she visited Philadelphia, and thence proceeded to New York, where the party spent a few days at the Astor House before returning to Washington.

Mrs. Madison was one of the guests on board the *Princeton*, at the time of the explosion of the "big gun" in 1844. The catastrophe occurred immediately after dinner, while most of the ladies were in the cabin, having fortunately lingered there to hear some merry songs by the young people. It was in the same year that the House of Representatives paid to Mrs. Madison an unusual and signal mark of respect, by offering her the privilege of a seat on the floor of the Hall, whenever she might desire to attend the sittings. This was a testimony of homage never before or since offered to a lady.

The noble qualities of head and heart which distinguished Mrs. Madison were crowned by deep and fervent piety. She was constant in her attendance, while resident in Washington, at the Episcopal Church of St. John's, which was built during Madison's administration; and on her return she found her old friend still the rector. She was confirmed as a member of the church by Bishop Whittingham, of Maryland.

In the last year of her life she suffered from extreme debility, but her mental faculties were not in the least impaired. Her memory was often busy with the past; she would have old letters read to her, and seemed to connect with them associations unknown to those around her. She took great delight in hearing the Bible read. It was while listening to a portion of the Gospel of St. John—the part of the New Testament which she most loved—that she sank into her last peaceful slumber. The sleep lasted so long as to cause alarm; and when the physician was summoned, he pronounced it slow apoplexy. For two days she lingered, apparently without suffering, and only occasionally roused to a consciousness manifested rather by loving smiles bestowed on those around her than by words. She died on the 8th of July, 1849. The funeral took place on the 11th. The body, incased in a sarcophagus, was temporarily deposited in a vault in the Congressional Cemetery. In January, 1858, the sacred remains were removed by Mrs. Madison's nephew, Mr. Richard D. Cutts, to the family burial-ground at Montpelier, and placed by the side of her husband. A separate monument was erected to her memory; a monument to Mr. Madison having already been put up the year previously by his friends in Virginia.

Eleanor Parke Custis was considered one of the most beautiful and brilliant women of her day. Her portrait is preserved with care among the treasures at Arlington House. She was the grand-daughter of Mrs. Washington, with whom she lived. She was never suffered to waste her time in idleness; being required, in addition to other studies, to practice the harpsichord four or five hours daily. One day, not hearing the music, Mrs. Washington came down stairs, and remarked that she had heard some one go out of the house, so that the young lady must have had a visitor. Noticing a blemish on the wall, which had been newly painted cream color, she exclaimed: "Ah, it was no Federalist!" pointing to the spot just over the settee; "none but a filthy Democrat would mark a place with his good-for-nothing head in that manner!"

In the beginning of 1798 Eleanor was a blooming girl, exceedingly attractive in person and manners, and a great favorite with General Washington. Lawrence Lewis, Washington's favorite nephew—the son of his sister Elizabeth—was at that time living at Mount Vernon, and learned to love Nelly Custis. But a seeming rival arose in the person of Charles Carroll of Carrollton, who had just returned from Europe, accomplished, well educated, and adorned with the social graces derived from foreign travel. Young Custis was pleased with Carroll, and, being anxious to secure Nelly's happiness, wrote to the General in April, 1798, that he thought it would be a desirable match. Washington wrote in reply: " Young Mr. C—— came here about a fortnight ago to dinner, and left us next morning after breakfast. If his object was such as you say has been reported, it was not declared here, and therefore the less said upon the subject, particularly by your sister's friends, the more prudent it will be, until the subject developes itself more."

Other suitors, meanwhile, came to Mount Vernon, and paid homage to the wit and beauty of Miss Custis. She wrote to a friend: "I was young and romantic then, and fond of wandering alone by moonlight in the woods of Mount Vernon. Grandmamma thought it wrong and unsafe, and scolded and coaxed me into a promise that I would not wander in the woods again unaccompanied. But I was missing one evening, and was brought home from the interdicted woods to the drawing-room, where the General was walking up and down with his hands behind him, as was his wont. Grandmamma, seated in her great arm-chair, opened a severe reproof."

Poor Nelly, taxed with delinquency, admitted her fault, and offered no excuse—but when there was a slight pause, she moved to leave the room. She was just closing the door behind her, when she overheard the General attempting, in a low voice, to intercede in her behalf. "My dear," he said, "I would say no more; perhaps she was not alone."

This intercession stopped Miss Nelly in her retreat. She opened the door again quickly, and walked up to the General with a firm step. "Sir," she said, "you brought me up to speak the truth; and when I told Grandmamma I was alone, I hope you believe I was alone."

The General made one of his magnanimous bows, and replied, "My child, I beg your pardon."

Eleanor was married to Lawrence Lewis on the birthday of the Chief, 1799.

It was a bright day in the early spring of the South. The flowers were budding in the hedges; the bluebird, making its way cautiously northward, gave out a few joyous notes in the garden; and nature seemed to sympathize in the hilarity that prevailed at Mount Vernon on that auspicious February morning. The bride was dearly loved by her relatives; Major Lewis was near his uncle's heart for the sake of his dead mother, who bore so striking a resemblance to the great Chief, that sometimes, when in sport she would put a chapeau on her head and throw a military cloak over her shoulders, she might easily have been mistaken for himself.

It was the bride's wish that the General should wear on that occasion the splendid embroidered uniform which the board of general officers had adopted; but Washington would not appear in a costume bedizened with tinsel; preferring the plain old continental blue and buff, with a modest black ribbon and cockade. The magnificent white plumes which General Pinckney had presented to him he gave to the bride; and to the Rev. Thomas Davis, the rector of Christ Church, Alexandria, who performed the marriage ceremony, he gave an elegant copy of Mrs. Macaulay's* "History of England," in eight volumes, telling him they were written by a remarkable woman, who had visited America many years before. She had crossed the Atlantic in 1785 to see General Washington.

Mrs. Mary Custis, of Arlington, the wife of Mrs. Washington's grandson, was the daughter of William Fitzhugh, of Chatham. Bishop Meade says: "Scarcely was there a Christian lady more honored; none more loved and esteemed."

Mrs. Marshall, the wife of Chief Justice Marshall, of

---

* Catharine Macaulay Graham.

Richmond, Virginia, was devoted to her husband. After her death, in 1831, he often repeated General Burgoyne's lines, substituting "Mary" for "Anna":—

> "Encompassed in an angel's frame,
> An angel's virtues lay;
> Too soon did Heaven assert its claim,
> And take its own away.
>
> "My Mary's worth, my Mary's charms,
> Can never more return;
> What now shall fill these widowed arms!
> Ah me! my Mary's urn!
> Ah me! ah me! my Mary's urn!"

An intimate friend of "Nelly Custis" was Mary A. Sitgreaves, the second child of Colonel Daniel Kemper, of the Revolutionary army. She was born in New York, in April, 1774. Her early associations were with persons distinguished in those times. When New York was threatened by the British, her father removed his family to Morristown, New Jersey. While the headquarters of General Washington were in the neighborhood, Miss Kemper was in the habit of playing about the Chief's premises, and now and then running into his marquée. Mrs. Washington one day was busy in arranging the camp-stools and putting things to rights, when the little visitor presented herself. The General seized her, placed her upon his knee, and had a long talk with her. This incident she often referred to with pleasure.

During the Presidency of Washington, Miss Kemper became prominent in the circles of the republican court for her great beauty and the fascination of her manners. In the Capital she attracted much attention, and was a welcome guest at Mrs. Washington's at all times. She was on a visit at the house of her uncle, the celebrated Dr. David Jackson, of Philadelphia, when she first met Hon. Samuel Sitgreaves, a member of Congress, in the President's drawing-room. Love at first sight ensued, and she was married to him in June, 1796.

Once hearing a sermon on the birthday of Washington, Mrs. Sitgreaves described a birthnight-ball she had attended, in company with him and Mrs. Washington, just fifty-six years before; Mrs. Washington appearing dressed in black velvet trimmed with silver lace, and Mrs. Knox in green velvet decorated with gold. She and Eleanor Custis had their hair arranged by the hair-dresser, long previous to the fête, and then had a frolic in the garden, on the afternoon preceding it; she plucking snow-balls from the tree and showering the blossoms over her friend's head. They stuck fast, and formed a most admired addition to the head-dress in the evening.

On the adjournment of Congress, Mrs. Sitgreaves accompanied her husband to Easton, Pennsylvania. He was appointed Minister to England during the Presidency of the elder Adams, and was in Congress several years. Their home was in Easton till the death of Mrs. Sitgreaves, who long survived her husband, and died in November, 1864. She retained her faculties unimpaired and clear to the last moment of her existence, and her firm faith in her Redeemer was a consolation to her bereaved children, and a bright example to all who knew her, as had been her life of active Christian duty and cheerful benevolence. The church was her beloved, and she was always ready for every good word and work.

Mrs. Susan Wallace, the mother of Horace Binney Wallace, was eminent for the noble grace of her deportment. Her mother, Mrs. Mary Binney, lived opposite Washington's house in Philadelphia. The daughter of Mrs. Wallace, who married John Bradford Wallace, died in 1849. The Rev. Herman Hooker said of her, "No praise befits the character of such a person but a truthful and grateful mention of her virtues. She was a model of a woman." She was born February 22d, 1778, and was just entering society in the last years of Washington's administration. Her husband was the nephew of Mr. Bradford, the second Attorney General of the United States.

XII.

One of the most distinguished and charming women who gave a character of elegance and high-bred grace to the best circle in Washington society, was the wife of General Van Ness. She was the daughter of David Burns, a gentleman of excellent family, who inherited a fine estate near the Potomac, in the District of Columbia, and held the office of civil magistrate while attending to the interests of his large plantation. He married Miss White, a young lady also of highly respectable family. Marcia was their only daughter, born on the plantation now embraced within the limits of the city of Washington. She grew up a lovely girl, light as a fairy in form, with a face of innocent beauty, and manners so arch and engaging that all who saw her were attracted. She was placed at school in Georgetown, where she received a good education, with the accomplishments necessary for a young lady entitled to move in the most refined society. After completing her studies, she was sent for "finishing" to Baltimore, where she lived in the family of Luther Martin, then at the height of his reputation as the most eminent jurist and advocate in Maryland. He was a friend of Mr. Burns. Marcia had formed an intimacy with his daughter at the Georgetown boarding-school, and the two enjoyed the best opportunities and were well pleased to go into society together. The conversation of Martin often turned on public affairs, and his enthusiasm kindled in the young girl the patriotic and philanthropic spirit which impelled her in after life to an earnest interest in public matters. Her brother at the same time studied law with Martin. This brother died young. Miss Burns returned to her home about 1799 or 1800, not long before her father's death. From him she inherited a large fortune.

The seat of National Government was removed to Washington in May, 1802. Miss Burns was much sought after and admired for her personal charms and intellectual acquirements, as well as for the endowment of wealth; she was, indeed, from the first, one of the most prominent belles of Washington, and received at her father's house all who were distinguished in the political as well as the fashionable world throughout the United States. Mrs. Madison was one of her most intimate friends. At the age of twenty she married Hon. John P. Van Ness, member of Congress for New York, a gentleman of ancient and distinguished family. He became a resident of Washington, and their home was one of the most brilliant and agreeable in the Capital. Youthful as she was, the beautiful and accomplished Mrs. Van Ness was regarded as a leader in the most select circle, and as a model of all that is charming in the character of a lady. The principal men in the national councils, and those who had gained distinction in political life, did homage to her varied powers, her grace and dignity, and the charms of her sprightly conversation.

Her splendid house on Mansion Square was surrounded by beautiful shrubs and evergreens, with flowers of the choicest variety; the woodbine and multiflora creeping up the sides of the building. This was her residence after quitting the cottage in which she had been born and passed her childhood. This house was noted for elegant hospitality, in small social gatherings as well as in more splendid entertainments, and the success of Mrs. Van Ness in drawing around her the refined and cultivated, superior to the frivolous butterflies of fashion, made it a most desirable thing to have the pleasure of her acquaintance. Chief Justice Marshall, Henry Clay, President Monroe, General Jackson, Mr. Calhoun, Mr. McDuffie, Daniel Webster, Mr. Hayne, and many other noted celebrities, were on intimate terms with General Van Ness, and were frequent visitors; the foreign ministers also sought the society of a lady whose receptions were so agreeable, and whose social gifts were so captivating. In the bloom of her loveliness Mrs. Van Ness was remarkable for a complexion of dazzling fairness. Her features were regular, and her face was bright with expression; her smile was most bewitching; her eyes, a soft hazel, were full of fire; her form, though she was not tall, was exquisite in symmetry. The great charm of her presence was her perfect ease and refinement of manner; a gracious affability combined with dignity that bespoke true elevation of mind. She was full of vivacity in conversation, possessing a rich fund of humor, and her poetic fancy gave a coloring to her thoughts and opinions. This taste for poetry led her now and then to metrical effusions; and her friends were accustomed to be facetious about her family name of Burns, averring that she was of kin to the poet; though probably no relationship existed.

The only daughter of Mrs. Van Ness—Ann Elbertina—was a lovely girl, and became, in her early bloom, the ornament and delight of society. She was not only the darling, but the intelligent companion of her mother, whose delight it was to teach her, and impress her mind with the solemn truths of religion. The two entered into each other's feelings with a sympathy not often seen even in that near and sacred relation. Mrs. Van Ness was not satisfied, in the midst of her social triumphs, with dominion over the world of fashion. She felt herself called upon to act a higher and nobler part in society than that of a minister to its fleeting pleasures. The charity which in her always abounded, had its root in that true love of God which leads to good works. Her piety was enlightened by the faith in the Redeemer that brings every thought into subjection to the obedience of Christ, and produces fruits such as He approved. Her influence was always genial; her example ever noble and elevating; her friendships were true and warm; but these were not enough to fill her ideal of Christian duty. The sympathy that takes in humanity, the benevolence that springs from earnest religious feeling, the beneficence that spreads its fostering care over all who need it, without respect of persons—the deep humility that disclaims all thought of merit—grew in her heart, regenerated as it was by the Holy Spirit. She became a ministering angel to the sick and suffering; the poor sought her aid and received both counsel and assistance; she found her greatest delight in comforting the afflicted.

> "Distress but gleaned from others' store,
> From hers it reaped a plenteous dole."

Her good deeds were unostentatious—her gentle and loving ministrations unnoticed, while they brought balm to many a wounded heart. Prayer and thankfulness were continual in her household, and she took part in social prayers for the diffusion of the Gospel. Her taste for the beautiful in nature and the arts was sublimed by her devotion to the good.

Her beloved daughter, so like her in all Christian graces, returned in 1820 from school in Philadelphia, and two years afterwards was married to Arthur Middleton, of South Carolina. The young wife went to visit her husband's friends in his native State, and then returned to Washington. She died of malignant fever shortly afterwards, giving birth to a child, who also perished.

Mrs. Van Ness never recovered from the shock of this bereavement. From the day of her daughter's death she bade adieu to the gay world, and mingled no more in fashionable assemblages. She selected a retired room in the cottage where her parents lived and died, and would often go to that venerated place for meditation. The allurements of society could no longer draw her from the remembrance of the happiness she had lost. But her faith was too firmly grounded to permit the Christian virtues that had taken root in her character to languish and die. The fountain of her affections continued to pour forth a stream of charity. She became resigned to the will of God, and sought consolation in a more earnest devotion to her duties, both as a wife and as the benefactress of the destitute. It was owing to her persevering efforts that an institution was established which became an honor to the Capital—the Washington City Orphan Asylum. With her husband's concurrence she bestowed on it four thousand dollars, besides many small contributions from time to time, and by her indefatigable exertions with friends in Congress she obtained an act of incorporation, and a donation of ten thousand dollars for its permanent support. She also gave directions that a legacy of a thousand dollars should be given to the institution after her death.

Mrs. Van Ness was thus the founder of the asylum, though she always acknowledged the efficient co-operation of other benevolent ladies. During the administration of President Madison, Mrs. Madison was First Directress of the Institution; but after her departure, Mrs. Van Ness was induced to accept the office, which she held till her death. She was truly a mother to the children thus saved, sheltered, and trained for heaven by her instrumentality. She did not wait for those "pelted by the pitiless storm" of adversity to present themselves at her door; night and day she sought them out.

The grave of her daughter was a holy place to her, and she resolved to make an offering there. She built the Alms House beside it.

The portrait of Mrs. Van Ness is still in the Asylum. She is represented sitting, with three little girls clinging to her as if claiming protection; one with its head in her lap.

The closing scenes of her life evinced the power of religion to give peace and joy in the hour of death. Her disregard of self was apparent, even in her last moments, and in her last words to her husband kneeling beside her. After a long and painful illness, she died on the 9th of September, 1832, at the age of fifty.

She was the first American woman buried with public honors. The funeral took place on the day following her death, and was attended by a large concourse of people. The mahogany coffin, inclosing a leaden one, was covered with black velvet without decoration. On the breast was a silver plate, engraved with the date of her birth, marriage, and death. As the procession began to move, General Van Ness, who was Mayor of Washington, received from a committee of the citizens a silver plate inscribed: "The citizens of Washington, in testimony of their veneration for departed worth, dedicate this plate to the memory of Marcia Van Ness, the excellent consort of J. P. Van Ness. If piety, charity, high principle, and exalted worth, could have averted the shafts of fate, she would still have remained among us, a bright example of every virtue. The hand of death has removed her to a purer and happier state of existence; and while we lament her loss, let us endeavor to emulate her virtues." Then followed dates; and the gift was accompanied by a copy of the preamble and resolutions.

At the gate of the burial-place the little girls of the Orphan Asylum stood in lines, the procession passing between them. The coffin was placed at the door of the vault, and the children came forward and strewed the bier with branches of weeping-willow, singing a hymn of farewell. The funeral service was then read, and the deceased was laid beside her buried child.

The Board of Managers of the Washington City Orphan Asylum passed resolutions expressive of deep and heartfelt sympathy, and testifying respect for the character of the departed. Similar condolences were offered by the Association of Beneficence of Trinity Church. Few ladies, indeed, have ever occupied a larger field of usefulness, or been more devotedly engaged for many years in those labors of love which the Saviour enjoined on his followers as the evidence of their discipleship.

One of the intimate friends of Mrs. Van Ness, and one called by her "the most popular woman who was ever in Washington," was the wife of Levi Woodbury, Secretary of the Navy during Jackson's administration. She was remarkable for her amiable temper and dignified elegance of deportment. The officers who came to her house on business were treated by her with uniform courtesy and kindness; the midshipmen with the same urbanity as the commodore. Mrs. Woodbury was the daughter of Hon. Asa Clapp, of Portland, the most wealthy man at that time in the State of Maine. His wife was Miss Quincy. Their daughter had the advantage of an excellent education, and was fitted to adorn a high position.

———

Mrs. Louis McLane is mentioned in the letters of Washington Irving, and in other publications, as prominent in fashionable society in Washington. She was the eldest daughter of Robert Milligan, and in 1812 married the son of Allan McLane, of Delaware. In 1817 he was elected member of Congress from that State; and his liberal, patriotic opinions made him the steady advocate of internal improvements and a just economy. The pendency of the celebrated Missouri question, and the legislation in reference to the admission of that State, gave extraordinary interest to that year's Congress; for a new discussion arose on a much agitated subject. Mr. McLane thought it a member's duty to vote according to his own judgment, without regard to instructions; and his wife approved his course. He took his seat as United States Senator in December, 1827; and was sent by President Jackson Minister to England in May, 1829. His diplomatic talents found aid in the courtesy, grace, and dignity of his accomplished wife. In 1831 McLane returned to take charge of the Treasury Department in Jackson's second Cabinet; and in two years he was called to superintend the Department of State.

While McLane was in England, Washington Irving was entertained at his house. His respect and admiration for Mrs. McLane were manifest in his conversation as well as his letters. One of her daughters married General Joseph Johnson; another the grandson of Alexander Hamilton.

Washington Irving mentioned a Miss Barney—the sister of "Beau Barney"—as a belle in Washington, and very graceful in her deportment.

Miss Butt, of Norfolk, the author of "Anti-Fascination"—published in reply to "Uncle Tom's Cabin"—was highly praised in the Norfolk journals as having maintained, at Washington, "the fame of the 'Old Dominion' for. charms and accomplishments, and for beautiful women beyond reproach."

Edward Livingston married, in June, 1805, the young widow of a Jamaica agent, Louise Moreau de Lassy, born Davezac de Castera. Her beauty was

12*

described as extraordinary, and to wondrous graces of person she added a brilliant intellect. Livingston's first wife was Mary McEvers. Eliza McEvers became the wife of John R. Livingston.

In 1834, when Edward Livingston, who had been Secretary of State, accepted the appointment of Minister to France, he was accompanied by Mrs. Livingston and his daughter. Mrs. Livingston was born in one of the West India Islands; her family, driven from home by the horrors of revolution, came to New Orleans. Her brother was Minister from the United States to the Hague. She was possessed of rare intellectual attainments as well as personal attractions; her manners were gentle and refined, and she was brilliant in conversation, for her well-stored mind and extensive observation fitted her to shine among the cultivated. Her daughter, Cora, inherited her mental qualities and her loveliness. She was in Washington with her parents when it was menaced by the British troops, in 1814. Amid the hurly-burly, says Parton in his Life of Jackson, "the grim and steadfast warrior found time to caress and love the little girl who sat on his lap and played around his high splashed boots at head-quarters while he was busy. For her sake he retained one of his horses from the public service."

When Edward Livingston did not return to New Orleans, Major Mitchell, the highest English officer in rank among the prisoners, was held as a hostage for the safety of the Americans in the British fleet. One day

General Jackson, calling on Mrs. Livingston, found her in great anxiety about her husband. Cora, the little girl, whimpered, "When are you going to bring me back my father, General? The British will kill him." The mighty man of war stooped, and patting the little one on the head, said, "Don't cry, my child; if the British touch so much as a hair of your father's head, I'll hang Mitchell."

Miss Livingston was famous as the belle of Washington in the time of General Jackson's administration. She was married to Thomas Barton, who went as Secretary of Legation on the mission to France. The party traveled through Switzerland and Germany. At Heidelberg, Professor Mittermaier, the voluminous and enlightened advocate of jurisprudential reforms (called the German Brougham) received the card of Mr. Livingston, with whom he had corresponded. He came to the hotel, and, on seeing him, rushed into his arms, clasped and kissed him, to the surprise and amusement of the ladies.

When Mr. Livingston returned home, Mr. Barton was left as Chargé des Affaires. He came to the United States in 1836, bringing water for the fire between Jackson and Louis Philippe.

Mrs. Barton continued to reside at Montgomery Place after her mother's death, in 1860. Mr. Livingston's rooms were kept in the same state as when occupied by him. She has for many years resided in New York.

A lady thus described an evening scene at the

Executive mansion in the early part of Jackson's administration. "The large parlor was scantily furnished; there was light from the chandelier, and a blazing fire in the grate; four or five ladies sewing round it; Mrs. Donelson, Mrs. Andrew Jackson, Mrs. Edward Livingston, &c. Five or six children were playing about, regardless of documents or work-baskets. At the farther end of the room sat the President in his arm-chair, wearing a long loose coat, and smoking a long reed pipe, with bowl of red clay; combining the dignity of the patriarch, monarch, and Indian chief. Just behind was Edward Livingston, the Secretary of State, reading him a dispatch from the French Minister for Foreign Affairs. The ladies glance admiringly now and then at the President, who listens, waving his pipe towards the children when they become too boisterous."

Brief mention of the wife of the military President may not be inappropriate, though she was no social leader. Rachel Donelson was a dark-eyed and dark-haired brunette; a gay, handsome, and spirited lass "as ever danced on the deck of a flat-boat, or took the helm while her father took a shot at the Indians." Her first husband was Lewis Robards, of Kentucky. She married Jackson in 1794. The last marriage was a happy one, their affection being elevated by mutual respect, sympathy, and unselfish kindness. Mrs. Jackson, in her husband's absence, took care of the farm and a hundred and fifty slaves. She had a wonderful memory for anecdotes and tales of pioneer adventure, and had not lost her merry disposition or her liking for old-fashioned dances. She was short and full in person, while the General was tall and gaunt. Having no children, they adopted nephews. The biographer of Jackson pays Mrs. Jackson a tribute of praise, as exemplary in all relations, with a warm, true, and excellent heart, frank and cordial manners; liberal in hospitality and overflowing with kindness. "Aunt Rachel" was loved by all the young people, and was "the stay and solace of her husband's life." At a ball given in New Orleans, after the peace of 1815, she mingled in the dance with the merriest. She wrote graphic letters descriptive of a journey to Florida, and a residence at Pensacola. A new "Hermitage" was built for her abode, where hung her portrait in white satin, topaz jewelry, low corsage, and short sleeves. She came to Washington with her husband, traveling with coach and four, in the autumn of 1824. Her health was in a precarious state. In 1828, she revisited New Orleans. Her reception was a splendid one; a brilliant circle was assembled to wait upon her, and fêtes were given in her honor. The huge old family coach, which afterwards was among the curiosities of the Hermitage, was there presented to her by the General; and the set of topaz seen in her portrait, by the ladies of the city.

When Mrs. Jackson came to the White House, the ladies of Washington took it on themselves to arrange the dresses suitable for her. The good lady, with her homely bearing and country manners, was both maligned and caricatured by the anti-Jackson party. One picture represented her perched on a table, with Mrs. Livingston lacing her stays. The General, however, was blind to any want of fashionable elegance, and always put honor on his "bonny brown wife."*

The high moral tone and pure taste prevalent in Washington society at this period was illustrated by the refusal of the ladies to visit or receive one whose conduct had been open to reproach, though influence was used in official quarters to induce them to relent. The President himself contended in vain with their determination.†

---

* See Parton's Life of Jackson.

† Mr. Parton, in his Life of Jackson, gives an account of the origin of the scandal about Mrs. Eaton. William O'Neal kept a tavern in Washington, at which several Senators and officers boarded. Major Eaton came first, in 1818, and stayed there ten winters; Andrew Jackson also was a regular boarder. O'Neal had a pretty daughter, lively, saucy, and full of repartee. She was married to Purser Timberlake; but in 1828 came the news of his death. There had been some scandal in regard to her and Eaton. Then the Major consulted Jackson as to the propriety of his wedding the pretty widow. "Why, yes, Major," replied the soldier; "if you love the woman, and she will have you, marry her by all means. Your marrying her will disprove these charges and restore Peg's good name." The marriage took place in 1829.

No sooner was it whispered that Eaton was to be a member of President Jackson's new Cabinet than the ladies at the head of society became alarmed. "Peg O'Neal" the wife of a Cabinet minister, would be, as such, entitled to admission into their sacred circle. Horrible! General

Jackson was remonstrated with by a reverend gentleman in writing, the letter being dated March, 1829. The President, in his reply, repelled the idea of judging his friend by common rumor; he believed Mrs. Eaton an innocent and injured woman. The story was fully investigated by Jackson's order; certificates of Mrs. Eaton's good character were produced, and a mass of confidential manuscript was laid open. The President brought to the cause the fire and resolution he had shown many years before in silencing the slanders concerning Mrs. Jackson. The matter got mixed up in politics; and suitors for Presidential favor were advised to attend Mrs. Eaton's receptions. She was beautiful, and full of graceful vivacity. Gentlemen were quite willing to visit her; but the lady leaders of society refused to be convinced of her worth by the President's showing the charges against her unsupported by testimony. They obstinately declined receiving her. Mrs. Calhoun would not, though Mrs. Eaton called in company with the Vice-President; Mrs. Berrien would not, though Mr. Berrien had been one of the guests at her wedding; Mrs. Branch would not, though Mr. Branch had been taken into the Cabinet at Major Eaton's suggestion; Mrs. Ingham would not, though gossip had not spared *her* fame. The wives of foreign ministers followed suit in their refusal. Mrs. Donelson, the mistress of the White House, though compelled to receive Mrs. Eaton, would not visit her. "Any thing, uncle, I will do for you; but I cannot call on Mrs. Eaton."—"Then go back to Tennessee, my dear." She went; her husband gave up his post of private secretary and went too; both returning in a month. Thus was the indomitable will of Andrew Jackson in collision with the will of woman. Three weeks after the inauguration came Mr. Van Buren as Secretary of State. He was a widower; had no daughters; and he was very happy to call upon and receive Mrs. Eaton, and even to make parties for her. For more than two years society was divided into hostile parties. "Bellona" was the sobriquet given to Mrs. Eaton in published letters. Baron Krudener, the Russian Minister, and Vaughan, the British, both bachelors, got up entertainments to keep "Bellona" afloat, and she was led by the British Minister to the head of his table. Mr. Van Buren appealed to Mrs. Huygens, the wife of the Minister from Holland, to be favored with an introduction to "the lovely and accomplished Mrs. Eaton." The lady avoided the advance, but finally accepted with reluctance, one evening, Major Eaton's arm to supper. Finding Mrs. Eaton seated at the head of the table, beside her own chair, Mrs. Huygens turned to her husband, took his arm, and walked out of the room. It was said that President Jackson threatened, for this, to send the Minister home to Holland.

Another similar failure occurred at a grand dinner, when Mr. Vaughan led Mrs. Eaton to the head of the table—the President allowing the guests to see how much he had her recognition at heart. Nothing could move the inflexible ladies of Washington. Even the Cabinet became divided on the subject; while Jackson threw the whole energy of his nature into the lady's defence. He was like a roaring lion at any attack upon her. Eaton finally had a quarrel with his old chief, and they never became reconciled.—*Parton's Life of Jackson.*

XIII.

The niece of Mrs. Van Ness, of Washington, was celebrated as a belle universally admired in the society of the Capital in the winter of 1828–9. She was Miss Cornelia Van Ness, the daughter of Cornelius P. Van Ness, the eminent Chief Justice and Governor of Vermont.

Mrs. C. P. Van Ness occupied a position not less distinguished than that of her sister-in-law. Her admirable performance of the duties pertaining to her position as the wife of the Governor of Vermont, added an elevating social influence to his political supremacy. Her house was the resort of distinguished travelers from every part of the United States as well as Europe; her hospitality was known throughout the State; and few, who had any claim to attention, passed through the beautiful village of Burlington, on their way to Boston or Canada, without stopping at the Governor's residence to pay their respects. Mrs. Van Ness was noted for personal beauty of a commanding order, as well as for uncommon powers of intellect, and attainments that in any time or country would be remarkable.

Her talents in conversation were improved by extensive reading; for she possessed a wonderful tenacity of memory, with a mental power of transmutation that enriches the mind with the products of what it receives. With these endowments, added to the most graceful courtesy, accomplished manners, and kindness of heart, it was not surprising that Mrs. Van Ness should hold an exalted place in the esteem of all her acquaintances. When General La Fayette revisited the United States, it was her part and privilege, as the Governor's wife, to receive and entertain him at her house. She accompanied her husband to Spain when he became Envoy Extraordinary at the Court of Madrid. Here a new sphere opened for the exercise of her talents, and new duties devolved upon her. At the christening of the present Queen of Spain, in the Royal Chapel, she represented America. When she came in, in a State procession, with other ladies of the corps diplomatique, her commanding figure, the dignity of her carriage, and the beauty of her face, caused many to fancy that her country must be remarkable for its lovely women.

Miss Cornelia Van Ness, when a very young girl, left her home in Vermont to visit her uncle, General Van Ness, in the Federal city. At that time there were many young ladies in society who had brilliant pretensions to belleship; but Miss Van Ness, on her first appearance, was acknowledged to possess superior claims, not only on account of her uncle's high position and the attraction of her aunt's fascinating social qualities, but for her own exquisite beauty, grace, sprightliness, and elegance of style, with accomplishments rare in one so youthful. Her admirers were not destined long to enjoy her society; in the autumn of 1829 she was taken to Spain by her father, who had been appointed Minister by General Jackson. The ambassador had his residence in Madrid, and his family was at once received into the most select of the court circles and of the society of the Capital. Immediately on her arrival, Miss Van Ness was introduced to the Duchess of Beneventi, one of the principal ladies of the court. The Duchess was charmed with her young American friend, and took pleasure in presenting her to the exclusive circles of the Spanish grandees; a favor seldom accorded to foreigners. The young lady was, of course, admitted to all State receptions and to the parties of the foreign Ministers, in virtue of her father's official position; but the old grandees of Spain are jealously exclusive, tenacious of their traditional grandeur, and averse to receiving into their social circles the most honored of any other nation. The distinction shown to the fair American was, therefore, a rare and valued one. Miss Van Ness had equal good fortune in being made acquainted with the persons of note in Madrid, and in being shown all that was recherché and distinguished in metropolitan society. Thus her time passed most agreeably, and the incidents of almost every day were treasured in memory as improving recollections.

The Marchioness de Casa Yrujo was an American; a daughter of Governor McKean, of Philadelphia. She had married the Marquis when he was Spanish Minister to the United States. The Marchioness had been in her day a celebrated beauty, and was, even at that time, an elegant looking woman. She possessed wealth, and lived in superb style, in Madrid, with her son and daughter. She had known the ambassador, Mr. Van Ness, in America; and both were happy to renew the acquaintance formed in a far distant country, to which both belonged by birth. This noble lady was well pleased to find a youthful countrywoman so accomplished and lovely in the daughter of her friend; one whom she could present to her friends with pride and satisfaction, and who would do credit to her regard and companionship. Miss Van Ness could speak both French and Spanish with fluency, and with two chaperones like the Duchess of Beneventi and the Marchioness, associating familiarly with those with whom they made her acquainted, she speedily found herself at home in Madrid. She was presented to Queen Christina, who made her entrance into the Capital, as the third wife of Ferdinand VII., the day after Governor Van Ness and his family arrived. The Queen received the young girl most kindly, and was particularly pleased with her; the sovereign honored her with special marks of favor, and, indeed, made quite a pet of her; showing a regard no American lady had ever yet won from a monarch of Spain. This distinguishing notice of royalty, of course, made the beautiful daughter of the western Republic "the observed of all observers." Her album contains numerous tributes in Spanish and French poetry signed by names of world-wide distinction. Fontaney sighs in verse—"Oh, that my eye was in itself a soul!" and there are records from Forcinet at Paris, Charles Nodier, Marie Nodier, Menessier, and many others. A Spanish poet, Don Manuel Breton de los Herreros, addressed to her some impromptu stanzas which have great spirit and beauty in the original.

During twenty months Miss Van Ness remained in Spain, partaking of all the gayeties and delights of the Capital, assisting at the court festivals, pleased with every thing she saw, and charming those who knew her. The last fête at which she was present was the baptism of the present Queen of Spain; a most interesting ceremony, celebrated with brilliant festivities. This appropriately crowned the series of stately pageants and entertainments, in which our fair subject had the rare privilege of mingling with noble and royal personages, honored as one of themselves, and endowed with grace and loveliness such as nature seldom bestows even on the favorites of fortune. After this she bade farewell to these bright scenes, and went to Paris. Here, in May, 1831, at the house of Mr. Rives—in the presence of many distinguished friends, among them General La Fayette, who gave away the bride—she gave her hand to Mr. James J. Roosevelt, of New York.

When La Fayette revisited the United States, Miss Van Ness—then at Mrs. Willard's school in Troy—had been selected, with Miss Cass, to present to the General the poetical tribute Mrs. Willard had written for the occasion. These daughters of the governors of Vermont and Michigan were chosen as representative young ladies for the office. La Fayette had never forgotten that pleasant incident, and thus agreeable recollections of her girlhood were mingled with his esteem for the charming maiden he bestowed in marriage. He invited her and her husband to visit him at his country home—La Grange. They passed several days there, welcomed with every mark of friendship by the General and his family.

In September, 1831, Mr. and Mrs. Roosevelt returned to the United States, taking up their residence in New York. On her return, Mrs. Roosevelt received a letter from the Marchioness de Casa Yrujo, giving her the gossip of their circle in Madrid: "The Duke of Ossuna," she says, "is rather triste on account of the absence of his friends. I had the pleasure of seeing your mamma a day or two ago; she looks very thin, and appears to feel the separation from you very severely. She is desirous of returning to America. It appears to me it would be for the happiness of all your family to return."

In a letter from La Fayette, dated July 25, 1831, he says:—

"In case you were still on this side of the Atlantic, I may assure you that Prince de Talleyrand will highly value the pleasure of your and Mr. Roosevelt's acquaintance; and should you think it requisite, these very lines, although addressed to you, would be considered as an introduction to him. But I think they will not be received before you have had the happiness to find yourself again in the great and good city of New York. Remember me to your sister, husband, and brother-in-law, and believe me forever,

"Your affectionate friend,

"LA FAYETTE."

In 1840, Mr. Roosevelt was elected Member of Congress, and took his seat in the following year, when his family accompanied him to Washington. During the winters of 1842-43, Mrs. Roosevelt remained in that city, her husband having taken a house. They were very prominent in society, and were among the first to introduce the new fashion of entertaining.

Mr. Ingersoll, giving an account of social matters in Washington at this time, wrote:—

"Washington's administration, with Jefferson's and Hamilton's concurrence, established some forms deemed indispensable for the new republican government, one of which was that the President was never to visit any one but the Vice President, nor ever to dine out. But Acting President Tyler sometimes, I believe, did both. When I first came to Washington, most of the hospitalities were done by the President and the several foreign ministers. But a great change has since taken place; and now many members of Congress give more and more luxurious entertainments than any of the foreigners who used to set the fashion. In 1842, one of the city of New York members, Mr. James J. Roosevelt, and his beautiful and accomplished wife, who had spent many years in Madrid when her father was American minister there, were among the earliest and most effective in that social revolution, by frequent and very agreeable dinner and evening parties. At one of these, where President Tyler was a gay and unassuming guest, I had the honor to play a rubber of whist with him, Lord Ashburton, and ex-speaker, and ex-minister to England, &c."

One literary curiosity preserved in Mrs. Roosevelt's

album is an original impromptu poetical conceit, written by Victor Hugo, with his own hand, in 1831:—

> "La Poesie, inspiré lorsque la terre ignore,
> Ressemble à les grands monts que la nouvelle aurore
> Dore avant nous à son reveille,
> Et qui, longtemps vainqueur de l'ombre,
> Gardent jusquo dans la nuit sombre
> Le dernier rayon du soleil.
> "VICTOR H."

A translation was written below by Mr. Adams:—

> "The bard is like yon hilltop high,
> At sunrise shining to the sky,
> While darkness reigns below;
> And when shall come the shades of night,
> Still on that hilltop's lofty height
> The sun's last beams shall glow.
> "JOHN QUINCY ADAMS."

JULY, 1842.

Another distinguished poet gave a more liberal version:—

> "Moorland and meadow slumber
> In deepest darkness now,
> But the sunrise hues that wakened day
> Smile on that mountain's brow.
>
> "And when ove's mists are shrouding
> Moorland and meadow fast,
> That mountain greets day's sunset light,
> Her loveliest and her last.
>
> "And thus the god-taught minstrel,
> Above a land untaught,
> Smiles lovely in the smiles of heaven
> From his hilltops of thought.
> "FITZ GREENE HALLECK."

The same treasury of art and poetry contains an

original drawing by Federico di Madrazo, of Apollo with his lute; and a drawing of our Saviour wearing His crown of thorns, by Vincentio Lopez, the great historical painter. There is also an extract in Washington Irving's delicate handwriting, from his unpublished essay on the "Self Dependence of an American," written in London, July, 1831; with some relics of Washington and Jefferson; a sonnet to La Fayette, in Mrs. Madison's quaint, old-fashioned hand; and the following sentiment:—

"The enduring record of departed goodness dwells in the soul, like the writing that is inscribed upon adamant.
"D. P. MADISON"

Mr. Clay wrote to Mrs. Roosevelt:—

"MY DEAR MADAM:
"You did me the honor to express a wish to possess some written memorial of me. I take pleasure in complying with it, and regret that I have not something to offer more worthy of your acceptance. But nothing could more truly testify than I now do, to the respect and esteem cherished for you by both Mrs. Clay and
"Your faithful friend
"And obedient servant,
"H. CLAY."

There is also a curious autograph of the Prince de Ligne, inviting Mr. Roosevelt to visit him.

Many letters were written to Mrs. Roosevelt by statesmen of the greatest distinction in American political life, touching affairs of national importance; but publicity cannot be given to what was written without any idea of publication. They serve to show the high personal esteem entertained for the lady by those friends, and their respect for her opinions and judgment in matters wherein a woman is not usually supposed able to decide. Some of the letters were sent to her while she was in Paris, on the eve of a contested nomination for the Presidency; and few ladies have been let so deeply into party secrets. One from Sir John Rowland Eustace, in 1854, showed how much he was indebted for his reception in America to the civilities of Mrs. Roosevelt. He wrote:—

"I recall to mind with very great pleasure my two very agreeable trips from Canada into the United States, into which I was ushered by you and Mr. Roosevelt; for, from the moment of my having the good fortune to make your acquaintance, in the steamboat upon Lake Champlain, every thing was to me quite '*couleur de rose*;' and when, after a very agreeable journey, you and Mr. Roosevelt so kindly presented me to your friends at Saratoga, I really felt quite as much at home as I should have done at any watering-place in England. And after that auspicious introduction, I never met with any thing in the United States but the greatest civility and kindness, and the most interesting scenery, and the most interesting people I have ever met. Indeed, I should like to revisit America very much; and I think I should have gone to your exhibition at New York last summer, but that we also had one in Dublin, where as an Irishman I was bound to attend. I was in hopes of seeing you and Mr. Roosevelt again in London before this time; but I suppose the high and dignified office which the Judge now holds—and upon which promotion I beg leave to offer my sincere congratulations—will prevent his being able to go so far from home."

Mrs. Roosevelt has for many years past been in reality "a queen" in the leading society of New York. Her regal grace and dignified deportment, her animated, intellectual countenance, her conversation, enriched with the treasures of a well-stored mind, and sprightly with brilliant fancies, adorn the drawing-room and give a charm to social intercourse wherever she is. Her entertainments have always been splendid, and marked by refined taste as well as lavish decoration. Flowers in profusion may be seen; the arts are worthily represented, and her guests are unanimous in their testimony to the enjoyment provided for them. Nor is the time of this lady, acknowledged leader of "the ton" as she is, altogether given up to fashionable gayeties; she is continually occupied with some good work, and is active and liberal in aiding many charities. In the great Sanitary Fair held in New York, Mrs. Roosevelt gave important assistance. The "Knickerbocker Kitchen" was especially under her superintendence. The "Herald" report said:—

"The high priestess of this ancient temple of cleanliness and comfort is Mrs. Judge Roosevelt, a lady of veritable Dutch descent, and a well-known leader in the best circles of New York society.

"If Washington Irving could now step forth from his summerhouse, he would put on his hat, take his cane, and quickly find his way to the Knickerbocker Kitchen. There, seated in some high-backed, broad-flottomed wooden chair, he would call for oly-koeks, kröllers, rollitjes, &c., with a cup of tea, and doubtless he would be served by Mrs. Roosevelt herself, in the costume of her great-grandmother, which becomes her so well that she looks more like a Duchess than a Dutchwoman.

"As you enter the door, the first glance conveys the impression that you have stepped across the ocean and are in a foreign country. The second is, that you have slipped backward two hundred years or more; and the middle of the seventeenth century, in the person of a pretty Dutch girl, stands before you.

"Grim old Dutchmen look down upon you from dingy canvas

on the walls; long-waisted, straight-laced old ladies, in remarkable head-dresses, and round-faced children, in wonderful clothes, greet you at every turn. The tables groan with blue china, steel forks, and all the good things that were found on the Knickerbocker bill of fare.

"Overhead, strings of dried apples hang in festoons from the heavy beams. Rows of dip-candles, large ears of seed-corn, and bright red-peppers adorn the ceiling. Above the deep fire-place, a shelf full of burnished pewter plates, copper sauce pans, bake-pans, kettles, and brass candlesticks, attest the devotion of the housewife to a godly cleanliness. The spinning-wheel is near at hand, the ancient dresser, and, above all, the corner china-closet, in which are displayed rare mementoes of the choice blue porcelain ware, once the pride of some old family table. In the chimney corner or bustling around the room, in old Dutch costumes, may be seen Mrs. Judge Roosevelt, Mrs. Ronalds, Mrs. Dr. Brown, Miss Roosevelt, and other ladies of the committee, which is composed exclusively of representatives from the oldest Dutch families in the State."

The account of this distinguished family would be incomplete without a brief notice of Mrs. Roosevelt's sister, whose lot has been to reside abroad most of her life.

Marcia, Lady Ouseley, says an English paper, "comes of a race of distinguished public servants of the United States." While the eminent diplomatist, Sir William Gore Ouseley, was at the British Legation in Washington, Marcia, then extremely young, was married to him, in 1829. Their residence afterwards was in different European courts, where Sir William was employed in a diplomatic capacity. He was a nephew of Sir Gore Ouseley, the famous Ambassador to Persia and St. Petersburgh, and the son of Sir William Ouseley, the not less famous historian of the celebrated Persian embassy. Entering the diplomatic career at a very early age, he filled important posts in various countries. He served at the Court of Rio Janeiro, whither his wife accompanied him, and was much pleased with the picturesque place and scenery. Here Sir William represented his queen and country at the coronation of the present Emperor of Brazil. Lady Ouseley accompanied him to Buenos Ayres in 1844, and subsequently to Washington, whither he went on a special mission, previously to proceeding to Central America. Some years before this he was specially accredited to Monte Video, during a most eventful epoch in the annals of the Eastern States of South America, in whose prosperity he ever continued to take a lively interest, contributing to it by his persistent antagonism to the military despotism and commercial restrictiveness of Rosas. The opening up of the affluents of the La Plata was mainly due to the preliminary expedition on which he dispatched Captain Hotham.

During Lady Ouseley's stay in Washington she was the object of universal attention, and took part in the gayeties of the season. A brilliant party was given at her house in March, 1858; at another was described her "winning elegance of manner, which could not fail to command attention;" at another, "Prominent in the throng we see Lady Ouseley's expressive face and engaging manners." Many such passing tributes show that she had a celebrity among the fairest in Washington for her personal loveliness, charming manners, and accomplishments of conversation; though her reign was but short, as she was called to appear in other and more courtly scenes, and in the sunshine of royal favor.

Sir William returned to England in 1860, from his mission to the governments of Central America and his visit to Washington. He died on the 5th March, 1866, leaving only one child, a daughter, who was married to the Honorable James Terence Fitzmaurice, of the Royal Navy, son of the Earl of Orkney.

Lady Ouseley was personally acquainted with many of the sovereigns of Europe; among them the late King Leopold, of Belgium—" the Nestor of sovereigns ;" Queen Marie Amelie and her husband, Louis Philippe, with their family; also the present emperor of France, Louis Napoleon. Her home of late years has been in England.

XIV.

The wife of General Winfield Scott was prominent in society where she lived. She was Maria Mayo, the daughter of John Mayo, of Richmond, Virginia; "a young lady more admired in her circle than her soldier husband." She had seven children, of whom four died young. She was not well known as a poetess; but she wrote some creditable verses in Paris to cheer her husband on his mission of peace to Puget's Sound, San Juan Island, via Panama. He sailed in the "Star of the West," September 20th, 1859. Mrs. Scott was present at a breakfast given to loyal American citizens in the Hotel du Louvre, Paris, in the May preceding her death. One hundred and fifty were present, one-third ladies. She was remarkable for pungent wit, and was often eccentric in her manners.

General Scott paid a high but just tribute to William C. Preston, of South Carolina, for many years a United States Senator, in saying he was a man "of the purest morals, with a wife worthy to 'glide double—swan and shadow'—down the stream of life with him. They were lovely and pleasant in their lives, and in their death not long divided." Both Mr. and Mrs. Preston were well known to the writer of this volume during her residence in South Carolina. Mr. Preston, as his friend observed, was "greatly gifted in genius and fancy; highly accomplished as a scholar, a gentleman, and a statesman, with splendid powers of oratory to enrapture the multitude and edify the intelligent; with a soul so genial and a voice so sweet as to win all who approached him—young and old, men, women, and children."—"Though at an unhappy period he was given up to nullification, his good genius triumphed in the end; for he lived long enough to make atonement to the Union, and to die faithful to the same allegiance that distinguished his grandfather Campbell, of King's Mountain, and his immediate parent, General Frank Preston, long member of Congress from Southwestern Virginia." He lived also to testify to his acceptance of the Christian's hope through a Redeemer, and to show the evidence of his earnest faith.

Frank Preston, the father of William Campbell Preston, by his marriage with Miss Campbell, obtained the salt-works and mines of Abingdon and on the Kenawha. His sons were William C.; John, who married Miss Hampton, of South Carolina, while in Louisiana; and Thomas, the present owner of the Abingdon property. His uncle had married Edmonia, daughter of Edmund Randolph, the first Attorney General of the United States, and the friend and legal adviser of Washington. Frank's daughters were Eliza, who married Colonel Carrington; Susan, who married James McDowell, Governor of Virginia, the brother of Mrs.

Benton; Sophy, who became the wife of Rev. Robert Breckenridge, of Kentucky;* and Sarah, who married her cousin, Governor Floyd of Virginia.† The sister of Frank married one of Madison's family.

William Preston, a brother of Frank Preston, married Miss Hancock, and settled in Kentucky on a grant of military land, now the site of part of the city of Louisville. Their only son was William Preston, afterwards minister to Spain, who married Margaret Wickliffe, the daughter of Robert Wickliffe, an eminent lawyer of Kentucky, and the owner of extensive lands and large fortune. He was distinguished for elegance of manner combined with determination and strength of will, being popularly called "The Old Duke." His home in Lexington, over which two of his daughters presided, was noted for hospitality, and was the center of social attraction for several years. The eldest daughter married Judge Wooley, an eminent jurist; Mary became the wife of John Preston of West Virginia. After Margaret's marriage, she went to reside in Louisville. She accompanied her husband to Washington when he became member of Congress for that district, and afterwards when he went as ambassador to Spain. Everywhere her beauty and intellect, her accomplishments and charming manners and conversation, and

---

* Dr. Breckenridge of the Presbyterian Church, uncle to John Breckenridge.

† His father was Dr. Floyd, United States Senator; his mother, the sister of Frank Preston.

her influence in society, gave her a leading position. Both she and General Preston were of majestic height and regal appearance. Since the late war they reside in Lexington, on Mrs. Preston's estate.

Mrs. Merrick, the wife of Judge Merrick, of the United States District of Columbia, was the daughter of Charles Wickliffe. She was a leader in Washington society, and gave superb entertainments.

I have heard Washington Irving remark, that William C. Preston was the most brilliant man in conversation he had ever known. His discourse, in fact, sparkled with illustration and wit, in which sarcasm was often blended. Sometimes, by a felicitous turn, he would rebuke an unjust or censorious remark. One evening at Professor Ellet's house, a gentleman known to have a stupid wife, looking at an engraving of Lady Byron, said: "I should not like to marry one of these clever women; they are seldom suited for it;" whereupon Mr. Preston coolly added: "Well, I like to see a man's practice in life correspond with his theory." His words were often pictures, and, in ordinary conversation, seemed to glow with the abundance of the treasures his fancy showered; it almost realized the fable of the fairy who dropped pearls and jewels from her lips in speaking.

The second wife of Mr. Preston was Louisa Penelope Davis, the daughter of Dr. James Davis, of Columbia, South Carolina. She was born in 1807. She improved the advantages of a superior education, having little taste for the occupations in which young girls generally delight; and became distinguished among her associates for the extent and variety of her acquirements. Her powers of conversation were remarkable; pronounced by Calhoun, Mitchell King, and others, superior to those of any other woman they ever knew. In girlhood she possessed great beauty, combined with graceful and winning manners, which made her a favorite with all. The soft melody of her voice, with its clear and rather slow articulation, added to the pleasing effect of her animated language, in which her delicate wit illustrated every subject.

In the autumn of 1830, Miss Davis gave her hand to William Campbell Preston. During his brilliant career in public life she was his inseparable companion, the star of beauty and wit in Washington, the leader of the most aristocratic society in her native town. Her health became very fragile, but she never relaxed in her devoted attentions to her husband, who suffered much from illness. To please him, she cultivated her rare mental powers, and read the works in which he delighted. The Bible, and Shakespeare's plays, were so familiar to her retentive memory, she was almost a living book of concordance to them. In Columbia she was the acknowledged queen of society. Her entertainments were marked by good taste as well as profuse liberality. The house had a large and well-shaded garden, in which the company was invited to wander on summer evenings, lamps being hung in the trees and shrubbery. Sometimes refreshments were served in the grove. I remember the visit of Baron von Raumer, who wrote a book entitled "America and the American People." He thus mentioned the occurrence:—

"We dined with an agreeable party at the house of Colonel Preston. After dinner we had a very interesting conversation upon Shakespeare and the Greek tragedians. Our host showed throughout a great deal of knowledge and acute judgment; others were not behindhand; and the ladies also took a lively part in the discussion. Seldom do we hear among us such sensible and coherent remarks."

The soil of that portion of South Carolina did not produce the grassy turf so beautiful in the Northern States; but Mrs. Preston, with great pains, had cultivated a square space where the grass was green in spring; and here, after dinner, her guests were invited to sit in the cool shade. She had a favorite peacock, with a gorgeous tail, which he was fond of spreading; but on this occasion the perverse bird chose to hide his brilliant plumage among the shrubbery, out of the sight of the distinguished visitor. Desirous of showing off her pet, Mrs. Preston whispered to me a request that I would drive the bird upon the green in front of her guests. The young baron, son of the elder, volunteered his assistance, holding a glass to his eye, for he was extremely near-sighted. The obstinate peacock seemed determined to balk our purpose; he ran into all manner of obscure by-ways; and when, after long pursuit, the chase became vigorous, and he was fairly cooped in to the desired locality, he fled, with closed plumes and frightened pace, across the Baron's feet, quite unnoticed. The learned German was discoursing on the topics he mentions, and would no doubt have despised the spread tail had he seen it. What made the failure more provoking was, that an ugly turkey buzzard, of whom Mr. Preston had made an uncouth pet, sturdily refused to be kept in the background.

Soon after Mr. Preston's retirement from the Senate of the United States, he was chosen President of the South Carolina College, which his reputation and talents raised to much prosperity. Here Mrs. Preston's influence was felt in a new sphere. Her benignity and kindness conciliated the respect and gratitude of the students; and her entertainments diffused a general spirit of courtesy and good-will, that promised to open a vista of increasing usefulness to the institution. But renewed attacks of illness constrained her husband to resign his position, and seek the restoration of his health in retirement. In March, 1853, they made an excursion to Louisiana, to visit the plantation of his brother, John S. Preston. Mr. Preston's health improved; but that of his wife gave way, and she was seized with a disease which for her medicine could not relieve. For weeks she suffered, anxious to return home, but unable to be removed, till a slight improvement induced her physicians to consent to her removal to South Carolina. She reached her beloved home a few days before her death. Her mother, her brothers and sisters, and many friends were near her, and calm in the assurance of a blessed immortality—for her life had for years been passed in the light of Christian faith—did she "like tired breezes fall asleep."

I cannot resist the temptation of including some notice of a beloved friend, whose influence, limited indeed within a select circle, was powerful over all who knew her. She was a native of Scotland, but the greater part of her life was passed in the city of New York, where, up to the advanced age of seventy-seven, she adorned a high position with all those qualities of heart and mind, all those sweet and captivating amenities of manner, which had in her youth, when joined to great personal attractions, rendered her one of the most fascinating maidens of Annandale, in Scotland. Her father was the Rev. Andrew Jeffrey, of Lochmaben, in Dumfrieshire. At his fireside the bright blue eyes of his daughter, the young and blooming Jeanie Jeffrey, then only in her fifteenth year, attracted the beauty-loving eye of Burns, who, under the impression they had produced upon his imagination, made her the subject of one of his sweetest songs:—

> "I gaed a woefu' gate yestreen,
> A gate I fear I'll dearly rue:
> I gat my death frae twa sweet e'en,
> Twa lovely e'en sae bonnie blue." &c.*

---

* A memoir of Mrs. Renwick, written by the accomplished Mrs. Balmanno, and included in her illustrated volume entitled "Pen and Pencil"—a volume which is a credit to American art and literature—enables me to give her reminiscences of our friend.

"Often in the familiar flow of friendly conversation has she described, with animation, the universal joy which prevailed among the younger inmates of the manse, herself included, when the step of their father's friend—Burns—was heard at the door; the joyful enthusiasm which his appearance never failed to create, and then the hushed quietness on their part which succeeded his entrance; while, with their creepies (low footstools) drawn as closely round him as possible, they sat looking up into his face, listening to his eloquent words, and never weary of watching the changes of his varying countenance. His powers of conversation, she said, were unequaled; feelings the most ardent, fancies the most brilliant, perpetually leaping forth, and rendering the commonest theme from his lips full of novelty and beauty. The pastor's hospitable fireside, independent of its own intrinsic charm, must for him have abounded in associations the most romantic; Marion Fairlie, the 'Fairlie fair' of Scottish song, being the ancestress of Mrs. Jeffrey, who herself was the direct descendant of 'Jonnie Armstrong,' the famous freebooter, and had in her maiden days formed the theme of song as the 'Nannie' of 'Roslyn Castle.'"

In a letter to her sister-in-law, Mrs. Renwick thus describes the occasion upon which Burns addressed to her the poem above referred to:—

"It was after dinner, in company with the poet, at the house of Mr. Nicol, who was living at Moffat for the benefit of his child's health, that Burns sent to me the two songs—'Willy brewed a

Peck o' Maut' and 'The Blue-eyed Lassie.' Mr. Nicol was the 'Willie' whose 'maut got aboon the meal' that night with the poet. I was then only fifteen, and sic a wee bit lassie, that Burns danced out with me in his arms, and put me into the carriage to my father, singing 'Green grow the rushes, O.'

"Poor, poor Burns! how often have I seen him in a cold winter's night, when he had been riding for hours over the moors and mosses after smugglers (what a task for such a spirit!), open our little parlor door, and stalk in with his great lion-skin coat and fur cap covered with snow, and his fine Newfoundland dog, Thurlow, at his side, looking stern and dour, as if at war with all the world. With what kindness he was welcomed by my dear parents, while my sister and self seated him in my mother's easy-chair, brought dry slippers, and prepared for him a warm, comfortable cup of tea; then, seating ourselves on our low creepies at his feet, watched his countenance brighten up into almost more than mortal beauty and intelligence, and listened to his inspired words, every one of which was absolute poetry."

Burns addressed to this "blue-eyed lassie" another song, beginning, "When first I saw my Jeanie's face," &c.

Mrs. Balmanno describes Mrs. Renwick in her later years:—"Of medium height, her features feminine and regular, with a benign, engaging aspect. Her complexion was still fresh, her brow unwrinkled, and her eyes still those of the 'Blue-eyed Lassie;' and when, a short time before her death, she was humorously describing the great number of her descendants, her cheeks were dimpled with pleasure, and she spoke with such a sweet voice, laughing at the same time so softly and yet merrily, that it seemed no wonder she should have made so many hearts her own in the days o' lang syne, some sixty years ago, when she was that most beautiful girl and elegant dancer described by Mr. Cameron. This gentleman, a Highlander by birth, passed much of his boyhood at Lochmaben, where he describes himself deeply enamored of 'Jeanie Jeffrey,' having a 'great jealousy' in those days of 'ane Wully Brown' (afterwards Sir William Brown), his powerful rival at the dancing-school."

"How delightful was a visit to Mrs. Renwick's house in Barclay Street, New York! The servants wore an honest, kindly look, as if glad to see their mistress's friends; while she herself, to whom time had given a grace for every one it had taken away, received her friends in a manner that showed she loved them, and spoke and smiled a thousand welcomes. Surrounded by objects of taste and vertù, of elegance and luxury, by pretty little tributes of affection and respect, by all that can delight the eye or charm the mind, the beholder experienced that sense of pleasure which arises from objects in just proportion and harmony with each other. In a conspicuous situation hung a fine old Andrea Ferrara, that perchance had given many a hard blow at Bannockburn, and beneath it stood a finely chased antique silver casket, containing a pair of the silk and silver-fringed long kid gloves of the lovely Mary Stuart, queen of Scotland. This interesting relic came into the possession of Mrs. Renwick from the representatives of her relative, Professor Kemp, of Columbia College, New York. In his family, in Aberdeenshire, it had been an heirloom, traced back more than two centuries.

"The two large bow-windows were filled with choice

flowers, one of the windows affording entrance to a long, narrow terrace, overlooking beautiful gardens and venerable trees, old Indian warriors of the woods, which had been saplings when New York was a choice hunting-ground; dear to her eye as shadowing the grounds of Columbia College and the house of her son, who was its distinguished Professor of Chemistry. This pleasant walk was always in summer crowded with exotics, large and small, among which she loved to walk, and from whose treasures she enriched the conservatories and drawing-rooms of her friends. There also might be found violets, daisies, Scotch heaths, bluebells, and the 'lang yellow broom,' cherished as mementoes of that far 'long ago' which spoke to her again in its old familiar flowers. Amidst these charming objects of innocent delight, she cheerfully pursued her needle-work or knitting, chatting vivaciously on old times or new, and managing to make people, when they retired from her presence, have a better idea of themselves, their friends, their neighbors, and the world in general. The elasticity and vigor of her mind were wonderful. Even to the last she read and enjoyed all the best publications as they came out, with the same keen zest and appreciative judgment for which she had ever been distinguished, taking the greatest delight in the fine passages and noble sentiments of her favorite authors, and often devoting many hours after she retired to her chamber in perusing them." Truly was she called "good, gentle, and true; possessed of all that gives loveliness to female character."

"The simplest souvenirs from her hand were accompanied by a tenderness, a tact, and a grace, that made trifles precious by her manner of bestowing them."

Washington Irving was an intimate friend of Mrs. Renwick, and spent hours in conversation with her whenever he visited New York. She gave him a root from her ivy, which had grown from a root brought from Melrose Abbey,* and covered the wall in her garden. Irving called her house his "Ark," as his favorite resort. Professor Charles Anthon called her "The Queen," in his epistolary and poetic compliments. Henry Brevoort and Mr. John Greig, of Canandaigua, were her devoted friends.

Maria Livingston, who married John C. Stevens, was for some years a leader in the fashionable society of New York. She lived in a splendid stone mansion, with pretty grounds, in College Place, and gave brilliant parties and masquerade balls, with select dinners, and general receptions once a week. She was remarkably clever, had an excellent memory, and was witty in repartee. The following description, from a letter, of one of her entertainments may illustrate them:—

"The great feature of the week in the fashionable world has been the ball *en masque* of Mrs. John C. Stevens. From ten till eleven o'clock long lines of carriages were delivering, at her magnificent portal, into the hands of that indispensable adjunct to all

---

* A root from the same beautiful ivy, given me by Mrs. Renwick, I planted in front of our house in the college grounds, Columbia, South Carolina. It has since covered the front of that and the adjoining house, and survived the devastation of Columbia in the late war.

parties, Mr. Brown, the fair denizens of New York—from the towering battlements of Murray Hill to the Italian villas of Fifteenth Street; from the Tuscan and Doric mansions of the Fifth Avenue and Union Square, to the sylvan shades of Chelsea. No one in New York entertains more elegantly than Mrs. Stevens; her tables groan with the choicest productions of the season; and on the score of wines, John C. Stevens yields the palm to none, and, like his famous yacht *America*, carries all before him. Among the ladies were Mrs. Parish, in a rich pink brocade, trimmed with antique lace and diamonds; Mrs. Hickson W. Field, in a sea-green velvet, trimmed with three flounces of very rich guipure lace, with head-dress to match, and a fine display of diamonds. Young Mrs. Pendleton wore a scarlet satin dress covered with point lace, her fair neck encircled with a chain of very large diamonds; a white wreath in her hair completed the beautiful toilet.

"Mrs. William Jones appeared in white lace trimmed with gold fringe, with cap and plume to match. Mrs. John Costar was in lemon-colored silk trimmed with rich lace, her brow encircled with a tiara of diamonds. Mrs. Haight wore a rich white lace dress, powdered hair, and long waving plumes. Mrs. William Schermerhorn wore a profusion of antique lace and diamonds."

The Mrs. Parish referred to was Miss Susan Delafield. She married Henry Parish, a prominent merchant, and was a party in the famous "Parish will case." She lived in Union Square, and gave splendid entertainments. Sixteen hundred invitations would be sent out for a morning reception. She is said to have been the first to introduce the ancient custom of birds dressed in their plumage at suppers. A peacock roasted, and adorned with its feathers and spread plumes, was a favorite ornament on her table. She was celebrated also for superior literary attainments and general culture.

The elder Mrs. Hickson Field was Katharine A. Bradhurst, and married first John McKesson, a noted lawyer. Her second husband was Hickson Field, who was also a widower. Mrs. John Jay is his daughter by his first marriage. His son, Hickson, married Mary Bradhurst, the niece of his second wife. Both these ladies have been abroad some years.

We have not space for the merest mention of leading ladies in different sections of the country of the present time. To do them justice would require another volume. A friend sends account of a lady residing in Syracuse, New York, whose social influence has been salutary and widely acknowledged. Mrs. Redfield—Ann Maria Tredwell—is not only noted for position, but known as the author of a popular work—" Zoological Science, or Nature in Living Forms "—a book commended by Professor Agassiz as one that would " do great credit to a majority of college professors in this department." She came of a distinguished family. Her grandfather devoted his entire fortune and best energies to the support of American independence in the great struggle for nationality, and served his country in Congress during its first sessions; while her father obtained distinction by his military services in the war of 1812. Ann Maria was born at the beginning of the century, at St. Crignal, Canada West, and passed the earliest part of her life on the banks of the beautiful Ottawa; afterwards residing at Plattsburg, a place named for her mother's family. She was educated in the school of Mrs. Willard, at Troy. Her intellectual culture was softened by native refinement and a sympathy that went forth spontaneously towards all who needed it or claimed her tenderness. The mother of a numerous family, she took pains with the education of children who, like her, are prominent in society.

Mrs. Leavenworth is identified in a measure with the prosperity of Syracuse, which town was founded by her father, Hon. Joshua Forman. Mary, his daughter, was born in the romantic valley of Onondaga, being descended from leading families on both sides. Her maternal grandfather was Hon. Boyd Alexander, member of Parliament for Glasgow, Scotland. As a young lady she was noted for beauty of person, elegance and refinement of manners, and mental powers that gave her extensive influence, and directed the judicious employment of an ample fortune. She married a professional gentleman who had been much in public life, and with the cares of a family and of liberal hospitality found time for the exercise of systematic charity. She was one of the first to establish a Home for orphan children; and while presiding over such an institution, she is manager of one for indigent women. During the war, she was president of the Christian and Sanitary Commission, and was indefatigable in her benevolent labors. Her attractive home is still the resort of the most intelligent and distinguished of the townspeople and visitors.

XV.

Otis is an old Revolutionary name, and "has the true patriotic ring." In that great charter of freedom, the Declaration of American Independence, it occupies an honored place, and has always been cherished as a household name in the United States. Mrs. Harrison Gray Otis is the daughter of a Boston merchant, William H. Bordman, who was largely engaged in the Northwest Coast, China, and India trade. He married Elizabeth Henderson, the daughter of Joseph Henderson, who was the first high sheriff of the county of Suffolk, in Massachusetts. The sword he once wore is now hanging in the City Hall of Boston, as a historical relic. It was his duty to read the proclamation of Congress, announcing "A Treaty of Peace between Great Britain and America," from the State House balcony, on the 23d of April, 1783.

The parents of Miss Elizabeth Bordman were devoted to their children, and gave personal care to their education, which was not only thorough in all branches, but elevated by all the salutary and beneficent influences felt only in a happy and religious home. The subject of our sketch at an early age married the eldest son of the Hon. Harrison Gray Otis, who bore the same name with his father. They were said to be the handsomest bridal pair in Boston. Her term of married life was short, and she was left a widow with young sons dependent on her care. Anxious to secure them the best advantages of education, and to improve her own mind by study and observation, Mrs. Otis took her sons to Europe, remaining abroad seven years. During that time she visited many friends of rank and distinction, and was received with marked favor among literary circles and the aristocracy of different countries, being presented at several courts. Thus her time passed agreeably; but the attainment of social distinction was never an object with her. As soon as she had accomplished her design in forwarding the studies of her boys, Mrs. Otis returned to America, and took up her permanent residence in Boston. Here she employed all her time that could be spared from domestic and educational duties in works of benevolence, lending ever ready aid to institutions of charity and temporary efforts to benefit those in need. She gave efficient aid to "The Blind Asylum Fair," "The Sailors' Snug Harbor," "The Washington Equestrian Statue," and other fairs, and devoted much time and labor to the enterprise of purchasing Mount Vernon. After the work was stopped by Miss Cunningham's departure for the South, Mrs. Otis persevered in her exertions, and had the pleasure of giving to the cause its crowning contribution—the last sum which secured the purchase of Washington's tomb. Thus the record of her life, almost from early youth, has been a chronicle of noble deeds for the benefit of the public and the country.

This last gift to the Treasury was from the proceeds of the Mount Vernon Ball, got up by Mrs. Otis at the Boston Theatre, March 4th, 1859. It was said to be "more splendid in its arrangement, more brilliant in its array of fair women and brave men, and nobler in its purpose, than any thing which had ever preceded it." The Boston Theatre presented a scene of unsurpassed beauty and magnificence. In the vestibule the flags of all nations covered the heads of the children of America, and hung in graceful folds at their sides, while the scene beyond was one more gorgeous than is often offered to the eye. An angel of mercy sounded forth upon his trumpet the new offering which those who had assembled were about to make to a noble object. The decorations were admirable. The sum realized towards the purchase of Mount Vernon was about ten thousand dollars.

It was due to the untiring exertions of Mrs. Otis, commenced about 1850, that the birthday of Washington was made by law a holiday in Massachusetts. It had been her custom to open her house for a public reception on that day, and the guests were coming and departing all day. The house was usually dressed with American flags. The rooms were fragrant with large bouquets and flowers of the choicest variety, sent by friends. The military bodies celebrating the day passed by the house, and the band paid the customary salute to this patriotic lady.

On the return of Mrs. Otis from Europe she opened her house for Saturday morning receptions and Thursday evening soirées, conducted on the foreign plan of tea and cakes. She did not vary this simple style of entertainment, even when strangers of distinction were her guests. On one occasion, at the opening of the railway between Boston and Montreal, the President of the United States, Mr. Fillmore, the Governor General of Canada, Lord Elgin and suite, an Indian chief, and many strangers of note were present at the same time. Her house was then kept open a week for the reception of visitors, but the same plain style of refreshments was preserved. The house standing at the corner of Mount Vernon and Joy Streets was the well-known resort of all the fashion and gayety of Boston, and of all distinguished strangers who came to the city. Many brought letters from the European friends of Mrs. Otis, and some were commended by sovereigns in the old world to her hospitable attentions.

Mrs. Otis's connection, by blood and by marriage, with the oldest and most distinguished families in the country, her command of wealth, her literary accomplishments, her sprightly humor, and her attainments as a linguist—speaking fluently four or five languages—with a personal power acknowledged by all who became acquainted with her as irresistibly charming, gave her an influence in society unrivaled in her own city or State. It was her delight to use this power in doing good, and especially by her example to lead others to seek opportunities of aiding worthy charities. Few left her after a long interview without enlarged views and more earnest aspirations in some good work; and many who were friendless and destitute had reason to be grateful for efficient aid. Mrs. Otis visited other parts of the United States, and spent much time in Norfolk, gathering information she was afterwards to make useful.

The time came when she resolved to relinquish her social honors, to give up visiting and receiving guests, to pack up and put away her books and her works of art, and to devote her whole time, her house, and her means to a needed public service. This was immediately after the commencement of the late civil war. The city government of Boston at that time was offered the use of a hotel, called the Evans House, as a place of deposit for goods and money for American soldiers and sailors and their families. The high position of Mrs. Otis, her administrative energy and untiring zeal, and her habit of leading projects of improvement, rendered her very name a tower of strength, and the authorities invited her to take charge of the new enterprise, and to carry out her own plans. One of these was the establishment of a Bank of Faith; and most successful did she make it. The following extract from her first report will give the best idea of her work:—

"Mrs. Harrison Gray Otis presents her compliments to His Honor the Mayor and the gentlemen of the Donation Committee of the City Government of Boston; and having entered the Evans

House, which was lent to the city by the liberality of William Evans, Esq., on the 29th of April, 1861, now begs leave to submit for their consideration a recapitulation of the work which has been done in that establishment. The plan of placing a woman in communication with the soldiery, outside of hospitals, having been entirely original as far as her knowledge extends, and being a novelty, it was naturally by many persons considered wholly impracticable, and various were the prognostications issued of its lack of duration, and even security from insubordination and rudeness. Mrs. Otis commences by stating that nothing can surpass the exceeding respect, deference, and boundless gratitude with which she has been treated—to such an extent that she feels warranted in asserting that, religiously, morally, and physically, she firmly believes the Evans House to have been most beneficial to the Massachusetts troops. It has been, in some sort, a home to friendless soldiers, sick, suffering, discharged and paroled. Soldiers of other States and from the South passing through Boston have derived benefit from this house. The names of fifty regiments and batteries are on its books, from which large numbers of men have participated in its stores, and are now daily sending, individually, from the army and hospitals, for comforts which they know will be instantly forwarded to them. Thousands of letters have been received from them, stating in glowing terms their gratitude on their reception. A few sailors have made their appearance at the house, and have been well satisfied with their visits. It has been believed to be a most important part of this novel plan, that the donations of wearing apparel, books, &c., should be personally made. It is proved that all articles so presented have acquired a far greater intrinsic value from the acquaintance made with the house, conferring a local habitation and a name on the source of the bounty.

"Now, gentlemen, it may well be asked: 'From whence proceeded the money and effects to answer these enormous demands on the Evans House, not one cent or one shred having been begged for the great cause—not even from yourselves, by the writer?' The answer is this: A Bank of Faith was established, and, under Divine Providence, it has grandly prospered. Noble men, women, young girls, and even little children of all classes and conditions—rich and poor—have contributed liberally after their means and fashion," &c.

The Committee on Military Donations, December 22, 1862, passed the following resolution:—

"That this institution, under the management of this most excellent and patriotic lady, has been of incalculable benefit to the soldiers of our army. By her untiring perseverance and benevolence, our volunteers have been supplied not only with substantial, well-made clothing, necessary for a campaign, but with many of those smaller articles calculated to render their camp life more comfortable, and which could only have been provided by womanly kindness and forethought.

"Without entering into details, some idea of her labors, and the generous donations which have been received and distributed by Mrs. Otis, may be derived from the fact that five thousand four hundred dollars have been received in cash, and two hundred and fifty thousand six hundred and seventeen articles have been distributed. Many donors presenting well-filled boxes and barrels, ready for hospital use, with the assurance that they were properly packed for transportation; the package, with its contents, having been considered but a single article in the enumeration."

Such labors, as may well be imagined, entailed on Mrs. Otis the severest self-denial and unremitting exertions. She gave her personal superintendence to every thing, and assisted in all that was done; never leaving the house for a single day, nor relaxing her labors long enough to visit a single place of private or public amusement. Her life had been a summer of joy, her youth renewed continually by the ever-gushing fountain of cheerfulness; the sympathy and love that filled her heart made her Religion's willing handmaid and almoner. But she was prepared to be still more disinterested, and to undertake tasks that might have repelled one less anxious to alleviate suffering and minister to the wants of the deserving poor. No small degree of heroic fortitude and firmness was required to carry out the great and beneficent objects of the organization. Mrs. Otis did so with an entire disregard of her own personal comforts, and a self-abandonment rarely found among the greatest philanthropists.

Another report says:—

"Mrs. Harrison Gray Otis presents her compliments to His Honor the Mayor and the gentlemen of the Donation Committee of the City Government of Boston, and informs them that on the 29th of April, 1864, she completed the third year of her most interesting work in Boston for the soldiery, having commenced it in the Evans House in 1861, and therein remained two years, and one year at 126 Tremont Street, opposite Park Street Church. During this period she has not left her post for one day, excepting on Sundays and religious festivals, and has found abundant occupation in the distribution of all manner of useful articles conducing to the comfort and welfare of the troops, as well as sick, suffering, and dying soldiers, in their tents and hospitals; and others in their own homes.

"Thousands of soldiers and their families have blessed the willing givers; for not one cent has been begged, Mrs. Otis's whole system having been based on voluntary donations; and you well know, gentlemen, she has not received any pecuniary assistance from yourselves. The original plan, a sort of Bank of Faith, has been thoroughly tested, with perfect success, and no deviation has been made from the opening of the house.

"During the seventeen months this report covers, there have been distributed four thousand dollars in money, and two hundred thousand substantial articles, comprising shirts, drawers, socks, mittens, soldiers' bags, containing implements for mending clothes, pocket handkerchiefs, towels, comforters, blankets, pillows, nightgowns, dressing-gowns, and all kinds of hospital garments and stores, of wines, liquors, spices, tea, coffee, chocolate, sugar, &c. Testaments, prayer-books, tracts, and reading matter have been abundantly supplied."

As an instance of the appreciation of foreigners, the following account of a Swedish compliment paid to Mrs. Otis may be mentioned:—

"By invitation of Captain Adlerspawe, Mrs. Otis visited the Swedish man-of-war *Norrkoping* yesterday afternoon. Her reception on board was most flattering. The marines were in line at present arms, the sailors then formed in line around the deck of the vessel, so that every face could be seen, and a good idea of the Swedish physiognomy obtained. The gun-deck and officers' apartments were next viewed. After that an entertainment was given in the Captain's saloon, when the Captain proposed a toast in honor of Mrs. Otis, stating that her patriotic life was a model for ladies of every nation, especially when harassed by war.

"Before Mrs. Otis left the ship, the sailors gave an exhibition of their national dances. One—the Weaver's Dance—is suggestive of the spinning of thread and weaving of cloth, and is very complicated and beautiful. The music is as weird, dolorous, and charming as the ancient lore of the country.

"On her departure the yards were manned, and three hearty cheers were given for Mrs. Otis, and a salute from all the guns of the vessel was fired in her honor."

As this will be, perhaps, the only connected memoir, in enduring form, of this wonderful charity, I offer no apology for occupying space in the history of it. Another report, dated April 29, 1865, says:—

"Mrs. Harrison Gray Otis presents her compliments to His Honor the Mayor and the gentlemen of the Donation Committee of the City Government of Boston, and informs them that on the 29th of April, 1865, she completed the fourth year of her interesting work for the soldiers.

"The furloughs which have been bestowed upon the men for bravery and good conduct, have resulted in pleasant visits to their well-remembered resting-place, from which their families have also derived support. Mrs. Otis can never forget the last touching request of a young and brave officer—Colonel Griswold. 'I have a favor to ask,' he said; 'two of my men have been promoted for bravery to lieutenancies, and, as I firmly believe in the beneficial efficacy of the gifts of Testaments and useful articles from this house, personally presented as they are by yourself, I beg I may give them introductions to you.'

"With regard to the outfits, it is undoubtedly true that the greatest care has been taken of them, and a certain degree of pride exhibited in their preservation. Many of the Testaments and prayer-books, with the signet of the House attached, and even garments, have been brought home drenched with the blood of their possessors, after a three years' service.

"The supplies of the House have not been confined to Massachusetts alone; no soldier with fitting testimonials has ever left it empty-handed.

"A corporal with six soldiers, accompanied by a drummer boy, went to bathe in a river near Boston, and, observing the little fellow carefully concealing under a pile of leaves something very precious, at least to him, their curiosity was aroused, and they questioned him. The boy replied it was an article he very much prized, and always carried with him wherever he went; they laughed, and teasingly suggested various childish things; whereupon he knelt, and, removing the leaves, exhibited a Testament, saying that Mrs. Otis had given it to him and begged him to preserve it. The next week the corporal and his six men all came to the house, asked for, and received Testaments.

"During the twelve months this report covers, there have been distributed three thousand dollars in money, and fifty thousand substantial articles. Testaments, Bibles, prayer-books, and tracts have been abundantly supplied, and newspapers of all sorts."

. At a council meeting, Alderman Clapp offered the following preamble and resolutions, which were passed:

"*Whereas*, During the war recently brought to a close, Mrs. Harrison Gray Otis, acting in behalf of the citizens, and with the approval of the City Council, has devoted her time for four years to the charge of the City Donation Room, laboring incessantly to provide comforts for the sick and wounded soldiers, and clothing to those in need; therefore

"*Resolved*, That the thanks of the City Council are hereby tendered to Mrs. Harrison Gray Otis for her labor of love, which has been productive of great good to the heroes of the war, and has reflected credit upon the city of Boston.

"*Resolved*, That a copy of this vote be sent to Mrs. Otis by the City Clerk."

"This remarkable lady," said a prominent journal, "has done more to alleviate the sufferings of the soldiers than is generally known. At the beginning of the war she expended largely of her own ample fortune. During four years she was never absent a single day from her post—not even on the Fourth of July (except Sundays) —from ten A. M. to three P. M. Her noble deeds have attracted even the notice of foreign countries. The Stockholm Daily, of Sweden, contained her portrait and three columns on the subject of her labors. She is a friend to all the hospitals. Soldiers in service, soldiers disabled and discharged, all go to see her, and come away happy. Her name will be prominent in history, and will be honored by future generations.

"We can call to mind no other instance of such exclusive, prolonged, uninterrupted devotion to the soldiers, carried on from day to day with undiminished enthusiasm and activity. Mrs. Otis's position in society helped her position as head of the Donation Room; for it drew to her large amounts of contributions in money and goods. But she not merely gave to sick, wounded, or destitute soldiers the comforts or clothing they needed, she also gave them counsel, sympathy, and encouragement, and delighted them with the genial kindness of her manner. She received the humblest private soldier as she would have received the Lieutenant-General, and cheered his heart as much by the courtesy of her address as by the warmth of her benevolence."

The flag of the Union Club was displayed in front of Mrs. Otis's house, and patriotic airs were played in compliment to her. She was named queen of the army and navy, and her house became a centre of attraction for military men. The New England Guard Regiment presented her with implements of war from Newbern.

When Mrs. Otis received her friends, as usual, on the Washington anniversary, all Boston seemed delighted to pay its respects to her public spirit and loyal devotion. Merchants, legislators, lawyers, artists, literary men, civil and military dignitaries, and strangers, came to acknowledge the credit due to her. At about three o'clock the Second Battalion halted in front of her residence, and paid her the compliment of a military salute. Major Rogers and his officers were invited into the house, and Mrs. Otis presented him with a beautiful bouquet, while the band played national airs. The Mayor and his wife were present, with Governor and Mrs. Banks, and many other persons of distinction. In the morning, Mrs. Otis was surprised by the gift of a richly framed cabinet copy of Stuart's Washington, from several gentlemen, who had caused it to be painted for the purpose.

Among the fine oil paintings for Count Schwabe's Gallery of Fallen Heroes, is a full-length portrait of

Mrs. Harrison Gray Otis. It is the only living person's having a place in the gallery. It was procured by the Volunteer Soldiers' Army and Navy Association, and presented to the owner of the gallery; Mrs. Otis's connection with the army and navy, during the late war, having created a desire to perpetuate her memory among those brave fallen ones, for whom she devoted so much labor and money.

The value and importance of Mrs. Otis's work was thus recognized. She won a place in the grateful remembrance of the whole country. It is not saying too much to assert, that she did more than any other woman in the land for the amelioration of the condition of American soldiers in the field. Nor were her kind ministrations confined to Northerners; she had ever as warm a welcome for the humblest of her Southern countrymen. How entirely she disregarded what usually is a woman's chief consideration, may be seen from the fact that she did not purchase a new dress, nor have any made up of those presented to her, nor any repaired, during the four years that her labors were in requisition. In all, it is thought not less than a million of dollars was received and expended in money and goods. So glorious a work will only be fully appreciated in after times. Mrs. Otis will have a place in our history, not only as "in her youth the most celebrated belle of her day, but in the ripeness of her mature years a true philanthropist, and a perfect model of American womanhood."

This patriotic and self-sacrificing woman, who has

also divided, it is said, tens of thousands from her own fortune among the soldiers and their families, does not find her mission ended. "My life's work," she says, "will not be finished so long as I breathe." Since she resigned her post in the city, she has been solicited, in various places, to give her energies and labors for all kinds of projects and plans. In testimony of gratitude she has received, from the generals down to the private soldiers, an immense variety of relics of the war. She resides still in Boston.

The brother of Mrs. Otis married Miss Emily Marshal, who has been called the most beautiful woman ever seen in the United States. She was accompanied by her father on her first visit to Saratoga. The people crowded to see her as she alighted from the coach; and whenever she passed from the hotel to her carriage or to the steamboat, they would stand in a line on either side, to gaze on the vision of surpassing loveliness, to the effect of which her gentle and graceful manner added.

Mrs. Richard Derby, the daughter of a physician in Maine, and the wife of a wealthy gentleman of Boston, is mentioned as a beautiful and accomplished woman. She spent much time in Paris, and was a favorite with the last king of France.

Lydia, the accomplished wife of Hon. E. F. Wallace, American consul at Santiago de Cuba, was born and educated in Boston. Her responsible position was adorned by the attractions that brighten and elevate society, and strengthen the influence of a husband distinguished for ability and classical scholarship. Her correspondence would fill a volume, most interesting to readers for its picturesque delineations of novel scenes.

William H. Prescott, the historian, once pointed out to me, in his library, two swords crossed; one belonging to his grandfather, Colonel Prescott, who defended the works cannonaded by Captain Linzee, of His Majesty's ship-of-war *Falcon*—the other sword to Captain Linzee. Prescott married that officer's grand-daughter. He wrote to Miss Preble, in 1845, of his wife: "She is a niece of Mr. Nathan Amory, and I do not think your sister did her any injustice. At all events, we have passed our quarter of a century together, and reached our 'silver wedding,' as they say in Germany, without as yet finding the truth of La Bruyere's maxim—'that the happiest couple find reason to repent, at least once in twenty-four hours, of their condition.'"

Miss Harriet Preble died in Manchester, near Pittsburgh, in 1854. She was deemed an ornament to society, and was in no ordinary degree esteemed and beloved. She was a niece of Commodore Preble, the first commodore of the Revolution. Born in England, and passing her childhood and youth in Paris, she received her education in the famous institution of Madame Campan. Her genius and literary acquirements were sublimed by ardent piety. In early life she became acquainted and associated with most of the leading and most brilliant scholars, and the most distinguished statesmen and writers of France, with whom she corresponded after her return to America. In this country she was on terms of intimate friendship with Ticknor, Prescott, and the most distinguished scholars and authors. Her varied mental stores made her conversation delightful to old and young; and all her gifts, with her property and her labors, were consecrated to her Redeemer.

XVI.

The ancestors of Mrs. Crittenden resided in Albemarle and Goochland counties, Virginia. Her great-grandfather, Colonel John Woodson, inherited from his father a large landed estate called Dover, on James River, in Goochland. He married Dorothea Randolph, of Dungeness. One of her sisters was the mother of Thomas Jefferson, the third President of the United States; another was Mrs. Pleasants, the mother of Governor Pleasants, of Virginia. Her only brother, Thomas Mann Randolph, was the heir to the large estate of Dungeness. A son of Mr. and Mrs. Woodson, Josiah, married his cousin, Elizabeth Woodson; and their daughter, Mary, in 1801, married Dr. James W. Moss, of Albemarle County, Virginia. These latter were the parents of Elizabeth Moss, the subject of this brief notice.

After a few years' residence in Goochland, Dr. and Mrs. Moss removed to Mason County, Kentucky. There Elizabeth was born. Great pains were taken with her education, which in her years of childhood and early youth was superintended by Miss Eliza Spencer, a lady of English birth. Before the young girl had arrived at womanhood, Dr. Moss removed from Kentucky to Missouri, then just admitted as a State into the Union. His home was at first in St. Louis, but, after a temporary sojourn there, he was attracted to the beautiful and fertile portion of the State in which the town of Columbia is situated. There, in the midst of a small settlement of families from Virginia and Kentucky, which at that time gave tone and character to the greater part of Central Missouri, Dr. Moss devoted himself to farming upon a large scale. Elizabeth, whose accomplishments in mind were heightened by the charm of youthful beauty, was soon after married to a young physician of great promise, Dr. Daniel P. Wilcox. He was a member of the State Legislature, but did not live long to serve his State, or to enjoy the happiness promised by his union with so lovely a wife. He died, leaving his widow with two daughters; the eldest of whom, Mary, married Mr. Andrew McKinley, the only son of Justice McKinley, of the Supreme Court of the United States. He was then practicing law in St. Louis with eminent ability.

The youngest, Anna, became the wife of the Hon. E. Carrington Cabell, a representative in Congress from Florida, the son of the Hon. William Cabell, late Chief Justice of Virginia.

In the autumn of 1832, Mrs. Wilcox was married to General William H. Ashley, then the sole representative in Congress from Missouri. His residence was in St. Louis, where he owned a large estate, and was distinguished for noble integrity of character, and for the benevolence of an amiable nature. Mrs. Ashley accompanied him to Washington immediately after her marriage, and at once became the star of general admiration, and the centre of a large circle of devoted friends. She led the fashion both there and in the summer resorts visited by her, without making the least sacrifice to the frivolity of a worldly life. Her natural grace and affability, the union of dignity and frank cordiality which formed the charm of her manner, the intellectual cultivation that enriched and elevated the most unstudied flow of conversation, and, above all, the genuine kindness of her heart, drew around her all who appreciated the true sweetness of woman's character, and made her truly "a queen" wherever she moved. "The allegiance of hearts" was hers by right divine. Many remember her at Saratoga; and the universal praise accorded to this charming woman was never mingled with the least breath of envy or disparagement. She was one whom all "delighted to honor."

General Ashley died, regretted and lamented, in 1838. Widowed, with only the solace of her children's society, Mrs. Ashley returned to her peaceful home in St. Louis. It was then a suburban residence, built on one of the Indian mounds, formerly used as burial-places, or forts of defence. The grounds were terraced, and ornamented with a variety of shrubbery and flowers, while majestic forest-trees here and there gave pleasant shade, and improved the beauty of the extensive view. Here the little family passed the days in seclusion; but for the sake of those in whom her affections were bound up, and of her circle of attached friends, Mrs. Ashley did not refuse all society. Her house was the seat of unostentatious hospitality, and reunions the more agreeable, that they were limited to friends who were interested in each other, and had not the ceremony and state belonging of necessity to the assemblies of the Capital. Mrs. Ashley had an object in life that absorbed her cares; the education of her lovely young daughters. To this she devoted herself; and when she deemed it necessary to give them advantages of instruction, then difficult to command in a Western city, she accompanied them to Philadelphia. She remained in that city till their studies were completed.

After this was accomplished, and the young ladies were able to join Mrs. Ashley, several of her winters were passed in Washington. It was with even improved beauty, and with matured intellect, and the refinement growing out of habitual association with what tends to elevate character, that she again appeared in society. Her former friends and admirers flocked eagerly about her, and her grace and loveliness were the theme of general comment. The resident society of the Capital was marked by elegance and refinement, and she was more than ever a favorite. Few of her sex could have withstood the allurements of the homage lavished upon her; yet she was unspoiled. Her greatest pleasure always consisted in promoting the enjoyment of others. It was her delight to dispense happiness; and many were her opportunities of bringing out merit from obscurity, and of placing in the best light qualities that needed but to be recognized to win popularity. With a tact rarely equaled, Mrs. Ashley was ever performing kind offices in a way that secured the best results without wounding the self-love of those she obliged. It would fill a volume to detail· the instances in which her liberal aid and her cordial kindness forwarded the views and contributed to the pleasures of those whom her delicacy caused to feel their obligation but lightly.

She always entered with interest and sympathy into the affairs of her young friends; and it may be conjectured that they often solicited her counsel and co-operation. In every part of the American Union one may hear persons of the highest social position speak of her with ardent gratitude and affection, and of the many kind acts and attentions by which she contributed to their benefit or enjoyment while at the seat of Government. It has been remarked, that she was never known to speak harshly or censoriously of any one; nor did she ever forget an acquaintance, or wound by any capricious change of manner. She was perfectly familiar with all the political issues of the day; but never advocated, as a partisan, either side of the question. Always intelligent and fluent in conversation, whatever the subject might be, she never assumed the slightest superiority by her manner, or seemed conscious that her own opinion or judgment was better than that of others. This modest reticence, notwithstanding the real superiority which those who knew her could not fail to acknowledge, was manifest in what might be called "a gracious way of listening." Many ladies who converse well do not listen with attention to persons less gifted than themselves; Mrs. Ashley had the faculty of doing so most charmingly. It was a part of the delicate tact springing from a disinterested regard for the feelings and the pride of others, which, scarcely less than her noble beauty and grace, rendered her the ornament of every social circle, showing the true dignity, blended with an indulgence for the claims of all classes, that won grateful regard while it commanded respect.

The Hon. John J. Crittenden, then Attorney-General of the United States under Mr. Fillmore's administration, in 1853 won this lady to be his wife. After the retirement of Mr. Crittenden from the Cabinet he was returned to the Senate, and continued in Congress till his death, in 1863. His history belongs to the country's annals.

Mrs. Crittenden always accompanied him to Washington, and remained there while his duties detained him. Admiration always followed her. A lady wrote, describing a party at Governor Aiken's, in 1857, and Mrs. Crittenden's appearance: "Nothing can harmonize better than the magnificent dress, ostrich feathers, and superb scarf of lace that falls over it with such a gorgeous levity. Between the dress and the light folds of the scarf, relieved by the one, and half hidden by the other, plays a diamond cross of rare beauty. This lady possesses more kind feeling than would serve a whole clique of the ordinary stamp of fashionables." She is again described as wearing "a superb moire antique, of the most delicate pea-green tint, with point-lace bertha." And again: "Here was the lady of the distinguished Senator from Kentucky, Mrs. Crittenden, with her perfect coiffure and air of society; all the political and diplomatic world flocking to compliment and congratulate her on the very able speech of her husband, made in the Senate during the day."

Mrs. Crittenden has more of the unconscious grace of repose, which invests one like a spiritual atmosphere, than any woman I ever saw. No intelligent person can fail to recognize it; no language can define or describe it. It differs from the grace of motion, or of mere form; it is felt as an emanation from the pure and benignant soul, whose expression gives beauty its chief and most lasting charm. Its influence is magnetic; always as a beneficent spell.

Mrs. Crittenden was in Washington during the stormy debates that preceded the outbreak of the Rebellion; and deeply did she sympathize with her husband in his anxious desire to preserve the Union without the devastation of war. She wrote, in one of her letters to her daughter, in a spirit with which all Northern people ought to sympathize: "Our Southern friends have made a great mistake—God bless them! I long to shake hands with them and welcome them back."

It is not often that a lady receives such a tribute as

was offered Mrs. Crittenden, in March, at a reception given to her in the parlor of the National Hotel. On that occasion the following address was presented by Mr Lovejoy:—

"MRS. CRITTENDEN:—

"While the whole nation is paying its tribute of willing and abundant honors to the venerable senator whose name you adorn and whose home you bless, we, the guests of the National, and some of your other numerous friends in Washington, come to pay our respects to your many excellencies.

"We bring no gifts of gold or silver taken from the cold earth, but we offer you the more precious treasures of our hearts—our affection, respect, esteem, and admiration.

"For many years you have held a conspicuous place in the best circle of Washington. Your exalted place in society has been adorned by grace, dignity, courtesy, and kindness universally manifested. These constantly flowing streams could have no other fountain than a heart full of goodness.

"It is the testimony of those who have been longest your friends, that they have never heard from you a word that could wound, nor seen a look that could give pain. Detraction you have always scorned; kindness and genial feelings you have cherished. You have thus been a nation's benefactress.

"The names of Cornelia, Portia, Madame Roland, and Lady Holland have become classic in history for their patriotism, high social qualities, and domestic virtues. Uniting the patriotism of the Roman matrons to the conjugal devotion of Madame Roland and the polished refinement of Lady Holland, your presence has diffused a charm wherever known. You have shown us that if political life is an ocean with its dark waves and angry storms, social life may be a calm, serene lake, reflecting bright images of purity and love.

"The names of Mrs. Hamilton, Mrs. Madison, and Mrs. Crittenden will always shine in the annals of social life in Washington.

"We pay you the homage of our sincere respect and esteem. We take your daguerreotype upon our hearts, and will keep it fresh while memory lasts.

"The hand of time has dealt so kindly with you thus far, that while you have the health and vigor of middle age, you still retain the freshness and vivacity of youth. May that hand still lead you gently on, till we all meet you in that better land, where youth is perpetual and beauty unfading!"

After the death of Mr. Crittenden, his widow remained for a time at Frankfort, Kentucky. She is now a resident of the City of New York, where her pleasant home is shared by the family of her eldest daughter, and where she still dispenses the elegant hospitality of one who delights in making others happy.

The graces of Miss Harriet Lane, the niece of President Buchanan, were mentioned in many journals during her domestic presidency at the White House. She entertained as a guest the heir to the British throne. She was with her uncle in London, in 1855, when he was the American Minister. She was described as " a stately, high-bred woman, composed and elegant in her manners, courtly and graceful in receiving; in conversation self-possessed and very cordial. She is rather above the middle height, with finely moulded person, complexion fair, with delicate color, blue gray eyes, and fine brown hair." She was married to Mr. Henry Elliott Johnston, and resides in Baltimore.

An entertainment given at the house of Governor Aiken, of South Carolina, in February, 1857, was pronounced the most brilliant of the season in Washington. "The daughter of one of the leading members of the

Washington Bar, Mr. Fendall, was there; a brilliant and versatile belle, who is a privileged wit in society here, expected to say what nobody else can say. Her face is full of a hundred laughing fancies, and a certain careless ease of expression denotes that she is not afraid of her own voice, and never hesitates to laugh or retort when the impulse is upon her."

At another party, at Secretary Guthrie's, Miss Windle says:—

"Conspicuous among the belles upon the floor was Miss Eliza Morgan, of Kentucky, a queenly looking girl, in black velvet and pearls, who walked through the figures like an empress at the Cobourg. This lady is chaperoned by the wife of the distinguished Senator from Kentucky—Mrs. Crittenden."

"The elegant looking wife of Judge McLean, of the Supreme Court, was there, in a gorgeous crimson dress, and one of those labyrinths of blonde, feathers, and velvet, which Madame Delaran says she is obliged to invent to appease the ravenous appetite for head-dresses of our Washington ladies."

Mrs. Slidell, the wife of the Senator from Louisiana, afterwards conspicuous abroad among ladies devoted to the Confederate cause, was described as wearing "a flowing dress of black velvet, with a superb bandeau of pearls, binding down her raven hair like a queen."

At Greenbriar Springs she was thus noticed:—

"Mrs. Slidell, of Washington, is here. Every one seems anxious to receive the law from her lips on all points of fashionable etiquette. Her influence in society is remarkable. Were she to appear attired in a tunic and zone, the ranks of fashion would swarm with Cordelias and Agrippinas. Were she to discover an eighth deadly sin in the vulgarity of robust health, chicken broth would suffice *pour tout potage*. Should she favor the fine arts, throngs of upper-tendom would bid for pictures they did not want, and statues they did not appreciate."

Mrs. Slidell was Miss Dalond, of Louisiana. Her home was on the Mississippi coast. She appeared at an entertainment given in January, 1857, at Secretary McClelland's:—

"We recognized the brilliant teeth and radiant smile of the lady of the Senator from Louisiana. Encircling her plainly parted hair shone a circlet of diamonds which might have been the ransom of a Great Mogul. The charm of this lady's conversation seems irresistible. There is an animation, a fascination in it, which we have rarely known equaled. The peculiarity of her phraseology, the 'abandon' with which she speaks, the grace of her gestures, excite a perpetual interest, and leave such a delightful impression, that all seem perfectly ready to do every thing reasonable and unreasonable that she may request."

At Governor Brown's ball given in January, 1858—

"Mrs. Slidell appeared in a Russian court-dress. It consisted of a coquettish crimson velvet cap, trimmed with rich lace and ostrich feathers, and black velvet dress, the little jacket of which was trimmed with gray fur of the most light and aërial description." This lady has met with much attention in Paris.

The wife of Senator A. G. Brown, of Mississippi, "was in a superb crimson moire antique, with point-lace trimmings. This lady's high-bred air gives great dignity to her appearance, while her hands and arms are those of a statue. She is universally beloved in our city."

Miss Windle wrote:—

"One of the most brilliant entertainments ever given in our city came off at the residence of the Postmaster-General, Hon. A. V. Brown, of Tennessee. He married a sister of General Pillow. The company composed the *élite* of Washington. The almost regal ball-room, a spacious and lofty apartment to the left of the entrance-hall, was lined with superb mirrors, extending from floor to ceiling, and divested of furniture to make room for the dancers. In the drawing-rooms opposite those who declined dancing might retire, and find cushioned lounges, chairs of any angle of inclination suggested by the fancy of elegance and ease, and jardinières bright with flowers from the hot-house of the Executive mansion. In the center of these rooms stand the host, hostess, and daughter, receiving the guests.

"Mrs. Brown, an elegant-looking woman, is dressed in rose-colored brocade, with an exquisite resemblance of lace stamped in white velvet on either side; a point-lace cape, a head-dress of fleecy whiteness, with a few ornaments tastefully arranged, completed her attire. But it is the lovely girl by her side we wish to draw your attention to, as she receives the salutations of her mother's guests. A white tissue embroidered in moss rosebuds, a circlet of pearls on her hair, and natural flowers on her bosom, present an appropriate and beautiful contrast to her mother's more elaborate and gorgeous toilet.

"The charm of Miss Sanders is her simplicity of character—of all qualities the most acceptable in the highly artificial society of Washington. This sweet girl performs on the harp beautifully with arms as white as those Venus might have lifted above the sea-foam, and little pink-tipped fingers, so delicate and taper that one feels that it is marvelous how they can pinch the cords so as to produce such full-sounding, pleasant notes as they do. Young, lovely, and an heiress, like Elizabeth of old, whichever way she turns, people will assume an attitude of devotion. Her fortune will insure her suitors of various countries.

"At about nine o'clock, the guests passed from the heated ball-room into the cool interior of the supper-room. In the center of the table stood a monster bouquet, composed entirely of japonicas and the rarest hot-house flowers, and reaching half way to the ceiling. Among the ornaments of the table was one which elicited general admiration. It was the exact imitation of a mammoth 'nest,' containing two harnessed swans, driven by a man. This ornament was made of the finest sugar, and spotlessly white.

"But here comes a lady with a regal look more remarkable in her than beauty. Rubies would well become her princely, pure and stately head, crowned with a braid of profuse black hair. This is a daughter of Duff Green. She was Margaret Green, who married Andrew Calhoun.

"Again we see Mrs. A. V. Brown, in a rich blue satin dress, superb flowers of point-lace—lace which a Pope, in his highest day of festival, might have coveted. But it is not on her richness of dress or her personal beauty that our pen delights to dwell when referring to this inestimable woman. We would like to speak of the personal qualities of one of the noblest and best of her sex—one who, as a mother, wife, and friend, stands, we think, without a rival. The women of Tennessee may well feel proud of her, for she reflects credit upon that noble State, and is rich in qualities of heart that truly place her above the majority of her sex."

At a party at Lord Napier's, April, 1858—

"One guest was strikingly conspicuous—a daughter of Captain Dahlgren, of the Navy. She was a slender girl, exquisitely graceful, with a lovely coral mouth, eyes of the softest, meekest violet, and a face shaded with long golden ringlets, like floating rays of sunshine. It was her first appearance in society, and she was simply dressed in white, with natural flowers on her bosom, so purely, freshly beautiful, that they were fit emblems of the one they adorned. By general acclamation, she was pronounced the loveliest of that brilliant crowd, and as such was selected by Lady Napier to open the festivities of the evening.

"Mrs. Pringle, of Charleston, appeared in a robe of very elegant material, the flounces edged with lemon-colored velvet." I remember the results of Mrs. Julius Pringle's fine taste and historical knowledge, in some splendid tableaux at a fancy ball given at Mrs. Roper's, in Charleston, South Carolina. In accuracy of costume and striking effect those tableaux could not be surpassed. She was noted for artistic skill in such matters.

One of the most brilliant and intellectual women in the South was the wife of Mr. Duval, a planter from Louisiana, and son of the former Chief Justice of Maryland. Her sister, a beautiful girl from Natchez, was the belle of the White Sulphur Springs in the summer of 1857.

Among the "social queens" of the late Confederate Court in Richmond, Virginia, Mrs. James Chestnut, of Camden, South Carolina, Mrs. Davis, and Mrs. Clement Clay have been mentioned as eminent for culture, wit, and colloquial powers. They won the admiration of foreign visitors, as well as the Southern people who had long known them.

In Baltimore, Mrs. Reverdy Johnson has long been prominent as a leader in society. She was very beautiful and queenly, and helped to advance the fortunes of her husband, as well as to train her daughters in every accomplishment.

Mrs. Douglas, the widow of the senator—a celebrated beauty—was long the pride of Washington society. She has a second time entered the matrimonial state—the wife of Colonel Williams.

Mrs. Myra Clark Gaines has been at different times prominent in society at Washington; but her life has been filled with too much of struggle and suffering to leave her much leisure. Her name is familiar to every one, and her romantic history is generally known. A full memoir of her life, occupying a large volume, is, we understand, in preparation. The history of her claim to her father's estates,—prosecuted under various discouragements for thirty-five years,—and of the judicial proceedings in regard to the claim, will hereafter be considered one of the most extraordinary, as well as the most interesting, in the annals of American jurisprudence.

Miss Lucy Crittenden, the sister of the great senator, possessed superior intellect, and had extensive social influence. Her husband, Judge Thornton, was member of Congress from Alabama, and the first land commissioner in California. Her residence is in San Francisco.

XVII.

Among the daughters of our country who have been distinguished in social life, a few have aimed at something above the mere triumphs of fashion, devoting their energies to make their homes a paradise and diffuse a happy influence on all around them. Of these, each has created for herself a distinct sphere of usefulness and benevolence. Mrs. White's peculiar charitable enterprise deserves special mention. Her method of realizing large benefits was almost a novelty in America, when her splendid success called forth on every side a spirit of generous emulation. Yet much as she has achieved for charity in these public undertakings, as well as in the thousand unknown instances in which she has been Mercy's angel to the poor and afflicted, what she has accomplished beneath her own roof, in the education of her children and the management of her household, ought to be still more widely known. At the risk of invading the privacy of domestic life while describing the woman of the world, we may hold up to admiration the wife, the mother, and the friend, justified by the object in view, to show the beneficent and extending effects of home education.

The grandfather of Rhoda Elizabeth Waterman was

one of three brothers, two of whom served as officers in the Revolutionary army. General Waterman, her father, one of the earliest settlers of Binghamton, New York, was a prominent lawyer, and, as such, was among the legislators who revised the laws and statutes of New York, in 1829. Her mother was the daughter of General Whitney, a wealthy landowner, distinguished as well for his sterling principles and high character as for his patriotism, hospitality, and public spirit.

Many venerable and respected persons of the olden time speak with heartfelt praise of General Waterman and his admirable wife, and describe their spacious and comfortable mansion at Binghamton as the abode of elegance and hospitality. Mrs. Waterman elevated all who came habitually within her reach, while training her children with jealous care for lives of exemplary usefulness. Hers was a rare and exceptional excellence. Brought up by such a mother, and gifted by nature with uncommon qualities of mind and heart, and graces of person, Rhoda Waterman, at a very early age, was admired alike by the old and the young.

The following letter from Daniel S. Dickinson speaks of one accomplishment of her girlhood, which has been a great charm in her home and in company:—

"BINGHAMTON, December 1, 1859.

"MY DEAR MRS. WHITE:

"Twenty-eight years since, this month, I came to reside in Binghamton, and the first Sabbath of my residence was deeply impressed with the funeral service and ceremonies of the Episcopal Church upon the death of Mrs. James McKinny.

"My attention was turned to the gallery by the rich, plaintive tones of a sweet female voice, rising above the choir and the organ in the 'Dying Christian'—'O Grave, where is thy victory? O Death, where is thy sting?'

"I inquired, and learned that the singer was a daughter of General Waterman, yet in her early and happy girlhood.

"Since then, I have passed from early manhood to age; have reared children and committed them to the dust; have stood amongst the honored of the land, and mingled in all the conflicts of life: but the notes of that heavenly song yet dwell upon my ear.

"That you may live long to cheer and bless those who love you, and to adorn society; and when it shall please a beneficent Providence to call you home, that you may experience the triumphs you sang so beautifully, is the prayer of one who is

"Sincerely yours,
"DANIEL S. DICKINSON."

At the date of the above letter, the lady to whom it was written had become the mother of children who adorned her home with the virtues and accomplishments that reward the fondest parent's most devoted love and unremitting labor. Mr. Dickinson, while visiting that home, could hear in the exquisite voices of the oldest daughters the echo of that which had "dwelt upon his ear" so many years.

At a very early age Miss Waterman became the wife of James W. White, a young lawyer of Irish birth and parentage, born in the County Limerick, and a nephew of Gerald Griffin, author of "The Collegians." He was of an excellent family, noted for the virtues as well as the talents of its members, and must have been distinguished by uncommon qualities to have won a prize coveted by many suitors of wealth and distinction.

The young couple took up their residence in the city of New York in 1834; and from that time Mrs. White made her home so bright and so attractive, that it has ever been the favorite resort of the refined and the youthful, as well as of the afflicted. We owe it to the mothers and daughters of our land to reveal some of the hidden causes which have made "Castle Comfort" (so the family and their friends delight to call her house) an enchanted abode, as well to its inmates as to all who are brought, even for the space of an hour, within Mrs. White's charmed circle. The good we mean to do by this revelation must plead our excuse for it with this estimable lady. From her own accomplished mother she early learned the science, not only of the most admirable domestic economy, but of increasing, day after day, the happiness of her husband, her children, and her servants. Possessing the unbounded confidence of her husband, and devoted heart and mind to the purpose of affording him, beneath his own roof, all elevating pleasures, and that repose of every faculty needed by a lawyer after his hard mental toil, his wife never, from her bridal day, relaxed her efforts to render his evenings delightful, and with the ever varying devices of womanly affection to keep his soul young and his heart fresh and full of its early happiness. Mrs. White, from the first, considered it her most sacred duty to God and to her husband to deepen, purify, and increase, in her own heart and in his, the conjugal affection which bound them together, and which she prized as Heaven's best gift. And God blessed the effort. Through storm and through sunshine, amid the severe and protracted trials with which Providence visits His best beloved servants, when sickness came and death snatched rudely away some one of the lovely children that bloomed around the doting parents,—no bereavement, no injury of fortune or injustice of men, ever could dim the sunny brightness of that home, nor stop the flow of that warm tide of love. To the stranger or the friend it was a touching and instructive spectacle to see these happy parents, so youthful in spirit, surrounded by their children and grandchildren,—as keen for the enjoyment of song, and dance, and tale, and joke, as the youngest and blithest in the circle. One was reminded of those beautiful trees growing amid the eternal spring-tide of the valley of Mexico, and covered the whole year round with unfading verdure, and the opening blossom side by side with the ripe mellow fruit.

In this blissful home, created by superior virtue and talent, the mistress delighted to dispense the courtesies and kind offices of true hospitality,—her own sunny and genial temper lending them a new charm, while her finished education and varied attainments rendered her conversation delightful, and enabled her to afford continual enjoyment to visitors of the most refined taste and intellect. It may be said of her, as of another of her sex, "to know her well was itself a liberal education." She alone was the teacher of her children. Certain hours of the day were set apart for study and instruction, with which she permitted no engagement to interfere. In the higher branches, and in music—for which they had extraordinary talent—she gave them lessons and carefully superintended their practice, allowing them the assistance of masters in foreign languages. Idolizing their mother as they did, they needed no stimulus but her love and their own keen appetite for knowledge. Thus her devotedness and their own loving zeal for study were rewarded by uncommon proficiency on their part,—every one of them laying the foundation of a solid education, to which were added all the accomplishments that embellish social life. " To what school do you send your children ?" was frequently asked by those who wondered at their progress.

With the careful training of their minds Mrs. White combined a diligent and happy tutoring of the heart; and not rarely were their domestic pleasures made to develope the affections as well as the mental powers. Home festivals on birth-nights, or on the return of absent members of the family, were frequently given, with private operatic or dramatic performances by the children, dressed in appropriate costume—the drawing-room decorated with garlands and floral mottoes. Short moral plays, written by the mother, were frequently acted by the little ones; and their musical parts were sustained to the admiration of the friends who listened. Three of the daughters possessed voices of extraordinary purity and power, and, with the excellent instruction they had received were capable of the highest vocal performances. Nor, while thus mingling with graceful and natural ease with the gifted and eminent in society, who came to their mother's receptions, were these children permitted to neglect the culture of any useful art or acquirement.

A friend who happened to visit the family, after a long absence and severe mental trials, could not help repeating to himself the sweet lines of Jean Ingelow:—

> "There was once a nest in a hollow:
> Down in the mosses and knot-grass pressed,
> Soft and warm, and full to the brim—
> Vetches leaned o'er it purple and dim,
> With butter-cup buds to follow.
> I pray you hear my song of a nest,
> For it is not long:
> You shall never light, in a summer quest,
> The bushes among—
> Shall never light on a prouder sitter,
> A fairer nestful, nor ever know
> A softer sound than their tender twitter,
> That wind-like did come and go."

Never indeed was "a prouder sitter" than she whose heart had made that nest so warm, and had reared into the maturity of all moral and intellectual excellence such a numerous brood. She sought on earth no other reward, and that was not denied her.

Mrs. White's untiring activity was not confined to the education of her children, the management of her household, and the entertainment of her numerous relatives and friends. Even when burdened with the care of a large young family, her thirst for doing good constantly led her to seek out among the poorest classes of the New York population, and in the most wretched haunts, the objects of her sympathy. And many an anecdote is still related of the personal risks she ran while thus endeavoring to reclaim the fallen or to succor the needy.

A soul like hers, gifted with an enlightened and tender piety, and not unacquainted with the bitterest pangs of suffering, could not but attract the afflicted and feel attracted towards them. She knew them to be dearest to the Saviour's heart, and such they ever were to herself and her children. Her daughters, partaking of their mother's piety, shared also her every good work undertaken for the poor.

In 1853, in conjunction with the writer of this volume, she arranged a private concert at Niblo's Saloon in aid of a charitable institution, at which Madame Sontag sang, and which proved "the great fashionable event of the season," and the most successful entertainment of the kind ever given in the city. In 1856, Mrs. White was solicited by the Sisters of Charity to use her influence in obtaining aid for the rebuilding of their hospital. A great idea occurred to her, and Archbishop Hughes approved her design. A meeting of the ladies representing the different Catholic Churches was called; but they were appalled at the daring plan, and were sure no possible success could repay the outlay necessary for a fair held in the Crystal Palace. Almost a storm of opposition greeted the proposal; but Mrs. White was determined to carry through her scheme, and alone assumed the direction of matters.

Four hundred ladies, representing thirty-one churches, were engaged, and their work was assigned to them. Their disapproval was manifest, even to the day of the opening; the tide, however, soon turned. The vast edifice was lighted from the dome, and the flags of many nations draped its alcoves. An immense variety of foreign goods were exhibited. The ladies in attendance were in full dress, and each department was picturesquely decorated, presenting a scene of unrivaled magnificence. The whole area was dazzling in its gorgeous beauty.

As the crowd poured in the first evening, and friends thronged to congratulate the queen of the occasion, she was affected even to tears. The amount cleared by this "Great Charity Fair" was thirty-four thousand dollars, a splendid memorial of the indomitable energy, practical wisdom, and noble zeal of her who had been the soul of the enterprise. This was, moreover, the first Ladies' Fair that had obtained a brilliant success, and the largest—except the subsequent Union Sanitary Fair (in 1864)—ever given in the United States. Visitors flocked from different cities, curious to see it; and plans for similar enterprises, inferior in extent, were discussed in other communities.

At the close of the Fair, the sisters begged Mrs. White's acceptance of a massive silver épergne, as a mark of their gratitude. But she declined the gift, persuading them to dispose of it for the benefit of the hospital.

It was not surprising that one who had achieved such a triumph, should be beset on all sides with entreaties to give her influence and energies in support of other undertakings. Inventors, teachers, managers of charitable institutions, &c., sought to enrol her among their patrons; and more private applications were incessant. One evening, a starving woman came to beg for needle-work, stating that she was the widow of a British officer, whose death had left her destitute, with a son ten months old; a deafness resulting from illness preventing her from making use of her education as a means of support. To help this poor woman, Mrs. White gave the first private charity soirée ever given in New York, and realized enough to take and furnish a room, and provide the widow with a sewing-machine, by which she afterwards gained a comfortable living.

In 1859, Mrs. White was president of an association for getting up a large fair in aid of the Sisters of Mercy. This was held in the Academy of Music. One of Mrs. White's contributions was a massive volume bound in velvet and gold, valued at twenty-five hundred dollars, of the rarest and most precious autographs ever collected. The book was drawn in a lottery, after a goodly sum had been raised by the sale of tickets; and the fortunate drawer presented it to the original donor. The Pope had been solicited for his autograph; but, replying through his secretary, he preferred to contribute a splendid stone cameo set in gold.

Of the amount of labor required to fill this book

with its valuable array of autographs, no one who has not tried the experiment can form any conception. The following letter from Archbishop Hughes is suggestive in more than one way:—

"NEW YORK, April 9, 1859.

"MY DEAR MRS. WHITE:

. . . "I must congratulate you on this one thing, that in your projects for aiding the charity you imitate nobody. Your plan may be successful; but, after a first successful experiment, it can never be repeated with success. I know your idea would be to have autographs of the few great living men, such as kings, emperors, prime ministers, &c., &c. These, I fear, it will be difficult, if not impossible, to obtain.

"Our ministers plenipotentiary are respected at the different courts of Europe on account of the prepotency of the United States which they represent. But, to my own knowledge, they are, as a general rule, held in personal contempt. They would not, therefore, be able to obtain the signatures of the European courts to which they are accredited. And, knowing the state of the case as I know it, I should be afraid to solicit from them any autograph, except it might be of distinguished individuals apart from court circles. . . . . I know the fastidious etiquette of European courts; and if there be any chance for such autographs, it must be in consequence of a letter from yourself, written as you will know how to write it, to our ministers and representatives. You may succeed as a lady, but I could not as an archbishop, except by the merest chance.

. . . "Besides, I will ransack further all Bishop Bruté's papers, and furnish you with such autographs as you may judge of interest for your book.

"I remain,
"Very sincerely, your friend and servant in Christ,
"✠ JOHN, Archbishop of New York."

One would be led to judge that these repeated labors for public or private charities, and the temptation to

external activity begotten by public triumphs, must have interfered sadly with the duties of domestic life, or rendered the repose of home a little irksome. It was not so, however, in this case. Mrs. White all the while continued to superintend with unrelaxed assiduity the advanced education of her children; studying with them, and making herself their companion as well as instructress. She was continually in their midst, perfecting herself in some already familiar branch of knowledge, or pursuing some new one with all the ardor of youth—hearing the lessons of her youngest girl, encouraging, by her presence and advice, the higher studies of her married daughters, and then giving herself up to her own appointed hours for self-improvement. All these studies were sanctified by the spirit of prayer, and made delightful by the sunny smile and loving words of the mother, as well as by the cheerful eagerness of those whom she thus trained by word and example. An hour every day was set apart for religious reading and devotional exercises. The spirit of generosity derived from the lofty views inculcated by their mother, not only led the children to apply with alacrity to their advancement in knowledge, but to seize and seek every opportunity of performing acts of self-denial for the benefit of others. This was made a governing principle of their conduct towards each other, and hence the continual and touching forgetfulness of self in the endeavors of each one to make all the others happy. Hence, too, their readiness ever to disregard present suffering or personal discomfort, where an effort on their part may be required, or may help to enliven the company in which they find themselves, or to advance any public or private good.

No opportunity was lost of impressing these golden rules of life on their minds. Few mothers, indeed, understand as she did the importance of detail and illustration in recommending Christian duties. It is one thing to inculcate them by theory, and another to point out the way to practice them. With the mother's self-sacrificing devotion and earnest perseverance in duty, she showed the habitual cheerfulness and serenity of soul and temper on whose ever equal surface no interior trouble or external tempest could produce a single ripple. This perpetual calm in her manner, and the bright smile she ever wore in the most trying circumstances, had a better effect on the young spirits around her than a thousand homilies. Besides, the house was always neat, and resounding with pleasant voices; the household (as we have said) managed to perfection; the indefatigable spirit and strictly disciplined energies always pressed into the service of duty; the warm atmosphere of affection filling the home thus made the happiest spot on earth. Could it then be wondered, not that husband and children should "rise up and call her blessed," but that to them, one and all, a single night spent outside of such a home should appear a privation hard to bear?

Home parties and amusements of all kinds were encouraged. On several occasions concerts, and an entire opera, were performed without professional assistance; many of the spectators possessing high musical culture, and all charmed with the wonderful artistic skill of the sons and daughters, who owed to the mother their rare attainments. I do not know of another instance of such an operatic performance in a private drawing-room as was arranged and prepared by Mrs. John Mack, one of the daughters, and in which she and other members of the family took the parts. It was universally voted a perfect success.

How, with this unwearied and all-absorbing activity, has Mrs. White found leisure to write books, or to keep up an immense correspondence by letters? Yet she has done both. She is the author of two popular works of fiction: "Portraits of my Married Friends" and "Mary Staunton;" both successful, but not to be here discussed.

A romantic instance of the ingenious benevolence of this lady's daughters was the experience of Kate De ——, a beautiful young Irish girl who lived in their family, and who, being wedded above her station, returned, after her husband's death, to his family abroad. She was only able to read and sign her name, and too mu ashamed of her ignorance to be willing to betray it to her proud connections. She sought aid from the three eldest daughters of Mrs. White. Though separated by the Atlantic from her, they educated her entirely *by letter*, instructing her thoroughly in the common English branches, and writing out an entire grammar, geography, and arithmetic adapted to her comprehension and use. These she could understand, but not the simplest school-books; and under this training she became a well-educated woman.

Mrs. White has had an extensive correspondence with the learned, the gifted, and the distinguished in this country and in Europe. She may well be called "the *Sévigné* of the United States." Archbishop Kenrick of Baltimore and Archbishop Hughes were her correspondents and intimate friends; so also were many of our statesmen, and not a few generals prominent in the late war. President Lincoln corresponded with her. Her influence is extensive as the Union, and over the finest minds in the country. Her eldest son, General Frank White, had a military career, and won a renown the bravest could envy. At the time when the Tenth Regiment, New York Zouaves, took their departure for Fortress Monroe, they marched to the residence of Mrs. White, in Fifth Avenue, where they were presented with a regimental flag by Miss Nettie White, with a charming address to the soldiers.

The eldest daughter married, in 1862, Señor Don Bernardino del Bal, and in June, 1863, left New York for their distant home in Santiago de Veraguas, in the State of Panama. On returning from the steamer which bore away her idolized child, the heroic mother, with her heart yet agonized with the parting, and her eyes still streaming with tears, accompanied her second daughter, Ellen, to the Convent of the Sacred Heart, and gave her up that very hour to the home she had chosen for herself among the Brides of the Lamb.

On her arrival at Santiago, Señora del Bal set to work to enlighten, elevate, and refine the numerous and long-neglected population, which unceasing civil strife and all its demoralizing influences had reduced to a sad state of spiritual destitution. In Santiago, besides finding every place of worship closed by the tyrannical decrees of that odious usurper and despot, Mosquera, she saw the Indian and colored people deprived of every chance of religious or mental culture. She put into execution every means which her experience, ingenuity, and zeal could suggest to remedy these evils, and obtain for her labors the sympathy and co-operation of the wealthy and educated. It would be hard to say by whom the young and delicate stranger is most looked up to and most revered, the native Indian and colored people in town and country, or the proud, sensitive, and quick-witted Spaniards. She has equally benefited both: the latter by her superior and enlightened piety, by the graces and virtues with which she adorns her home and her conduct; the former by making her blessed influence felt far and wide, in Sunday-schools established by her, in hospitals, at the sick-bed of the plague-stricken, as well as in the remotest and most wretched hovel where extreme want or extreme suffering called for her presence. Everywhere she is hailed as a ministering angel, and bishop and priests and people, the high and the lowly alike, sound the praises and bless the name of the sweet American lady, "La Niña Jenny," as they delight to call her in their heartfelt gratitude.

Mrs. White performed an important part in the great Fair for the Orphans' Protectorate of New York, in 1867. Presents from General Grant, Colonel P. G. Washington, Colonel James A. Hamilton, Chief Justice Chase, and many other personal friends, adorned her table. One splendid set of Magelica ware was the gift of the Marchioness of Londonderry, who has been for years the friend and correspondent of Mrs. White.

Thus does the current of that life of devotedness gain depth and width and strength as it approaches the ocean, diffusing, as it goes onward, a still wider beneficence. None of life's painful experiences—and the saddest of all, in the death of her husband, has fallen upon her as these lines are printed—have chilled the warm heart where Christian faith and love are ruling principles. Her noble deeds are a bright example for her countrywomen; the sweet poem of her life illustrating the truth of the lines:—

> "We need not go abroad for stones to build
> Our monumental glory; every soul
> Has in it the material for its temple."

On the 5th of February, 1854, two charitable ladies who were conspicuous in the best society of New York were conversing together of the great suffering among the poor. One of them, Mrs. Thomas Addis Emmet, who had long been a manager of the Marion Street

Lying-in Asylum, spoke feelingly of the miseries of neglected infants, and of mothers compelled by poverty to give the children of the rich the nourishment intended by nature for their own. She mentioned an instance of a nurse weeping over her charge, to think what comforts she was enjoying in a good home, while her own child, to whom she could not attend, was exposed to unknown sufferings. One who pitied her distress, going to see after her child, stood at night in a small, dirty basement room, by the bed of a sick woman, who replied to her questioning: "My baby died yesterday of small-pox." —"And where is the nurse-baby?" asked the visitor. "Oh, if it's that you want, here it is," said the woman, leaning over and drawing from under her bed a basket of soiled clothes, among which lay the forlorn infant. The visitor took off its rags, wrapped it in her shawl, took it home, bathed and dressed it, sent for a physician, and, by the Divine blessing, saved it from death. This incident, related with the eloquence of Christian feeling, gave rise to the first conception of an institution which soon became an honor to New York. In a few weeks ten thousand dollars were subscribed, and in less than a month from the first inception of the idea, the "Nursery for the Children of Poor Women" was organized and chartered. Before this refuge was provided, Mrs. Dubois, the lady to whose energetic efforts it owed its existence, had been in the habit of looking up the poor children of wet nurses among her circle of friends, and, until rooms could be provided for them, of giving them shelter in her own beautiful house on Gramercy Park. The building soon became so full that more extensive accommodations were required. This was the first attempt made in New York, or the country, to provide an asylum for the shelter and care of infants. The first idea was to form an asylum for the children of wet nurses, or those otherwise deprived of a mother's care; and for the daily charge of those little ones whose mothers were obliged to labor away from their own homes to gain a subsistence. When it was found that the institution had been commenced on too small a scale, applications were made both to the State Legislature and to the city authorities for assistance; and the result was a grant from the city of a perpetual lease of a plot of ground one hundred and forty feet wide, and one hundred feet deep; while the State gave ten thousand dollars towards the erection of a suitable building.

The necessity of a "Child's Hospital" became apparent; and on application to the Legislature in March, 1857, an act was passed changing the name of the Institution to "The Nursery and Child's Hospital." A new building was erected in 1858, and the funds necessary for the support of the charity which voluntary contributions did not supply were raised year after year by public entertainments given by the lady managers at the Academy of Music. Thus the Institution was linked with associations of fashionable amusement. Not long afterwards another noble charity was added to this—a Foundling Hospital for the admission of illegitimate children whose mothers were previously of good character. In December, 1865, it was leased to the "Nursery" as a Lying-in Asylum—a place for the reception of young women who had borne irreproachable characters till overtaken by one fault, and who had no other refuge. The three institutions are now blended, and under the care of the same directress, Mrs. Cornelius Dubois, who had given up the triumphs of fashionable life to have her time and her heart engrossed by the claims of this charity. She has made it so popular among the leading ladies of the metropolis that the Institution is generally regarded as a favorite with them. The most gorgeous public balls given at the Academy of Music under their patronage have been for its benefit; and at many concerts for the same object, year after year, those ladies have contributed by their amateur singing and instrumental music.

Mrs. Dubois was Miss Delafield. She has also been distinguished for her skill in sculpture and cameo-cutting. Her works in this line have been mentioned with high praise.*

Another noble charity to which the most distinguished ladies of New York gave their co-operation, and in aid of which many brilliant entertainments were given, was that for the benefit of the soldiers' orphans. A later one, which has enlisted the warmest feelings of sympathy, is the "Southern Relief Association," appeal-

---

* See "Women Artists in all Ages and Countries."

ing for aid to the suffering women and children of the South. No public charity has ever been so popular. The winter of 1866-67 was crowded with amusements for it, and it is believed that none have been so unfeeling as to oppose its triumphs.

Mrs. Emmet is the widow of Thomas Addis Emmet, the son of the distinguished Irish patriot, and a lawyer of high standing in New York. She is the daughter of John Tom, one of the firm of Hoyt and Tom, noted East India merchants. Mrs. Emmet was an admired leader in the best social circles of the metropolis, as a youthful matron, and her influence was most useful in promoting public and private charities. She was the devoted benefactress of the poor, to whom she gave the time that could be spared from the cares of a large family. Their residence was a beautiful estate on Fifty-ninth Street, between the old Boston Post-road and Third Avenue. There was an elegant mansion, with extensive grounds and gardens, and a private cricket-ground. A fête was given there in 1844, which created a great sensation. For seventeen years Mr. Emmet's family lived at this beautiful country-seat, till the advancing city encroached upon it. Then they removed to New York.

XVIII.

It is not often that a celebrity which may be called historical is gained by leadership in the fashionable circles of a large city without beauty or attractive personal qualities, and without association with any great social event or institution. Such was the celebrity of Mrs. Rush in Philadelphia. Her attainment of preeminence in spite of many disadvantages argues rare powers of intellect. She was Ann Ridgway, the daughter of Jacob Ridgway, who rivaled Girard in the acquisition of great wealth by commercial pursuits. Ann was born in Philadelphia, and inherited a goodly share of her father's fortune. Her income was a large one for that day; her husband having also an independent property. Her education was completed in Europe, where she spent several years, and acquired more than the usual share of accomplishments then deemed essential to a lady. In those days mental culture was more thorough than at present, if the facilities were less. Miss Ridgway mingled in the best society, and acquired that taste for the elegancies of life which was afterwards shown in her days of sovereignty over the society of Philadelphia. She was married to Dr. James Rush, the son of the celebrated Dr. Benjamin Rush, one of the signers of the

Declaration of Independence, the fame of whose genius and scientific attainments spread throughout Europe; whose works were quoted by Lord Byron, and rewarded by the first Alexander of Russia. Having his origin in such noble intellectual stock, the son maintained the celebrity of the name by his original and profound work on "The Philosophy of the Human Voice," which has furnished material and guidance to so many treatises on elocution.

Though abroad a long time, Mrs. Rush passed most of her life in Philadelphia, and did not take the lead in social life till her return from Europe. Her latest residence was in West Chestnut Street, Philadelphia. The building was erected about 1849, and was magnificent in its proportions, and the splendor of its internal plan and decorations. Here the mistress of the mansion was accustomed to dispense those enlarged hospitalities which "have given her an unsurpassed eminence in American society." She had a genuine love for the arts, and was invariably a liberal and impartial friend to artists of every grade. At her weekly receptions it was her delight to assemble them around her, to introduce them to persons who might appreciate their talents and promote their success; and not unfrequently to assist them in a more direct manner. Her annual balls were magnificent; the drawing-rooms of her house were more spacious and more sumptuously furnished than those of almost any other private residence in Philadelphia, and there was unstinted outlay in both the decorations and the entertainment. A gentleman who was her guest, described, on one occasion, "her superb dress of Genoa velvet and lace, and the exquisite gems that adorned her person. Feathers drooped from her hair, and she carried in her hand a fan made of plumes of the richest dye, ornamented with a bird-of-paradise with diamond eyes and claws set with rubies." Mrs. Rush always gave her visitors a cordial greeting, with unaffected kindliness of manner. She was pleased to show her plants and the choice flowers in her conservatories. These, as well as the halls, dancing saloons, and corridors, were always thrown open—and the light, alternately brilliant and subdued, the clear, pealing music at intervals, from the band playing on the staircase, the company of splendidly dressed women, the dancing and promenading through the different rooms, the lavish and gorgeous supper, with the charming manner and lively conversation of the hostess, put the most timid at their ease, and made her parties ever agreeable. While she presided thus over the festive scene, her husband, it was said, often sat alone in his library, absorbed in study, or enjoying the contrast of perfect quiet with the bewildering gayety of the rest of the house.

Mrs. Rush was, by universal consent, acknowledged to be the queen of Philadelphia fashionable society. "This community," said a resident, "requires despotism to move it from its frigidity. There must be one sovereign—the appointed of fashion, the layer down of law. Partly from charity, partly from ambition, this large-hearted and energetic woman took into her own hands the reins of government, and has shown herself a second Semiramis." It was well for those over whom she reigned, that none could say she did not use her power with generosity. At the parties given by Mrs. Rush, the most prodigal splendor was exhibited in the services of china, glass, and gold and silver plate, and in the profusion of flowers. Yet in the more strictly artistic adornments—such as pictures—there was rather a deficiency of the best works; and there were comparatively few antiques or articles of vertù.

A lady who had been entertained in the aristocratic circles of Europe, described one of Mrs. Rush's parties as excelling any she had seen in sumptuous appointments. The tables were set the entire length of the supper-room, with cushioned seats of blue damask, and a service of the costliest china, for the accommodation of two hundred and fifty out of the eight hundred guests invited. The servants at the foot of the tables, wearing broad blue ribbons, interdicted the entrance of more guests at a time. The hostess walked through her rooms, wearing a robe of pompadour velvet, with an under dress of white satin covered with lace; the robe looped with marabout feathers and diamonds; with low corsage.

Mrs. Rush seemed to consider her parties as a necessary duty to society, yielding her, however, little gratification. The attractions of intellectual cultivation had no play in such crowded reunions. It was a yearly sacrifice to fashion. She rarely gave small parties, except to gentlemen. Besides these annual balls, Mrs. Rush had morning receptions every Saturday, when she always had something attractive or curious to amuse her guests. Sometimes it would be a fashionable tenor; sometimes children who recited verses; and on one occasion the Aztecs were shown, before they became common in public exhibitions. Of course many persons desired to attend these parties who were not acquainted with the lady, and she was frequently annoyed with applications for cards of invitation. An invitation was once taken through mistake to a Miss Patterson, a stranger, who was advised to accept it. Fancying a degree of coldness in the manner of her hostess, Miss Patterson requested a friend to inquire if the card had been meant for her, and ascertained that it had been intended for a vocalist. She insisted on leaving the house, notwithstanding Mrs. Rush's request that she would remain. The next day an article appeared in the papers stating that Mrs. Rush had sent a lady out of her house who had received an invitation by mistake.

These receptions had decidedly a musical character. Grisi and Mario were at one, and many celebrated artistes who were visiting Philadelphia had here an opportunity of being introduced to those who might become friends and patrons. Actors of merit were welcome as well as vocalists, and those who excelled in painting; yet the assemblages were generally select. Attractive ladies were sure of invitations, perhaps that they might render the house agreeable to gentlemen;

for Mrs. Rush was well known to have no partiality for her own sex. Sometimes she pressed an invitation with great kindness; once ordering a pretty dress sent to a South Carolinian lady who had not come prepared with a costume suitable for her ball. Yet she would perhaps turn coldly in the street from a woman who presumed, on an invitation to one of her receptions, to join her in a walk. A Philadelphia lady asked for a card for a female friend; it was refused, but permission was verbally given to bring her. Mrs. Rush was said to be tyrannical in social ethics, though indulgent to her gentlemen friends. A New York paper called her "one of the few relics of the old school." She had steadfast ideas of democracy, and was independent enough to carry them into her drawing-room. Above all things she had a hatred of "snobs." It was a pleasure to her to break down conventional distinctions which had no ground in reason. Inviting whom she chose to her parties—always persons of good character—the son or daughter of the tradesman or retailer found a warm welcome to her reunions, if known to possess personal worth. This was a noble trait of character; and when her inviolable fidelity to the few friends she trusted, and her liberal charities and many kind acts are placed in the account, it must be conceded that hers was a generous nature, true, strong, and earnest in its aversion to all meanness or falsehood. She always manifested a deep respect for intellect; and it was her reverence for mental gifts and culture, and sternly disciplined character, that caused her preference for men. Notwithstanding the endless gossip about her with the stronger sex, those who knew any thing of her were constrained to admit that her intimacy never bordered in the least on flirtation. She had no personal attractions, and never desired admiration. Her taste for the ornamental seemed to expend itself in a passionate love of flowers. Her conservatories were something royal. "You ought to be a happy man," said a Philadelphia lady to Dr. Rush, when she was admiring this floral magnificence. "I have always been a happy man," was his reply.

It was Mrs. Rush's custom to go to Saratoga almost every summer. Her example there might well be followed by fashion's votaries, so far as moderation in dress was concerned. She took but few dresses; usually one of black silk, one of grenadine, and a poplin for morning wear; and one trunk sufficed her. She always appeared in black, reserving her rich colored dresses for home wear —and always gave away on her return those she had worn at Saratoga.

The following letter mentions a fancy ball at the Springs in August, 1849:—

"All around the different wings of the hotel was in a blaze of light, and the company might be seen gathering in costumes before the dancing commenced. Turks, flower-girls, Quakers, goddesses, nuns, and court ladies, all gracefully and gayly threading their way among the crowd, were seen in the porticos of the windows, and along the illuminated walks. In the full blaze of the ball-room, some of the costumes could not be surpassed for costliness of material and exquisite design. Laces delicate as gossamer, and of rare value, seemed to take new delicacy from the jewels. Mrs.

Rush, of Philadelphia, wore a scarf of rich lace worth its weight in—gold will not answer here—its weight in diamonds. The jet and jewels upon her bosom seemed absolutely sparkling through a wreath of mist."

On either side of Mrs. Rush at table were always seats for gentlemen chosen by herself. When one chanced to be vacated by the departure of the friend, she selected another occupant, and signified her pleasure to the fortunate individual; always making two conditions, to which the gentleman was obliged to assent before she would name them. Of course he promised compliance, sure that the lady would stipulate for nothing unreasonable. The first promise he was required to make, and keep absolutely inviolate, was, that whenever he thought proper to order any special delicacy from the restaurant, he would never invite Mrs. Rush to partake of it. The second was, that whenever *she* chose to order any such dainty, and to offer it to him, he would not refuse to accept. These conditions were always insisted on, and always observed. At the next meal, the new occupant would be formally installed in his place. Mrs. Rush often drove to Saratoga Lake and took dinner, inviting one or two favored friends to accompany her. The banks of the lake were a favorite walk with her. While at the watering-place she did not remit her studies, taking a lesson in German and one in music nearly every day. When asked why she continued her musical practice in this way, while she was never known to play in company, she replied that she took the lessons in that and German in fulfilment of a promise to a deceased friend. She was fond of reading, and a great linguist; and was always exact in properly filling up the hours of her day. Much of it was devoted to out-door exercise. She walked a great deal; not only in summer, but in winter, without heeding inclemencies of weather.

Her last ball was given in January, 1857, and was of great splendor. It was about six in the morning when the last guest had departed, and Dr. and Mrs. Rush retired to their rooms, which communicated by a door. Mrs. Rush removed her diamonds and left them in their caskets on her table, the outer doors of both apartments being fastened. It was afternoon when she arose and took breakfast. Being still overcome with fatigue, both she and her husband went to bed very early, and she did not put away her jewels. In the night she fancied she heard the door leading from her room to Dr. Rush's open or shut; but, supposing that he was passing through, paid no attention to the circumstance. He too heard the noise, and "wondered what Ann was up for," but took no heed of it. At daylight the next morning—it was Saturday—Mrs. Rush recollected that she had not left on the ledge or table outside some money for an article she was always accustomed to send for to market on that day, and which must be purchased very early. She rose and went to her bureau, in a drawer of which she had put a thousand dollars in gold to pay tradesmen's bills. The money was gone! She opened the jewel caskets; they were empty! She instantly aroused Dr. Rush, who bade her keep still, while he examined the doors of the house. All were locked; and the outer hall door was duly fastened. The new-fallen snow showed no trace of footsteps. He went out and called a detective. By this time the servants had risen; they were called together, informed of the robbery, and told they must submit to examination. Not a trace of the thief or the booty could be found; not a single fact was elicited whereon to hang suspicion. The jewels were valued, it is said, at twenty-one thousand dollars. The police of Philadelphia did their best, but discovered nothing. The matter created a great sensation, and was the subject of newspaper comment in other cities. The public insisted on suspecting a young man who had been a guest at the ball, and soon afterwards had gone to New York, and sailed for Europe. The impression on the minds of those who remember the occurrence still is that this young man was guilty; but Dr. and Mrs. Rush thought otherwise. The detective had fancied something suspicious in the manner of the cook, who was engaged to a jeweler in New Orleans, whom she afterwards married. Nothing could be proved to justify her arrest; but Mrs. Rush always thought it likely that the woman had stolen both the money and jewels, entering the chamber at night or during her temporary absence the day after the party.

The summer following this occurrence Mrs. Rush was at Saratoga, at the United States Hotel, unaccompanied by her husband. She was detained by indisposition after the departure of other guests. A friend whose society she had much enjoyed—Mrs. Macgregor, of New York—was about to leave Saratoga; but when Mrs. Rush expressed regret at her going, she offered to stay with her. Mrs. Rush would not, however, permit her to remain on her account. She was not accustomed to receive visitors in her chamber, and did not usually like being called on when suffering from illness. She spoke with her friend as she stood outside the door, and begged that she would not stay at the hotel. Her maid, she said, was trusty and efficient; she had no need of further care; she would be well in a day or two. The hotel was then nearly empty. Mrs. Macgregor returned to her home in New York in some anxiety about Mrs. Rush, though not anticipating any danger. Her complaint was supposed to be erysipelas, followed by a general breaking up of the system. When she did not regain strength, Dr. Rush was sent for, and it was still hoped that his wife would soon be able to travel homeward. Mrs. Macgregor wrote from New York, inviting them to stop and rest a day or two at her house in passing through the city. Dr. Rush answered that they intended postponing their departure from Saratoga for a few days, to allow Mrs. Rush time to recruit her strength; but that, when able to set out, she would prefer making the whole journey in one day. It was but a few days later that news came of the death of Mrs. Rush, at Saratoga, on the 23d October, 1857.

Her remains were placed in a coffin and conveyed to

Philadelphia. She was buried according to instructions contained in her last will. Her death produced a wide sensation in her native city; saddening the hearts of many who remembered how ready her sympathies had always been with true merit, and how liberally she had dispensed her means for its advancement. She had not yet reached a very advanced age, and appeared uninterruptedly in society till the beginning of her last illness.

Mrs. Macgregor was Miss Ely, of Connecticut. She has been conspicuous for many years in New York society. Her receptions at her pleasant home in Washington Square, are attended by numerous friends of the really choice and elevated spirits, who would not mingle with such as had no claim but wealth to their association. She is noted for wit and humor in impromptu effusions. Some of her light sketches have been published by stealth.

The wife of the great statesman, Daniel Webster, was Caroline Le Roy. She was born in New York, and married in 1829 to Mr. Webster, who was a widower with children. In May, 1839, she went abroad with her husband, and was well received at the courts where they were presented; but remained only nine months. They passed their winters usually in Washington, and the summers in Marshfield, their country-seat on the Massachusetts coast—that beautiful Marshfield on the ocean shore—with Webster's "herds of noble cattle, his broad productive fields, his yachts, his fishing, his rambles in the forests planted by his own hands, his homely chats with neighbors and beloved dependents." He was wont to say, "If I could have my own will, never, never would I leave Marshfield!" But he was led away, by the advice of friends, to the protracted stay in Washington that undermined his health. Mrs. Webster shared his wanderings, and was always a helpmeet to her distinguished husband, both in domestic and public affairs. She read to him and for him, saving him time and labor by culling and arranging such facts and ideas as might be useful or available; she assisted him in his extensive correspondence, and was relied on by him in all matters where sound judgment and discretion were required. During his Secretaryship, which began in President Tyler's and continued in Fillmore's term, she was his efficient aid. At the same time she made his house the center of a brilliant society, drawing around them the finest spirits of the century, and those of high repute in the country's history. In Boston, Mr. Webster's house was in Summer Street; a noble residence, and the resort of the most cultivated society.

Mrs. Webster accompanied her husband on his celebrated Southern tour; visiting the principal cities and towns, where both were welcomed with distinguished honors.

Since her widowhood, Mrs. Webster has for the most part resided in the city of New York, though a home was offered her in Boston, suited to the style in which she had always lived.

Mrs. Henry D. Gilpin is the widow of an eminent man, and has a ruling influence in the society of Philadelphia. This is due not more to her intellectual superiority, and her culture in the arts that refine social life, than to her noble qualities of heart and true Christian benevolence. She is the daughter of Doctor John Sibley, a distinguished surgeon, who resided until the close of his life in Louisiana, exercising a wide-spread influence in that State. She was born in North Carolina, and received her education at the well-known school of Mr. Mordecai, in Warrenton. Leaving school at an early age, she joined her father in Louisiana, and was married to the Hon. Josiah S. Johnston, then Judge of the Western District Court of the State. He was elected to the House of Representatives, and afterwards, for three terms, to the Senate of the United States. As an able judge, a distinguished statesman, and leading legislator, his fame belongs to his country's history.

Mr. and Mrs. Johnston resided in Washington, and their house was celebrated for its hospitality. It was the resort of the most distinguished persons in the Capital, many of whom continued their friendship with Mrs. Gilpin through life. The celebrated Edward Livingston was not only an associate of Senator Johnston in their public career, but a close and intimate friend; and their friendship was never interrupted. Mrs. Livingston, one of the most distinguished ladies of society in Washington, survived her husband many years. Mrs. Gilpin commemorated her talents and virtues in an eloquent tribute, full of truth and feeling.

After some years of widowhood, Mrs. Johnston became the wife of Hon. Henry D. Gilpin, at that time United States Attorney for the District of Pennsylvania. When Mr. Van Buren was elected President of the United States, he induced his friend, Mr. Gilpin, to accompany him to Washington as Solicitor of the Treasury. Subsequently, the office of the Attorney-General of the United States becoming vacant, it was offered to and accepted by him. A close and confidential friendship existed between these gentlemen, which continued without interruption through life.

Some years after the return of Mr. and Mrs. Gilpin to Philadelphia, they accompanied Mr. Van Buren and his son to Europe.* In London they were received with marked attention. Mr. Gilpin soon became associated with the most distinguished literary men, his own reputation having preceded him. Numerous "breakfasts" were given to him, where he met persons of congenial tastes, and largely extended his acquaintance. Mr. Joseph R. Ingersoll, so well known and honored in Philadelphia, was at that time Minister to England. By him, a personal friend, they were received with great kindness, and through him were presented at Court.

Among their earliest visitors in London was Mr.

---

* A journal kept by Mrs. Gilpin while abroad, to which the writer has had access, furnishes the facts mentioned here.

George Peabody, who extended to them every courtesy as friends, and as visitors to the great metropolis. Mr. Peabody was then as well known for his hospitalities to his countrymen as he has since become to the whole world by his noble acts of munificence.

The first entertainment given to Mr. Van Buren and Mr. and Mrs. Gilpin was a brilliant assembly at the American Minister's; the second, a dinner by Mr. Peabody. Among the distinguished guests assembled on this occasion, were Mr. Gurney, brother of the celebrated Mrs. Fry, and his accomplished daughter, Lady Buxton, and Lady John Somerset, whom they afterwards met in society in London. Subsequently they received numerous invitations to dine with persons of distinction; among others, from Lord and Lady Ashburton, at Bath House, a noble mansion, celebrated for its fine collection of pictures and statuary. Here they had the gratification of meeting many of the distinguished literary men and nobility of England; Mr. and Mrs. Monkton Milnes, Mr. Carlyle, Mr. Kinglake, author of Eöthen, Mr. Thackeray, and others. From a large dinner-party at Mr. Hume's (member of Parliament), Mr. and Mrs. Gilpin, with other guests, attended a ball at Buckingham Palace, to which, by command of the Queen, they had had the honor of being invited. Among the hospitalities extended to them were those of Mr. and Mrs. Cobden, Mr. and Mrs. Bright, Mr. and Mrs. Grote, Sir Charles and Lady Fellows, and Miss Burdett Coutts, the latter receiving them at her beautiful villa, Holly Lodge, near London. One of the greatest gratifications they experienced while in England was their visit to the ancestral homes of Mr. Gilpin's family, to Kentmere, where Barnard Gilpin, called "the Apostle of the North," was born (three hundred years ago), and to Scaleby Castle, a few miles from the Scottish border, now occupied by one of the family. After visiting the most interesting places in England and Scotland, Mr. and Mrs. Gilpin made an extensive tour on the Continent, visiting the principal capitals, and seeing every thing of interest to strangers. They passed Holy Week in Rome, and had two interviews with the Pope; the second by his own appointment, when he received them in his library.

Among numerous hospitalities offered to them in Rome, were those by the Prince and Princess Doria Pamphili, through a letter of introduction given to them in London by Lady John Somerset, a relative of Princess Doria. In the magnificent Doria Palace they had ample opportunity for examining the galleries, celebrated as containing one of the richest collections of Art in Europe.

From Naples Mr. and Mrs. Gilpin embarked for the East; ascending the Nile as far as Thebes, and spending three months among the great monuments of antiquity. From the top of the great pyramid of Cheops they beheld the valley of the Nile, with its picturesque groups of camels with their Arab drivers, and groves of waving palm-trees. Afterwards they visited Asia Minor, Turkey, and Greece, with some of the Grecian isles. At

Athens they remained several weeks, where they were much interested in the Mission Schools of Mr. and Mrs. Hill and Dr. King. They there formed the particular acquaintance of the late Earl of Carlisle, with whom Mr. Gilpin made frequent excursions into the interior of Greece. Their friendly relations were interrupted only by death. On their return to England Mr. and Mrs. Gilpin were invited by Lord Carlisle to visit him at Castle Howard, where they found assembled many of the distinguished members of his family; among them his aged mother, whose death, some years after, was communicated to Mrs. Gilpin by Lord Carlisle, in a letter touchingly evincing his reverence and filial love.

Mrs. Gilpin's residence in Philadelphia is the resort of all distinguished strangers. Artists and connoisseurs are especially welcomed, and find material for the gratification of their taste in the works of art collected with so much care in Europe, which occupy one floor of the dwelling. The library of Mr. Gilpin is, perhaps, the largest private collection in America. It includes the best selection of books in the English and foreign languages, the classical portion being particularly rich. This library was left by Mr. Gilpin for the use of his wife during her life, and bequeathed to the Historical Society of Pennsylvania at her death; the works of art were left to the Pennsylvania Academy of the Fine Arts in Philadelphia, to which collection Mrs. Gilpin has desired that the portraits of Mr. Gilpin and herself shall be added.

Mr. Gilpin died in 1860. His accomplished widow prepared and printed for circulation among her friends a memorial volume of his useful life and public services, including various tributes to his memory from eminent statesmen and scholars at home and abroad, with letters of condolence and friendship to herself. The monument which Mrs. Gilpin has erected to the memory of her husband is a noble work of art.

Her sympathy in the misfortunes of others induced Mrs. Gilpin to take a prominent part in the great Sanitary Fair of Philadelphia. She was appointed chairman of the Ladies' Art Committee, by which department alone was realized thirty-five thousand dollars.

Mrs. Gilpin, in resuming the hospitalities of her house, has been liberal in her welcome to the lovers of art and literature. Accustomed herself to these high and pure enjoyments, she has sought to give the same pleasure to others. Music by the best amateur performers is always a marked feature of her entertainments (as dancing is never introduced). Her receptions have a more elevated character than those of mere fashion. Her private charities are active and incessant, and she gives her personal attention to many whose sufferings require the solace and friendship of sympathy.

XIX.

CHARLOTTE AUGUSTA SOUTHWICK was the daughter of Jonathan Southwick, a successful merchant of New York, who accumulated a large fortune in business, though he died at the age of thirty-five. The ancestors of the family—the Worthingtons and Elys—were prominent at an early period of Colonial history. A curious relic preserved is a heavy gold seal-ring, antique in pattern, and engraved with three fleurs-de-lis; said to have been presented by Charles IX. to one of the ancestors of the Ely family, with instructions that it should always be worn by one of the descendants of the name of Robert. It is still so held. Richard Ely came first to America about 1660, and settled at Lyme in Connecticut. John Ely was a colonel in the Revolutionary army and a surgeon of great celebrity. His military career was detailed in the statement of the Committee on Revolutionary Claims to the House of Representatives, in 1853. In 1777, he was commandant of Fort Trumbull, his regiment having been raised by his own exertions and at his own expense entirely fitted out. His wife was Sarah Worthington, a great beauty, and the daughter of Rev. William Worthington, brother to another colonel of the American army. Mary, her sister, also a distinguished beauty, married the father of John Cotton Smith, Governor of Connecticut, the ancestor of the eloquent Rector of Ascension Church in New York. Samuel Goodrich ("Peter Parley") was a grandson of Sarah Worthington. These sisters were descended from Hugh Worthington, who held the Lordship of Worthington under Edward IV., in 1474. Some of the family afterwards intermarried with the descendants of Awley O'Farrell, remembered as the last king of Commerene, in 1207. The eldest son of John and Sarah Worthington was Worthington Ely, the grandfather of the subject of this sketch. He was also a surgeon and a colonel in the Revolutionary army, having graduated at Yale College in 1780. It is said that at the age of twenty he captured two British officers, and retained them as hostages till he obtained the release of his father, then in the enemy's hands. At the end of the war, finding his resources crippled, he resumed the medical practice, and settled on the Hudson, near Albany. His wife was Miss Bushnell, of Connecticut. Their youngest daughter, Lucretia, was the mother of Mrs. Waddell.

At a very early age, Miss Southwick was sent to Mrs. Willard's school at Troy, where she went through a thorough course of education. Soon after leaving school she was married to Mr. McMurray, who lived but a few months, leaving her a widow at the age of eighteen. She afterwards married Mr. William Coventry Waddell. He is connected with noble English families, being directly descended from Lord Daubeney, of the time of

Henry VII., 1485,* and from the earls of Coventry. He has kept up an interesting correspondence with the representatives of these families in England. Possessing high literary attainments, Mr. Waddell had held many important trusts under government, and was at that time in an official position, and possessed of wealth. Their residence was fixed in New York. Mr. Waddell built a splendid mansion at the corner of Fifth Avenue and Thirty-seventh street. "Murray Hill," with its grounds, occupied an entire block. It was a Gothic villa, with tower, and large conservatory; the grounds were laid out in walks and divided by hedges, and vines were trained along the walls. From the broad marble hall a winding staircase ascended to the tower, whence a view of the city, the river, and distant hills could be obtained. The picture-gallery, well stored with valuable paintings, always attracted the attention of visitors. In the winter of 1845, several lots had been put into a wheat-field by the gardener, so remote was the place from the city. For twelve years Mr. and Mrs. Waddell lived in this delightful villa, while the city gradually approached nearer to their home. The winters were passed here, while the summers were spent at Saratoga, where the remarkable beauty of Mrs. Waddell, her graceful manners, her good-humor and winning kindness of heart, and the intellectual charms of her brilliant conversation,

---

* See Burke's Dormant Peerage. That Lord Daubeney was in the direct line from William de Albini (1168), eldest grandson of the standard-bearer of William the Conqueror.

gave her indisputable supremacy in social circles. It was in her power to give happiness to those around her by her ample means for promoting enjoyment, and she took pleasure in doing so. Her parties in the winter, at "Murray Hill," were the admiration of the New York fashionables; and one might be always sure of meeting there any really worthy celebrity. When the frigate "*Prince of Orange*" came to the United States, Mrs. Waddell gave the Dutch officers a ball; and the decorations of her rooms and conservatory were magnificent. The lights in the tower, seen through stained windows, had a very fine effect. Sir William Boyd, in his work on America, wrote:—

"One esteemed friend I can neither omit nor fail to praise; charming in person, elegant and amiable in manner, considerate and kind in disposition, she honors the Fifth Avenue by her residence. So perfectly did her style of beauty resemble that of a lovely English woman, that, in the well-bred though liberal hospitality of her house, an Englishman could forget that three thousand miles separated him from his own dear country."

At Saratoga, in August, 1849, she was thus described in papers of the day:—

"Mrs. Waddell, of New York, was generally admired. A complexion pure and brilliant as the roses and lilies of childhood, large blue eyes, sparkling with vivacity, and lips always rosy with smiles, well became the superb dress of 'a bride.' A veil of exquisite lace fell from a tiara of pearls that confined her bright brown ringlets; a string of large pearls on the neck, a cross of brilliants on the bosom, diamonds twinkling on her arms and amid the folds of a superb lace dress, completed a costume distinguished for its costliness, its cloud-like purity, and that exquisite adaptation to the person which so few understand."

One morning, at Saratoga, she came late to the breakfast-table, where Washington Irving and J. P. Kennedy were seated. "Here comes Aurora!" said Mr. Irving, gayly. Mrs. Waddell asked him if he spelled it with an " A," or an " R." He laughed heartily, and said her question was the best joke he had heard in a long time.

A visitor wrote :—

"On Thursday, the ball of the season took place at Mrs. Waddell's Gothic villa on Murray Hill, Fifth Avenue. The beauty of the house, its corridors and halls, its towers and oriels, gave an attraction with which other establishments cannot vie; while the affability of the fair hostess, and the occasion—the début in society of a daughter of Mr. Waddell—added to the interest. We noted a greater array of city fashionables than we have seen gathered together this season; and, as is usual at this lady's parties, every one appeared to enjoy it. The beautiful conservatory was thrown open, and the flowers, the bay-windows, the winding stair-way through the towers, the oriels, the corbels, the tapestries, the music, the ball, the supper, the fair hostess, and the concourse of gallant knights, could not well be surpassed. There were about five hundred present. Mr. Brown the guard's arrangements were excellent, especially the fine large tent he erected to keep off the night air between the carriage-drive and the hall-door."

At a masquerade ball, given in College Place, by Mrs. John C. Stevens—

"Mrs. Waddell wore, in the early part of the evening, a black mask and domino; afterwards, white satin trimmed with rich black lace, with corsage of diamonds, and flowers in her hair. This lady, from her agreeable and affable manners, commanded much attention, and received the flattering encomiums of a large circle of admirers. Mrs. Waddell, at her villa, 'took up' the *bal poudre* of Mrs. Stevens, when that lady was compelled to relinquish it at her residence, in consequence of a death in her family. At Mrs. Schermerhorn's *bal costumé de rigueur* of the reign of Louis XV., a journal reported Mrs. Waddell's dress as Marie Antoinette, 'crimson moire antique, jupe flowered with point-lace. The Louis Quinze brocade trimmed with point-lace; the corsage ornamented with diamonds, and rose *de Chine* ribbon, fluted; powdered head, wreathed with diamonds.'"

Tributes of a higher kind were not wanting to this accomplished lady, as the following letter will show. It was elicited by Mrs. Waddell's sending a basket of fruit from her conservatories to the distinguished author:—

"UNITED STATES HOTEL, SARATOGA, August 2, 1858.

"MY DEAR MRS WADDELL:—

"Had it pleased the gods to make me poetical, what a choice copy of verses your most dainty present would have inspired! I should have wrought out some capital similitudes to yourself in the choice fruits of which it consisted. I should have made something of the peach with its damask cheek and nectared sweetness; of the grape, with its potent power to lead the senses captive, and 'make glad the heart of man.' But having no gift of weaving immortal verse, I can only make my acknowledgments of your kindness in humbler prose, which is the more sincere for not being labored into rhyme or turned into couplets.

"Believe me, very truly,
"Your obliged and admiring friend,
"WASHINGTON IRVING.

"MRS. COVENTRY WADDELL."

Here is a fragment from one of many tributary poems:—

"Let Dryden sing divine Cecilia's days,
  And Alexander's Feast in verse be sounded;
Be mine a greater glory still to praise
  The queen whose conquests yet no world hath bounded.
He wept for worlds to conquer; thou beguilest
  Realms which he never knew, thy sway to greet;
He *wept* for other conquests; thou but *smilest*,
  And all the world lies vanquished at thy feet."

The following is another specimen:—

"CLARENDON, Friday, January 23th.

"DEAR MADAM:—

"My friend, Mr. ——, who has just returned from London (where he was your Secretary of Legation, and danced in a most distinguished manner at our court and other balls), ought surely to see a beautiful ball at New York, and I shall be very thankful if you will favor me with a card for him. I am so glad that I shall be in New York on the night of your party, and that you kindly remembered that I wanted to see it.

"Believe me very faithfully yours,

"W. M. THACKERAY."

Mr. Thackeray first saw Mrs. Waddell at a party, and as she came into the room exclaimed, "Who is that lady!" expressing astonishment at her beauty. After his introduction, while looking at some paintings, he remarked to Mrs. Waddell: "You should have sat to Sir Peter." She replied that she did not admire Sir Peter Lely's pictures. Thackeray pretended, laughingly, that he had meant Rubens. A few days afterwards, while walking with Mrs. Waddell through her gallery, he remarked: "I still think, Mrs. Waddell, you should have sat to Sir Peter. None of these do you justice." Thackeray, during his stay in the United States, became a frequent visitor and a warm friend of Mrs. Waddell.

Her playful wit was sometimes exercised in reproving ill-breeding, but in a kindly way. A bigoted English nobleman, well known in fashionable circles (as something of a bore), who detested every thing American, and ridiculed the celebration of the Fourth of July, was kept firing off rockets on that anniversary till he was tired out, by his fair hostess.

In the monetary crisis of 1857, Mr. Waddell lost a splendid fortune. His reverses compelled him to sacrifice his home on Murray Hill; the house, grounds, and furniture were sold, and the march of "improvement" has now effaced every trace of the once beautiful villa; covering the site with stately brown stone houses. Mrs. Waddell submitted cheerfully to this change, and smiled as she read the notes of sympathy and regret sent by her neighbors. In Charles O'Conor's words: "In bending so gracefully and cheerfully to adverse circumstances, she won more laurels than were gained in prosperity." When, after removing from the house, she took possession of her rooms at the St. Denis Hotel, she found them filled with bouquets and baskets of flowers; welcome offerings, as delicate expressions of kindly feeling from those who had known her in the sunshine of affluence. After a few months, she retired to a country home upon the Hudson, two miles north of Newburgh. A tourist thus describes it:—

"A large stone mansion, wreathed with ivy, stands on an elevation overlooking the majestic landscape. It is the residence of Mr. and Mrs. Waddell. Her exquisite taste has already beautified the place, supplied by nature with every requisite for adornment; and her cheerful spirit makes it a paradise indeed. Those who visit her in her rural home will find her as charming as in her princely suburban residence. The pearly freshness and delicate rose-tint of her complexion, and the luxuriance of her rich brown curls, have not been impaired by the air of the Highlands; while the ease and grace imparted by perfect culture, mental accomplishments, and familiarity with the best society, are blended with the most winning frankness and elastic gayety of spirits, and with a genuine cordiality which, emanating from true kindness of heart, cannot fail of the response of heartfelt admiration and regard."

After living a few years among the mountains, Mr. and Mrs. Waddell returned to the city of New York; but her taste for flowers and fresh rural scenery could not be satisfied without a suburban residence. A neat ornamental one has been built, under her directions, at "West End," on the (proposed) grand Boulevard drive in course of being laid out by the Central Park Commissioners upon the northern part of Manhattan Island, a short distance above the unrivaled "Central Park."

Mary Wharton was born in Philadelphia, and became a celebrated belle in that city, being one of the most beautiful women in America. She was married when very young to James S. Wadsworth, who became a distinguished general in the Union army, and lost his life in the service of his country. He was the son of James Wadsworth, and the nephew of the bachelor, General Wadsworth, who was conspicuous in the war of 1812. Mrs. Wadsworth went with her husband to Europe for a bridal trip, and remained abroad nearly a year. Their home was then in Geneseo, New York, where the summers were spent; the winters being passed in different cities. During a few years they retained a house in New York; afterwards in Philadelphia. Mrs. Wadsworth had six children. Her daughter Cornelia married Montgomery Ritchie, a grandson of the elder Harrison Gray Otis. She was noted as a belle in New York, of a brilliant and stylish beauty; with dark hair and large, full dark eyes. She lived in Geneseo with her parents during Mr. Ritchie's life; in the widowhood of her mother passing most of her time with her. After her husband's death, Mrs. Ritchie went to England, and resides in London. Mrs. Wadsworth lives in Philadelphia, but spends her summers at her favorite country home. Her sister-in-law was Miss Elizabeth Wadsworth, who married Hon. Charles Augustus Murray, and died in Egypt.

Miss Emilie Schaumburg is a Philadelphia celebrity in society, who has added the fascinations of rare skill in vocal music, and still rarer powers of dramatic expression as an amateur comedienne, to the attraction of great beauty. Her grandfather, Colonel Bartholomew Schaumburg, of New Orleans, was a ward of the Landgrave of Hesse Cassel, and closely connected with him. Educated under the auspices of Frederick the Great, at the German Military School, he was commissioned an officer in the Grenadier Guards, and at the time of the American Revolution was sent to this country as adjutant and aid-de-camp to General Count Donop, who, in conjunction with General Kniphausen, commanded the German forces subsidized to England. Colonel Schaumburg never joined Count Donop, however; for the transport ship upon which he and other officers and soldiers had embarked, became separated from the fleet in a storm, off the American coast, and came up the Delaware, anchoring at Newcastle, where they learned from the people the nature of their struggle for independence, and that General Washington was at no great distance, on the Brandywine, daily expecting an attack from the British forces under Cornwallis. Preferring to fight for an oppressed people rather than for England, with whom they had no sympathy, they determined to join him, which they did, and were incorporated into General Sullivan's German Legion, serving under General Washington throughout the Revolutionary War. Colonel Schaumburg also served with great gallantry through all the early Indian wars, under Generals Wayne and Sinclair, and afterwards held the rank of Deputy Quartermaster-General during the war of 1812. The site of Cincinnati was chosen under his direction; and, as an accomplished artillerist, he superintended the casting of the first cannon ever made in the United States. Colonel Schaumburg had sacrificed his title and much of his property by espousing the American cause, but some years later he was earnestly solicited by his relatives to return to Germany, which he unhesitatingly refused to do. He married a lady who was a lineal descendant of the principal Indian chief or king Secane, of the Leanape tribe, who signed the treaty of 1685 with William Penn, selling him the large tract of land in which Philadelphia is situated. Su-sa-he-na, his daughter, had been married to Dr. Thomas Holme McFarlane, a nephew of Thomas Holme, the first Surveyor-General of Pennsylvania. Miss Schaumburg is the eighth remove, in a direct line, from this aboriginal princess, and was born in New Orleans, although she has always resided in Philadelphia. From childhood, her great musical talent was evident, united to a voice of uncommon power, purity, and sweetness. Its natural advantages have been fully developed by the late Signor Perelli, who considered her his most brilliant scholar; and she combines the finest dramatic appreciation with the most remarkable compass and execution. The "*soirées*" *musicales* at her residence gather together all that Philadelphia society affords of most elegant and most accomplished. The earlier portion of her education was chiefly directed by the late Hon. H. D. Gilpin, one of the most elegant scholars of America; and she has had all the advantages in cultivation which his magnificent library can afford. She has added the accomplishment of speaking several modern languages. She has also a graceful gift of versification, frequently, though unpretendingly, exercised for the entertainment of her immediate circle.

Miss Schaumburg's appearance in the first social circles was followed by general admiration. When the Prince of Wales with his suite visited Philadelphia, he spent the only evening of his stay at the Academy of Music. He saw Miss Schaumburg in another box, and his attention was at once attracted by her beauty. She was dressed with simplicity, in white, with gold ornaments in her hair. The lorgnettes of the royal party were turned in her direction long enough to show the whole house the object of their admiration. The Prince declared her "the most beautiful woman he had seen in America."

Her great dramatic talent was first developed during the patriotic exertions made for the Sanitary Fair. A number of gifted and energetic ladies and gentlemen fitted up a little private theater, to hold about three hundred persons, the performers to be all amateurs, selected from among the élite of Philadelphia society, and the proceeds to be devoted exclusively to the wounded soldiers. The enterprise was eminently successful in a financial view; and it also proved Philadelphia unsurpassed in the possession of amateur talent. Many plays were brought out, but "The Ladies' Battle," in which Miss Schaumburg sustained the principal rôle of the "Countess," took society by storm. Those who witnessed that exquisite rendition, combining the most perfect grace and highbred elegance with the most delicate shades of emotion, remember it as a piece of acting unrivaled on the American stage. A year or two later, the comedy of "Masks and Faces" was produced by the same association, for the benefit of the Chicago Fair, under the immediate supervision of Mrs. Aubrey H. Smith, a daughter of Judge Grier, of the Supreme Court, and a lady noted for her vivacity, energy, and spirit. Miss Schaumburg sustained in this the great rôle of "Peg Woffington," and again created a furore. It seemed difficult, indeed, to decide in which she most excelled—the dash and brilliancy, or the pathos and emotion of the impulsive, warm-hearted, and fascinating Peg; whilst her Irish "jig" was inimitable in its spirit, lightness, and grace. The play altogether was so superbly put upon the stage of the little theater, or "Amateur Drawing-room," as it is called, and so admirably rendered in each of its parts, by gentlemen and ladies of cultivation, that to those who witnessed it, all professional performances of it since have suffered by comparison. A melodrama, called "The Wife's Secret"—in which Miss Schaumburg sustained the rôle of "Lady Evelyn"—was afterwards produced, with great éclat, at the "Drawing-room," for charitable purposes. In this—probably the most trying rôle ever attempted by any lady amateur—Miss Schaumburg achieved fresh laurels. Madame Ristori, who was then in Philadelphia, and who witnessed one of the performances, expressed herself surprised and delighted at the genius of the brilliant amateur. So remarkable a talent should be frequently exerted in the noble cause of charity; and as it is becoming more and more the fashion for ladies in private life to exercise their gifts for the benefit of the poor, it is to be hoped that Miss Schaumburg may be induced to contribute her aid to them in other cities than her own.

XX.

"THE most charming woman in the world."

The phrase has often been carelessly used, under a fleeting impression. But when deliberately and universally applied to one person by all who know her, it acquires a significance deeper than common. Madame Le Vert is perhaps the only woman who has reigned as a belle in both hemispheres,—has received the homage of chivalrous admiration, alike in the Northern and Southern sections of the United States, as well as in the courtly circles of Great Britain and Continental Europe, and who, at the same time, has never been assailed by the shafts of envy or calumny. She has had a remarkable experience in wearing the crown of beauty and genius,—that it has been without a thorn. Such an anomaly argues an uncommon character. To receive tributes from the lowly and the exalted, the humble and the gifted, the obscure and the brilliant, all breathing the same heart-incense, is something remarkable. Calhoun called her "the gifted daughter of the South." Irving said of her: "She is such a woman as occurs but once in the course of an empire." Another eminent author said: "There is but one such in America." Miss Bremer named her "her Magnolia Flower of the South," and "Sweet Rose of Florida." A distinguished writer said: "I defy any one to spend an hour in her company without rising up a wiser and better man, having a sense of musical joyance in his heart, because of her words." Lamartine said to her: "You can fill with pleasure the hearts of your nation by describing what you have seen to them, as you are now delighting me." She is more widely known as a "social genius" than any American woman; for her fame has spread from the Atlantic to the Pacific, and in various countries beyond the seas. A key to this extraordinary popularity may be found in the observation of a little child, who whispered, after sitting by her, "She isn't a fine lady at all; she is just like *me;* and I love her." This is her specific charm; the spirit of love that goes out from a great and good heart, and meets everywhere response and recognition. The adulation received from every quarter could not mar a nature so gifted with good sense, simplicity, and earnestness. Living in the sunshine of fashionable life, and distinguished by the smiles of the fickle goddess, she never lost her tender humanity; always proving herself as genial as gay, as sweet and courteous as brilliant; as true and appreciative as fascinating. She was always "a social harmonizer." Her sunny spirit was like a stream

"In whose calm depths the beautiful and pure
Alone are mirrored."

"She was made without antipathies," says one of her

friends. "She receives, as it were by intuition, the idea of the ancient Greeks, that the whole universe is a 'Kosmos' of beauty and order." The world has smiled on her, because she was gracious to the world, and she has faith in the goodness of human nature. She has never, it is said, uttered or admitted an ill-natured suggestion, and never tolerated uncharitableness or scandal. Once, when the beauty of her feet was mentioned, Henry Clay remarked, with feeling, "She has a tongue that *never* spoke an evil word of any one." Her womanly sympathies, too, have remained keen and warm amid all the splendors of worldly distinction. "The belle of the Union," never weary of doing good, could preside at the bedside of suffering, as well as in the fashionable drawing-room. Her feelings were never deadened by association with the gay. The blessings of the poor and griefladen followed her. Shortly after her return from Europe, when her society was in great demand, hearing that a neighbor was ill, she came and spent the afternoon with her, while her own house was crowded with company; afterwards sending her carriage and taking the patient to her own house. When the pestilence raged in Savannah, and nurses were sent for to Mobile, she was the first to volunteer her services.

General George Walton, her grandfather, a signer of the Declaration of Independence, in early life resided in Prince Edward County, Virginia. He removed to Georgia before the war of the Revolution, in which he took part, being wounded in leading a regiment at the siege of Savannah. He was a member of the first Congress, and was afterwards Governor of Georgia and Judge of the Supreme Court. His wife was Miss Camber, the daughter of an English nobleman, to whom the crown had granted large estates in the colony. This lady chose to remain with her husband in the conflict, and suffered for her devotion, being taken prisoner and sent for a time to the West Indies. Letters of Washington, La Fayette, Adams, and Jefferson to General Walton are still preserved, and testify to their high appreciation of his character. He died in 1808, at his country-seat near Augusta. In the principal street of that town is a granite monument, erected by the State in memory of him. He left two children. One of them, the father of the subject of this sketch, was a millionaire when he married Miss Walker, the daughter of an eminent lawyer of Georgia, and a woman of brilliant accomplishments and large fortune. In 1821, Colonel Walton was appointed Secretary of State under General Jackson, the governor of Florida, whom he succeeded in office. Afterwards he was chosen to the legislature, and in 1835 he removed to Mobile, Alabama, where he was mayor, and filled other important offices. His fortune was lost by becoming security for friends; and large manufactories and houses, in Augusta, now occupy his lands.

Octavia was born at "Belle Vue," near Augusta, but when very young was taken to Pensacola, where her first recollections " were of the orange and live oak trees shading the broad veranda; of the fragrant acacia, oleander, and cape jessamines which filled the parterre sloping down to the sea-beach; of merry races with her brother along the white sands, while the creamy waves broke over her feet, and the delicious breeze from the Gulf played in her hair; of the pet mocking-birds in the giant oak by her window, whose songs called her each morning from dream-land."*

Pensacola, on its bay, was the rendezvous of United States vessels of the Gulf station. When they returned from their cruises, balls and parties were given in honor of the officers at the Governor's house, and entertainments on board the ships; there were moonlight excursions on the bay, and picnics in the magnolia groves. Thus the little Octavia became early familiar with society. Her father took great pains with her education. Before she was twelve years old she could write and converse in three languages, and often the Colonel took her into his office, to translate from the French or Spanish, letters connected with important affairs of State. Perched on a high stool, the little girl interpreted her foreign dispatches with great exactness. The Governor, who had located the seat of government in Florida, permitted his daughter to give it a name; which she did in kindness to the Seminole king, who struck his tent-pole there. She called the place "Tallahassee," signifying "beautiful land." The Indians were often indebted to

---

* See Miss Forrest's "Women of the South."

the young girl's intercession, and named her "The white dove of peace."

When La Fayette visited the Southern States, he wrote to Octavia's grandmother, requesting her to meet him in Mobile; but on account of infirm health she sent the little girl in her stead, to welcome the illustrious Frenchman. She was presented, with her mother, and handed her grandfather's miniature to La Fayette. Gazing upon it, the veteran shed tears, snatched the child to his breast, and exclaimed: "The living image of my brave and noble friend!" Octavia sat on his knee during a long interview, and talked in French. La Fayette solemnly blessed her at their parting. "A truly wonderful child!" he said. "I predict for her a brilliant career!"

Octavia never went to school; being taught by private tutors in all branches in which she did not receive instruction from her mother and grandmother. She and her brother were for years the pupils of an old Scotchman, a fine classic scholar and linguist, who had lived in the family since their birth. This careful instruction, with her indefatigable industry, gave the young girl that extraordinary proficiency in classical and scientific studies, as well as music, and in the modern languages, which so distinguished her. "She can speak five languages well," exclaimed a French gentleman, in rapture; "I have heard her converse at the same time with a Spaniard, a German, and a Frenchman, holding lively conversation with each in his own tongue, with remarkable precision of pronunciation and elegance of phraseology." In Italian she was equally fluent. In all, said Dr. Nichols, "Full of spirit and vivacity, she was simple as a child and charming as a fairy; she seemed like a choice goblet of sparkling champagne wine, surrounded by roses."

Soon after the removal of the family to Mobile, Octavia, with her mother and brother, made the tour of the United States. This was the commencement of her bright career. The name of Miss Octavia Walton became familiar to the fashionable world as "the belle of Saratoga." Her wonderful colloquial powers, her tact in bringing out the best qualities of all within her influence, and the light and warmth diffused by her sunny temper, joined to an indescribable faculty of captivating hearts, won her a popularity shown by innumerable tributes from poets and from grave critics. In one of her journeys by stage, her party formed the acquaintance of a middle-aged gentleman who had traveled much, and possessed a large fund of humor and anecdote. Elegant in manners, cultivated in taste, gifted in conversation—who could the distinguished stranger be? When Octavia was talking to her brother in Spanish he joined in the discourse, and described a bull-fight, dwelling particularly on a singular incident. This Octavia had heard before, and it was a clue to discovery. "You are Washington Irving!" she exclaimed. The gentleman who had related the incident to her had said Washington Irving stood by him when it happened. Thus commenced a friendship which continued till Irving's death. A correspondence was kept up, and Madame Le Vert was a cherished guest at Sunnyside. When they parted, the last time she saw Irving, he said to her, "I feel as if the sunshine were all going away with you, my child." She kept a journal, at his advice, and chronicled therein her impressions of Washington, which she visited during Jackson's administration; especially reports of the speeches of Calhoun, Webster, and her warm friend Mr. Clay.

Miss Walton's marriage with Dr. Henry Le Vert, of Mobile, took place in 1836. He was the son of Dr. Claude Le Vert, who came with La Fayette to the United States, as fleet-surgeon under Rochambeau, and after peace settled in Virginia. It is a curious fact that it was in honor of his wife's uncle, Admiral Vernon, that Lawrence Washington, who had served under him in South America, named his country-seat "Mount Vernon."

Dr. Le Vert was a leading physician in Mobile, and was not averse to as much society as pleased his accomplished wife. When he proposed building a house, she stipulated only for a library. This she filled with choice books and works of art. The house was in Government Street—the most pleasant in Mobile—and had beautiful grounds in the heart of the city.

It was in 1849 that her first sorrow clouded Madame Le Vert's life, in the death of her only brother and two lovely children. These misfortunes were the more keenly felt for her previous unbroken happiness. It was shortly after these afflictions that Lady Emmeline Stuart Wortley, the daughter of the Duke of Rutland, came to Mobile. She, too, was a mourner for her noble husband and child; and at the very commencement of her acquaintance with Madame Le Vert, a tender and holy sympathy bound together the hearts of the two stricken mothers. Lady Emmeline remained some weeks the guest of Madame Le Vert; and the friendship thus formed continued unchanged till Lady Emmeline's death. She was the faithful correspondent and devoted friend of Madame Le Vert, who at their parting secured her, through the Spanish consul, a passage home in a Government steamer. Lady Emmeline addressed to her the following stanzas on leaving America:—

> "I seek mine own fair land, but, ere I part,
> Some farewell words I fain afar would send;
> To whom but thee? thou friend of my true heart,
> My ever lovely and beloved friend!
>
> "Thou chosen sister of my soul! methinks
> Our friendship had a high, immortal birth;
> Beyond the stars were twined its deathless links,
> 'Twas born in heaven, to bloom awhile on earth.
>
> "Yet strange! 'twas born of death. Our joy, our pride,
> We both had seen snatched from us at a blow;
> Our morning stars of life, our darlings died,
> And both have drained the self-same cup of woe.
>
> "Ah! how alike both felt that deadly wound,
> With what congenial pangs, what kindred smart;
> What semblance in our sorrow's vein we found,
> E'en in the wildest storm-bursts of the heart.

"Say, sweetest friend, if, wandering by the wave
   That breaks like dawn on Alabama's shore,
Thou still dost dwell, with thoughts serene, though grave,
   On all that we together felt before?

"Friend, whom my changeless heart most dearly loves,
   .In all this radiant Western World, so wide,
Fair are thy Southern home's magnolia groves,
   Whose stately shades are glassed along the tide.

"But fairer, lovelier, dearer, heavenlier far,
   One little spot to memory's gaze appears;
A grave! yet gleamed it like a distant star
   Through the interposing medium of our tears.

"Locked were thy jewels in that treasure-cave,
   Where angels leaned, and watched the sleeping flowers;
My *pearl* slept far beyond the Atlantic's wave,
   New planted for the glad Elysian bowers.

"We stood beside that grave, in silence stood—
   'Twere vain to speak where human speech must fail;
We gazed not then on the emerald-tinted wood,
   Nor marked the varied pride of hill or dale.

"Then memory did to England's shore revert,
   Where keeps its precious charge another grave;
Ay, but with feelings glowing at my heart
   Which seemed death's darkness and its dust to brave.

"Now let me turn once more to thee! to thee!
   Sweet Rose of Florida—'twas there thine eyes
First opened to the light, the earth, the sea,
   And all the sparkling beauty of the skies.

"Most dear to thee are Alabama's shores,
   Though still thou own'st, while life's dark seasons roll,
And time thins fast the heart's own treasure-stores,
   'Tis no true Alabama* of the soul.

---

* "Alabama" signifies, in the Indian language, "Here we rest." There is a legend of a tribe of Indians who fled from a relentless foe to the forests of the Southwest. Weary and travel-worn, they reached a

"Bold was the proud red warrior, vainly bold,
   Whose lips pronounced the daring "Here we rest!"
Though bright as Hesperian groves of old
   Spread the fair land its calm and beauteous breast.

"But who can rest on earth, until no more
   Tossed on life's sea-like surface? 'Tis in vain.
They rested not, that race which passed before;
   Ye rest not, dwellers on this flower-lit plain.

"But they, our children, o'er whose graves we mourned,
   Sleep well. Rest, folded flower and buried gem!
By angels summoned, they to God returned,
   And all is "Alabama" now to them.

"Oh! lost and loved ones, lead us in the way,
   And be our sorrowings o'er your joys forgiven;
Warn us, ye tender teachers, not to say
   That "here we rest" in any home but heaven.

"Farewell! Yet surely friendship such as ours
   Dreads no farewell! It sprang from out the tomb,
To know no death. It flings off earthly hours
As rocks the spray. Eternity's its home."

In the summer of 1853, Madame Le Vert, with her father and daughter, visited England. The family of the Duke of Rutland showed her the greatest attention. She visited Belvoir Castle, the splendid home of the Duke, and was called upon and entertained by all the relatives of Lady Emmeline, who had delighted in describing the charming hospitalities of Madame Le Vert's house in Mobile. Never, perhaps, had an American a more brilliant success in the way of access to the

---

noble river, flowing through a beautiful country. The chief of the band struck his tent-pole in the ground, and exclaimed: "Alabama! Alabama!" ("Here we rest! Here we rest!") From this exclamation comes the name of the State and the river.

highest class of society, and notice from royalty. But if her first reception and welcome were due to Lady Emmeline's friendship, her own social gifts and accomplishments opened the way to further triumphs. The Queen herself honored the American belle in a remarkable manner, by sending her a card to a State ball without a previous presentation. This was an exception to the rule of court etiquette, and made quite a stir in aristocratic circles. Madame Le Vert was at dinner when a package bearing the royal arms was handed to her, containing an invitation never before extended even to a crowned head without the preliminary of an introduction. She procured a dress in all haste, sent for Mr. Ingersoll, then ambassador, and was escorted by him to the ball. The royal circle was composed of the Queen and Prince Albert, the Duchess of Kent, the King and Queen of Prussia, Prince Frederick William, the King and Queen of Hanover, and other royal personages. The Lord Chamberlain presented her, and bade her welcome in the Queen's name. Madame Le Vert made her obeisance, which was returned by the Queen and Prince Albert. The Queen then asked her how she liked England, and if she had been pleased with her new friends. This special distinction, of course, rendered Madame Le Vert a star in the court circles. Her fascinating qualities, frank gayety, and wonderful tact, went far to satisfy curiosity as to how this brilliant and fortunate lady could win such honors. She received the homage paid to her with the same simple grace as in her own home. A London critic speaks of the surprise and admiration of the foreign ministers at hearing her fluent utterance of their different languages. Even the Turkish Ambassador, being told she was a Georgian, exclaimed: "Ah, Madame, I can well imagine you are a Georgian—for no other women possess such beauty."

Frederika Bremer, an attached friend of Madame Le Vert, did all she could to contribute to the pleasure of her European visit. At a party at Lord John Manners's she met D'Israeli, and other celebrities. She also visited Stafford House, the residence of the Duchess of Sutherland, was at a conversazione given at the Lord Mayor's, and met the German poet Freiligrath, Mr. and Mrs. S. C. Hall, Mrs. Mary Howitt, and Mrs. Crosland. Returning to America in 1854, in the following year she went again to Europe, with her husband and lovely daughter Octavia. Some weeks were spent in Havana, whence she went to Cadiz, and traveled through Spain and France to Italy, arriving at Rome in time for the ceremonies of the Holy Week. The summer of the "Great Exposition" was spent in Paris, where she witnessed the pageants in honor of Queen Victoria's visit. She described particularly a ball at the palace of the Count de Walewski, Minister of Foreign Affairs, where twelve rooms were opened. At a ball given by the Prince Napoleon, she was presented to the Countess Montijo, the mother of the Empress Eugenie. This noble lady proved a kind and attentive friend to her; accompanying her to the palace, where she was presented to the Emperor and Empress. Lamartine, Dumas, Ristori, and others, figured in her record. On her return home, her house on the broad, imperial avenue became more than ever the abode of splendid hospitality. A genial welcome was extended to every worthy stranger, and a place of reunion was offered for all distinguished visitors. Her receptions were "the boast and pride of the citizens." A genuine republican in her feelings, Madame Le Vert respected and cherished genius and merit, however humble their condition. Whoever had talent and moral worth, with minds expanded by education, had a claim upon her; but she could not enjoy the society of commonplace money-grubbing people, unable to appreciate art or the best tone of conversation. Artists, poets, and actors she welcomed. After her first visit to Europe, she had receptions every Monday, from eleven in the morning to eleven at night; and the house was crowded all day. One day a plain old country planter called, and pointing to a picture, requested her to read to him from her book the description of a celebrated grotto on the coast of Naples. She readily complied. Lover visited her, and sang for the pleasure of her circle. When Kossuth visited Mobile, Madame Le Vert met and conducted him to her house to lunch; walking, while the carriage drove alongside, through the people who came to see the illustrious stranger.

Miss Bremer thus wrote of Madame Le Vert:—

"It is so strange that that little worldly lady, whom I had

heard spoken of as a belle, and as the most splendid ornament of society wherever she went, has yet become almost as dear to me as a young sister. But she has become so from being so very excellent; because she has suffered much; and because under a worldly exterior there is an unusually sound and pure intellect and a heart full of affection, which can cast aside all the vanities of the world for the power of gratifying those whom she loves. This fair daughter of Florida is surrounded by a circle of relatives who seem to regard her as the apple of their eye; and if you would see the *ideal* of the relationship between a lady and her female slave, you should see Octavia Le Vert and her clever, handsome mulatto attendant, Betsey. Betsey seems really not to live for any thing else than for her mistress Octavia."

Another friend writes:—

"North, south, east, west, goes Betsey with her mistress; through bristling ranks of Abolitionists, up the Rhine, over the Alps, everywhere goes Betsey defying prejudice, and scorning fanaticism. On one occasion, Betsey was thrown out of a railway carriage, and her mistress gave her the tenderest care."

A writer in the "New Orleans Delta" described an entertainment given at Madame Le Vert's house in Mobile:—

"From early starlight till the roses of morning began to lighten the eastern waters, the elegant mansion was a blaze of light in its drawing-rooms and halls; the surrounding parterres, with their thick foliage of orange-trees, oleanders, and magnolias, were illuminated with multitudes of many-colored lamps in the form of fruits and flowers, shining as though an emerald vail had entangled swarms of fire-flies, or flowers of flame and fruits of gold from fairy orchards were imprisoned within the clustering branches. About ten the 'goodly companie' began to fill the spacious rooms, which were decorated with works of art and fine paintings brought from foreign lands. The walls of the principal drawing-room, adorned by portraits of distinguished persons, were wreathed with garlands of the rich flowers then in luxuriant blossom; and in the midst of

the roses stood the accomplished lady, receiving her guests."—
"What sculptured beauty in that rounded form! She is not tall, but such perfect symmetry, such undulating grace, such decorous dignity, such cordial courtesy, such infinite adaptiveness of manner, you have never seen before. Her face is Madonna-like, brown waves of hair parting from a high, broad forehead; her eyes are blue, and seem to melt with thought, and her chiseled lips are tinted like the delicate sea-shell."—"She has made you think, just by her manner and her few felicitous words, that you are the very being she is most delighted to see. Such is the mysterious spell of her grace and courtesy."—"Look how yon stairway is crowded! You may see the loveliness of Mobile gliding through the dance. The stars crowd upon each other. Close by her mother's side is a fair young creature just entering on her teens—it is the eldest daughter of our hostess; and near her is the noblest specimen of a Southern matron, elegant, amiable, and intelligent—Mrs. Walton, the mother of Madame Le Vert. That splendid-looking man in the door-way is Dr. Le Vert, who always enjoys the social success of his wife. All the élite of our city were present, many from the interior of Alabama, and some from New Orleans. Two thousand invitations had been issued, and the preparations for the entertainment were extensive. In our Queen City of the Gulf there has never been a fête so magnificent."

The author of "Life in Washington," describing Madame Le Vert, said:—

"Lively and brilliant, she appears the favorite of every society she enters."

Another fair writer:—

"She was surrounded by visitors, of course; but she greeted us with great warmth, and we had not been five minutes in her presence before she found the direct road to our heart. She wore a light blue silk, covered with clusters of white roses, and her jewels were a set of turquoises. We listened to her delightful conversation in silence. In a short time, some of her visitors retired. Then she drew a chair close beside us, opened the book she held, and read us a few pages from her unpublished journal."

Another wrote of her at Newport, Rhode Island:—

"No queen could have met with a more enthusiastic reception. She has enchanted alike the grave and the gay, the old and young, by her exquisite grace of manner and kindness of heart. She may justly be called a female Crichton, for she excels in every thing she attempts. At the fancy ball given at the Ocean House, she appeared as Nourmahal, the Light of the Harem. Her costume was perfect in its oriental magnificence, absolutely blazing with jewels. She wore a closely-fitting bodice of silver lama, over which fell a net-work of pearls; around her waist was a girdle of glittering gems—the topaz, amethyst, emerald, and diamond mingled their splendors. Her dark glossy hair, simply parted upon her white forehead, was gathered beneath a turban of white and silver lama, adorned with a diamond crescent of rare value. The short dress was of satin, embroidered with pearls, and the Turkish trousers, of the same material, were fastened by silver anklets. Her feet were cased in gold and crimson slippers, and long oriental sleeves shaded her beautiful arms, which were decorated with armlets, her wrists being encircled by costly bracelets; while on her neck gleamed a superb diamond necklace. A gorgeous fan completed the dress, which might have been that of Lalla Rookh, when Moore wrote the lines:—

> " 'Illumed by a wit that would fascinate sages,
> Yet playful as Peris just loosed from their cages.' "

At Saratoga, where she had been so admired as a girl, Madame Le Vert was again a reigning belle by acclamation, "still wearing the chaplet of beauty, with many a fresh flower; even more lovely, more brilliant, more graceful than ever."

" Amid the charming representatives of the various States she stands the most distinguished, having no rival. Her colloquial talents, her tact, emanating from a kind heart, captivate all who approach her. She floats through the rooms, with a radiant smile for her acquaintances; now the object of admiration to a group of Americans, now with silver-toned voice and perfect Castilian accent describing the gay scene to a Spaniard, now in conversation with a Frenchman, an Italian, and a German, speaking in his own language to each, and changing one for another with lightning rapidity. Then we find her in earnest conversation with some distinguished scholar, and note the stores of erudition, the vigorous grasp of intellect, and the rich mental culture which are among her resources. We do involuntary homage to those matchless powers, such as in other lands made the undying fame of a De Staël, a De Genlis, or a Maintenon. At the same time, the grace and high-bred manner with which she receives homage remove her as far from the hackneyed every-day belle as the stars are above the earth. It is easy to see that a pure and noble heart, with a highly cultivated mind, brightens that soul-lighted face. Last night, at the fancy ball, she was brilliant in the costume of Haidée, in 'The Oriental Dream.'"

Society being the natural element of this gifted lady, she has always manifested an interest in benevolent undertakings which her influence could aid. She gave an eloquent address on the laying of the corner-stone of the monument to Henry Clay in New Orleans. Few had better opportunities of studying Mr. Clay's character, for he was to her a dear and honored friend. She was the Vice-Regent of the Mount Vernon Association for Alabama, and addressed an appeal in its behalf to her State, which met with a hearty response. On the 4th of July, at her own house, she received seven hundred dollars in small contributions to the fund.

Madame Le Vert was in New York in the autumn of 1860, during the visit of the Prince of Wales, and was one of the select and brilliant party at the superb breakfast given to the Prince by Mayor Wood at his villa—"Woodlawn." She and her daughter were treated with special attention by the royal guest, who expressed great pleasure in meeting with a lady known to his august mother, and who had been so kind to his countrymen.

The summer of this year had been a happy one to Madame Le Vert, and full of joy and hope she returned to her Southern home. There sorrow was hovering, as clouds were gathering over her country. Her idolized mother was in failing health. This lady has been mentioned as a woman of brilliant gifts. She lived near her daughter, and usually spent her evenings with her. "Frequently," says one of her friends, "the mother, daughter, and grand-daughter attend the same party, dance in the same quadrille, and attract their own separate coteries." After an illness of two months this estimable woman breathed her last in the arms of her daughter, who was so crushed by affliction that for many weeks she lingered in the shadow of the grave. God willed her continuance in life, and she slowly returned to health. The health of Dr. Le Vert had been failing, and his wife devoted herself to him day and night. In the midst of this distress Colonel Walton died. The accumulation of sorrow was overwhelming, but for her stricken husband's sake, the bereaved daughter struggled for strength to do all that his condition required, while she also gave relief in many cases of suffering brought to her knowledge. Dr. Le Vert died a year before the close of the war, having been an invalid four years, tenderly nursed by the wife whom he blessed with dying breath.

Thus was Madame Le Vert left alone in the world with her two young daughters. In 1865, her numerous slaves were emancipated with all others. They were in consternation on hearing that they were to be separated from their mistress. Gathering around her in a body, they implored her to keep them. "Let us stay with you," they entreated; "we will work for you as we have always done. We do not want freedom, if it takes us from you!" With tears of gratitude for their devotion, their mistress explained to them that they were now free; but she promised always to be their friend. Her maid, Betsey, positively refused to leave her.

Five years of trial and grief had left their impress upon Madame Le Vert's health, and her friends in Mobile urged her to revisit the North. She came to New York in the summer of 1865, with her daughters. They were received by their former friends with such cordiality and delight, that they found it necessary to have reception-days every week at the Fifth Avenue Hotel, where they stayed. The autumn and early portion of the winter were spent in the enjoyment of the fashionable gayeties of New York; in January they went to Washington. Here they were most warmly welcomed, and received flattering attentions from the President and his family, the members of the Cabinet, and the Foreign Ministers. Madame Le Vert's reception was, indeed, no less brilliant than in the days of her happy youth. Many of the friends of her girlhood came to greet her. Among these was Rev. John Pierpont, who exclaimed, on seeing her:—

"Octavia—what—the Eight! If gracious Heaven
Hath made eight such—where are the other seven?"

The summer of 1866 was spent at Saratoga and other places of rural resort—the party returning to New York in September, to prepare for the journey southward in November. On the way to Mobile, they lingered some weeks near Nashville, the guests of Mrs. Acklen. She gave them a brilliant reception, at which Madame Le Vert wore lilac-colored moire antique, with a Grecian head-dress; her daughters, rose-colored satin trimmed with Brussels lace and silver cord. The next stopping-place of Madame Le Vert was at "Bellevue"—the place of her birth, "the sweetest cottage in the world"—near Augusta, now the residence of her aunt. Its groves of oak, and bowers of jessamine, clematis, and Cherokee roses, its parterres of flowers, exhibit the luxuriance of nature in that sunny region. The lady of the place was in her youth called "the beauty of the South;" and enjoys a distinction few Americans can boast, in living, in advanced age, on the spot where she was born.

In 1867 Madame Le Vert and her daughters spent some time in New Orleans. Two of her former slaves, who were established in that city, left all other employment, and insisted on being permitted to wait upon their idolized mistress, refusing all payment for their services. Madame Le Vert was obliged to promise all her house-servants to take them back whenever she should return

to her old home in Mobile. Their attachment to her amounts to adoration. Even the little children, brought by their mothers to see her, would kneel before her, crying: "Oh, pray, Miss 'Tavie, come back, and live with us!" Such touching incidents prove that negroes have grateful hearts. Some Southerners, reduced to penury, have been supported by the free and loving offerings of their former slaves.

MRS. ACKLEN, distinguished for graces and accomplishments in the society of Nashville, Tennessee, is the daughter of Oliver B. Hayes, a native of South Hadley, Massachusetts. He was among the pioneers of the middle division of Tennessee, and at twenty-eight married Sarah C. Hightower, the daughter of Richard Hightower, a wealthy farmer of Williamson County. Mr. Hayes was for many years one of the most eminent lawyers in the State, acquiring a considerable fortune by his professional success. Thus he gained time and opportunity to devote himself to study in other branches. In after years he became a clergyman, distinguished for ability and eloquence. Mrs. Hayes was noted for personal beauty, grace of manner, and sweetness of disposition. She was never forgetful of the poor, and made her home a paradise. Reared by such parents, their lovely daughter, Adelicia, grew up surrounded by all the advantages of fortune and of judicious culture. She was educated at the Nashville Female College, the best seminary in the State. Possessing great beauty and every charming accomplishment, she graced an elevated circle of society. In the bloom of early youth she was married to Mr. Isaac Franklin, one of the most opulent planters of Louisiana. He lived but a few years—adoring his wife, to whom he bequeathed his immense fortune.

When the youthful widow reappeared in society, it was with even more brilliant loveliness, softened by a gentle grace and dignity that won more admiration than ever. Her hand was a prize coveted by many distinguished admirers; it was won by Colonel Joseph Acklen, of Huntsville, Alabama, an eminent member of the legal profession. Possessing refined taste and cultivation, he made improvements in their large estate near Nashville, building a magnificent house, Italian in its style of architecture. It stands on the summit of a hill; the grounds surrounding it are highly ornamental, and the spacious greenhouse and conservatories are filled with choice flowers. This villa—called "Bellemonte"—is one of the centre spots of attraction in the State, and is said to be the most beautiful in the Southwest. Mrs. Acklen was the light of this abode—the pride and joy of her husband; but he lived only a few years to enjoy the happiness that crowned his union with so charming a wife, in a home full of the sanctities of love.

Shortly after his death, Mrs. Acklen, with her children, spent two years in a European tour. She was invited to the Imperial ball given at the opening of the

National Assembly, and was received with marked consideration by the French Emperor and Empress. Her beauty, grace, and courtly manners, with her rich and tasteful dress at all times, and the superb style in which she lived, created a sensation in Paris, and in social circles she was universally admired. Returning to her princely home, she brought with her some of the finest works of art in statuary, painting, and engraving, with rare articles of vertù—a variety such as few American homes can boast—as contributions to her splendid galleries. No expense was spared in the adornment of this beautiful place. The drawing-rooms, halls, and lofty corridors contain specimens of the great sculptors of the old and the new world. In the centre of the grand, hall lighted by windows of stained glass, stands the matchless "*Peri*" of Mosier, pronounced quite equal to the "Greek Slave;" "combining angelic attributes with the charms of the human face." The sculptor has chosen the moment when the Peri, standing before the opening gates of Paradise, exclaims:—

"Joy, joy forever! my task is done!" &c.

In the front hall is the "*Ruth*" of Rogers; and in the large drawing-room, the exquisite "*Sans Souci*" of Ives, expressing, in its perfect beauty, the abandon and grace of a child. "*Rebecca at the Well*," by the same artist, is there; and the group of "*The Twins*," by Reinhardt, with a number of choice paintings from the old masters. At the close of 1866 Mrs. Acklen gave the reception "complimentary to Madame Le Vert," preparations for which caused no small excitement in the business streets of Nashville. It was called "the forerunner of a new régime of entertainments, combining intellectual and artistic enjoyment with perfect taste." The observatory, groves, and parterres were illuminated, and the effect of the light among the statues, shrubbery, and flowers, with music from the portico, was fairy-like. The beautiful hostess wore the dress of pearl-colored satin, trimmed with richest point d'Alençon, in which she had been presented at the French court, with a coronet of diamonds, and diamond necklace and bracelets. Ladies were there from Memphis and from Kentucky; and the sister and nieces of the hostess were greatly admired.

Mrs. Acklen has lately married Dr. W. A. Cheatham. She is no less distinguished for her generous charities than for her brilliant social graces. Hers is the home of cordial hospitality, to which resort all the celebrities who visit Nashville; and the poor partake of the profuse liberality that marks her entertainments. She has four beautiful children. Three of her brothers are living; they are gentlemen of high respectability and ample fortune. Her two sisters—Mrs. Shields and Mrs. Lawrence—have a share of the same personal loveliness, and are like her in all engaging feminine virtues.

Mrs. Robert Stanard—Miss Martha Pierce—was a celebrated leader in fashionable society in Richmond,

Virginia, where she lived thirty years. She was educated in Baltimore, and married at a very early age. Her house was the last burned when Richmond was in part destroyed, and at the close of the war she went to Europe. There she received the most devoted attention from Sir Henry and Lady Bulwer, whom she had entertained at her own house, and had taken to visit "Shirley," a noted plantation on the James River, belonging to Dr. Carter, and regarded by foreigners as "a show place." She was treated with great attention by other noble friends in England; was invited by the Duke of Wellington to Apsley House, and introduced to his friends. This charming woman illustrates the best social phase in the city where she resided—where wealth was no passport to distinction, and the golden-calf worship, which too often disgusts sensible people in our great metropolis, was unknown. With a simplicity and grace that bespeak high mental culture, an elevated nature, and familiar acquaintance with the most refined society, she unites a spontaneous cordiality that can only flow from a warm and generous heart. In the midst of trials and misfortunes, her sympathy with suffering friends has been deep and constant. The attachment of her servants to so kind a mistress, their sorrow at the parting which their freedom rendered inevitable, and particularly the devotion of her maid Patty, who put off her own marriage because she would not leave her lady alone and sad, are worthy of being chronicled. Mrs. Stannard has been for some time a resident of Baltimore, and expects to make her home with her son, in Fredericksburgh, Virginia.

Mrs. Wickham, who was Miss McClurg, and was born in Richmond, is well known through a portion of Virginia as prominent in society. Her daughter Ella was celebrated for beauty; another—Betsey—for intellectual attainments.

A daughter of Mrs. Wickham became the wife of Benjamin Watkins Lee, of Virginia.

Another distinguished lady, prominent in all noble works, as she has been in society by right of intellectual gifts and charming manners, is Miss Emily Mason, of Kentucky. Her parents were Virginians—descended from the best stock in the "Old Dominion." Her mother was of the Marshall and Nicholson families: her paternal grandfather and uncle were both United States senators from that State. Her father, General Mason, removed to Kentucky some years after his marriage, and Emily was born in Lexington. Her only brother being elected Governor of the Territory of Michigan, the family followed him to Detroit, and the young girl was thence sent to Mrs. Willard's school. The pressure of affliction, separating the members of the family, shortened her time at school; her parents went to Mexico, and at the age of seventeen Emily presided in the Governor's mansion at Detroit, where she entertained a great deal of company, and exercised unlimited sway in the world of fashion. Her sprightly wit and remarkable powers of conversation, even at that early age, gave her a social ascendency unrivaled by any in that fair western city, and her brilliant style of beauty attracted general admiration. After the death of her brother she rejoined her parents in Virginia, spending some time in different cities of the Southwest. In New Orleans and elsewhere she became a celebrity in society. Too earnest in purposes of usefulness, and too intent on the cultivation of her mental powers for the frivolous career of an ordinary belle, she had a far more elevating influence, and commanded attention much more enviable. It was the sway not merely of beauty, but of varied accomplishments, rare perception and adaptation, and a "social genius" few women have possessed in this country, combined with the magnetic power of a generous and sympathetic nature. In her impulsive, fresh, cordial manner, and what may be called heart-speaking, she illustrated a peculiar charm of Southern character; having always an object in her pursuits beyond the amusement of the hour. Her mother died in 1839. The death of her father was followed by utter loss of fortune. Many of her friends wrote to entreat the orphaned girl to reside with them; at one time no less than seven homes were offered, where she could still have had the enjoyment of affluence. But she preferred independence at the cost of privation and labor. She purchased a small market farm in Fairfax County, Virginia, to which she removed a widowed sister and her family. This little home was soon beautified by her own hands. With the children's help she papered and painted the house; and together they worked in the garden, digging and planting as if they had been accustomed to toil, while the boys went to market and mill after working hours. Often did Miss Mason labor in the hot sun for seven hours at a time, getting in her hay and fodder. On one occasion a carriage full of elegantly dressed ladies, from Washington—only ten miles distant—came to the house. The visitors found Miss Emily in the stable-loft, putting away and salting down the fodder; but she came in blooming from her work with a pleasant greeting for her friends, and, like true Southerners, they did not admire her the less for doing what was needed with her own hands. At another time, a fashionable lady, approaching the house at a distance, saw her occupied in sowing grass-seed, as she walked to and fro across her lawn. Mistaking her action, the affrighted lady exclaimed: "I have often heard it said Emily Mason would go crazy working about this place! and do look at the frantic way in which she walks up and down swinging her arm!" A young gentleman of her acquaintance was wont to declare that the hatchet and nails were handed round whenever he went to pay a visit, as cake and wine would be handed at another house! Thus was the energetic girl determined to carry on her enterprise, to the astonishment of her aristocratic friends; and, with the co-operation of her young relatives, their happy home became a little paradise, content and abundance smiling on their exertions. But war came; their home was taken from them for "military purposes," and the innocent inmates were driven out shelterless, being forced to leave behind them clothing, stores, and all the cherished tokens of days of prosperity. At the breaking out of hostilities Miss Mason was on a visit to a sick relative in the North. She became suspected, and was denounced as a Southern spy; was hunted by the authorities, hidden by her friends—and finally compelled to fly from pursuit. She fled homeward, and had a dreadful journey alone through West Virginia; finding no place of refuge where her home had been. Her property was entirely destroyed. She then went to the hospitals, and particularly devoted her energies to active usefulness in the Winder Hospital, near Richmond. Here, and in the prisons, she took care of the sick, wounded, and dying, wherever her ministrations were necessary; and many a Union soldier had cause for grateful remembrance of her good offices. Her spirit of benevolent enterprise survived the war. Since its close she has worked even more indefatigably than ever in the cause of humanity. She has been the benefactress of Southern orphans, solicitous to provide for them the means of education, that they may be enabled, in time, to earn their own living. Her widely extended influence, and the confidence of all who know her in her excellent judgment, faithful care, and generous charity, have enabled her to find temporary homes for twenty-five destitute little creatures, while she gives herself a respite of a few months, taking a tour in Europe with an agreeable party.

Miss Sallie Carneal, the daughter of Davis Carneal, of Kentucky, was the most celebrated belle of Cincinnati, not only for beauty, but for her rare musical attainments, her powers of song, and her accomplishments as a linguist, with marked and noble traits of character. Her fame spread widely through the Southwest, and in Cincinnati she was identified with all that was elegant and fashionable; being truly the pride and queen of the Queen City. She married Mr. Glendy Burke, a noted merchant of New Orleans, and did not long survive her marriage.

A prominent belle in Kentucky, and called "the belle of the Southwest," was Miss Louisa Bullitt. She married Mr. De Kantzou, a Swede, and went with him to Sweden, but returned to live in this country, with vivacity and social attractions undiminished. A wonderful charm of her manner was the faculty of putting those at their ease who conversed with her.

Mrs. ROSA VERTNER JEFFREY has a distinguished position in society and a reputation as one of its leaders, in many Southern States and at the North, as well as an enviable literary fame. The influences surrounding her in early childhood were such as to foster her genius and refine her poetical tastes. Her father, Mr. Griffith, possessed literary culture, and was much admired as a writer. His gifted daughter, born in Natchez, Miss., passed her early years at a lovely country-home near Port Gibson, Miss., where she was tenderly trained by her maternal aunt, who supplied the place of her lost mother, and gave Rosa the instruction best fitted to develop her talents. At the age of ten, she was taken to Kentucky, her father superintending her education at a celebrated seminary in Lexington. At seventeen she was married to Mr. Claude M. Johnson, a gentleman of fortune and elevated character. Their residence was in Lexington and on Mr. Johnson's plantation in Louisiana. Mrs. Johnson's first volume of poems was published in Boston in 1857, and at once secured her the very highest rank as a poet in American literature.

Her second marriage was with Mr. Alexander Jeffrey, a gentleman descended of a noble Scottish family, and celebrated for scientific and literary attainments.

This is not the place to speak of Mrs. Jeffrey's merits as an author: but we may mention the fact that many of her exquisitely beautiful poems, become "household words" by their popularity, have so endeared her to Southern readers, that her social influence has been greatly extended thereby. Her charming qualities of character, her brilliant powers, her fascinating conversation, and the evidences of a pure, noble, and generous nature, united to her remarkable beauty, have made her a queen in every circle where she has moved. A brief residence at the North gained her "troops of friends;" but the South claims her with peculiar pride, as one of its most accomplished and loveliest daughters, more widely appreciated than any other, because of her double title to admiration and esteem.

XXI.

THE influence of Mrs. Frémont has been very peculiar. Without entering personally into the arena of politics, or using any machinery of partisanship, she has sent forth an animating spirit, acting on eminent minds. Living in the whirl of social excitement, she has found time to maintain relations with leading statesmen in every part of the country. Her influence seems to have been exercised, not in the furtherance of schemes, but simply by the force of a powerful nature and a singular clearness of mental vision. In France she might have ruled openly in the councils of the nation; in America she merely gave suggestions and advice to those who controlled the people's destiny. Her father was the distinguished Colonel Thomas H. Benton, of Missouri, who sat thirty-one years in the United States Senate. She was born in Virginia, on the family estate of her maternal grandfather, Colonel James McDowell, to whose father, a lieutenant-colonel in the British service, the crown grant for military services was originally made, and who was killed there by Indians in 1742. The domain was in Rockbridge County, and extended "from the valley to the tops of all the hills in view;" the point of view being a lakelet formed by the meeting of two streams that crossed the valley. There was another grant of ten thousand acres of pasture land in Greenbriar County, adjoining; with yet another, called "the military," of some thousands of acres in Kentucky; and another on the Ohio side of the river, on which a part of Cincinnati was built. These grants of "wild lands" were made by the English government, instead of payments in money, to their young officers. The inheritor of this magnificent estate was distinguished not only by noble aspect and dignity of manner, but by uprightness, justice, and liberality, with a temperance rare in those days. He divided his patrimony with his mother and sisters, who, like him, bestowed on the lands the most careful cultivation, such as only those born on the soil they expect to transmit to their children are willing to give. It was a section where the chief crops were tobacco and wheat, and where the Scotch settlers had introduced a thorough system of farming. The best imported stock and horses always belonged to the property; and thrift, order, and abundance reigned. Colonel McDowell married into the Preston family, and held a commanding position during life. He was a private court of appeal on questions of property and honor among the neighbors. It has been recorded that but ten cases on which he had pronounced an opinion had afterwards been taken into court.

In this region stands the "Washington College," endowed by Washington, of which General Lee is now president. On the same "College Hill" is the Military Institute, of which Stonewall Jackson was for eight years the head. There stood also the "Ann Smith Academy," where the daughters of prominent families were sent, attended, in their own carriages and on horseback; their brothers at the adjoining school having their special servants, dogs, guns, and horses. Besides the ordinary branches, the girls were taught fine embroidery and the care of their complexions. No high-born Virginia maiden would "spread her hand" by turning a door-knob, or touching the tongs, or handling a heavy object. Long gloves and deep sun-bonnets were constantly worn, and they ate little meat or butter. It is now more rationally believed that sunshine and a nourishing diet are essential to health. Every girl was taught her duties as head of a house. The homely, hearty English middle-class country-life formed the model, to which greater breadth was given by the larger extent of the estates and number of laborers to be managed. The Scotch elements of diligence and conscientiousness, modified by a more liberal scale of living, created a form of rural life almost peculiar to the true Virginia home. It was the pleasure and pride of other proprietors besides Colonel McDowell that they lived on land which had never been bought or sold, and that in sixty years no negro had been transferred to another owner. Each plantation was a little kingdom, producing within its own limits every thing needed except groceries and fine cloths, which were brought from Richmond in the wagons that carried the harvest of flour and tobacco.

The central portion of Virginia, cradled among her

glorious mountains, where lie the Sulphur Springs, the Hawk's Nest, the Natural Bridge, and other wonders of scenery—not far south enough for the operation of planting interests, was the region where the old ancestral pride and contempt of mere moneyed aristocracy subsisted in sternest purity. Its farming, rather than trading or planting interest was first broken in upon after the invention of the cotton-gin, which revolutionized Southern interests. Among the leading families, such as the Randolphs, Wythes, McDowells, and others, a logical head and clear conscience led them to one result on the question they had to meet hourly in their lives—that of slavery. Most of them did not believe in its continuance; some went further, and emancipated their slaves by will; while others did so during their lives, giving them also a start in life, while they could lend them a helping hand. Of this latter class was the mother of Mrs. Frémont.

In those days there was a classified, sifted, and solidly established order of society. Everybody and everybody's family was known; and "pedigree" was a prized qualification. It has been lately the fashion to laugh at the phrase, "a Virginia gentleman," for the title has been usurped. Then simplicity of character, good faith, honesty of purpose, loyalty to a conviction, a liberal hospitality, and a life spent in the honorable discharge of duties, were indispensable traits. Thackeray has given us George and Henry Esmond as types of the best class in Virginia society. Could he have painted a loveable woman, he might have given the feminine side of the character. But Madame Esmond is but the colonial English woman, losing the calmness that marked the caste, through the wear and tear of managing ignorant servants and tenantry. The hospitality so often mentioned as one of the traditions, was never ostentatious; there was no imposing by false appearances, and no sudden increase of wealth; the capital of the residents being in land and crops. Thus there was a solid foundation for prosperity and homely abundance, with a frank truthfulness in the mode of life, in beautiful contrast to the often deceptive display in commercial communities. A temporary show of splendor, at the cost of real inconvenience, would have been regarded by the staid, honest inhabitants as a kind of forgery, for the purposes of an adventurer. Travelers who came even from the South, in their old-fashioned massive carriages, drawn by two or four horses, and attended by mounted servants, would stop at any plantation in perfect assurance of a welcome, with no other introduction than the name of a mutual friend. Northern travelers usually took the mail-coaches by the day, with relays of horses every ten miles, stopping where they pleased. This posting was called "taking the accommodation line." Richmond was the little London of that provincial world, and pleasant circles were there formed to meet with accession of gayeties at their Saratoga, the White Sulphur Springs.

Colonel Benton's family was also of English extrac

tion and Virginian birth. His maternal grandfather was the younger brother of the Sir William Gooch who was deputy governor of Virginia under Lord Dunmore. This younger brother died a few months before the elder, missing the inheritance of the title and estate in Northumberland. His daughter, Anne Gooch, was married to Jesse Benton, at the house of her maternal uncle, Colonel Hart—the father-in-law of Henry Clay. Her son was named for that uncle, who had been her guardian during her long orphanage. In the early records of Kentucky, her husband's name occurs as one of a surveying party of sixteen who explored that State. He had the tastes and education of a scholar, but the breaking up of the colonial governorship in North Carolina changed his plan of life. He was private secretary to Governor Tryon, whose chaplain was his intimate friend, and his widow's, when she was left at thirty-one with a family of eight children, the eldest, Thomas, only eight years of age. The great Senator often spoke of this friend's taking him by the hand when coming out of the church, leading him home through the grove, and reading aloud from the Greek Testament—translating as he read—and telling the boy he must be a classical scholar, as his father had been. The boy's course of study was planned by him and the mother, who was a woman of rare mental endowments and force of character.

It should be mentioned that the Harts had married into the Preston family, one of the largest and wealthiest in the State, and so enlarged by marriages into other distinguished families, that the subject of our sketch finds herself somehow related to half Virginia. In near connection by birth and marriage were the families of the Campbells and Patrick Henry; of the Marshalls the Randolphs, the Madisons, the Daniels, the Peytons, the Floyds, the Breckenridges, the Hamptons, the Carringtons, Harts, &c. These were all people of large property and kindred tastes. It was a custom with them to send the eldest son on a four years' tour in Europe, accompanied by a clergyman as tutor.

Henrietta Preston, the sister of William Preston of Kentucky, was a favorite cousin of Mrs. Benton's. She became the wife of General Albert Sidney Johnston. Mrs. Benton's aunt married one of the Madisons. The sisters of William C. Preston of South Carolina were beautiful women, much admired in society. Margaret, the youngest, was the wife of General Wade Hampton. Their son, Frank Preston Hampton, was killed in the late war.

Such were the ancestors and relations of Miss Jessie Benton, who, passing her early years in the settlement described, and familiar with the beautiful scenery surrounding her birth-place, where four generations of cultivation had spared the time-honored oaks of the primeval forest, remembers no rural picture with greater delight. At that period, the intermarriages of the Richmond families with those of the southern portion of the State, had softened the rigid sternness of manners formerly prevalent, leaving undistorted the clean lines of right and wrong, with which no effacing of boundaries was allowed. Mr. Benton kept his family in Washington every winter. The journey to St. Louis requiring three or four weeks, it was only taken at the close of the short sessions, when they could spend the time from March to November in their Western home. From March to May they were sometimes in New Orleans, where Mr. Benton had many clients among the old French and Spanish landholders. That city was a provincial Paris, far removed from the social laws that governed the Virginians. Its French language, usages, and costumes, its Roman Catholic churches, its Sunday theatres and places of amusement, were themes of serious discussion and apprehension, on the score of danger to the children, among the old-fashioned relatives in Virginia. The changes of moral atmosphere, with the travel to and fro through the liberal and growing West, the polished and luxurious life of the Crescent City, with the varied experiences of Washington, where Europe as well as the United States was represented, no doubt contributed to enlarge the ideas of the young people, and teach them a more liberal judgment than usually belongs to a puritanical and secluded community. Mrs. Benton's winter circles in Washington were composed of the most distinguished persons in the Capital. Chief Justice Marshall, Mr. Randolph, Chief Justice Taney, Mr. Mason of North Carolina, Mr. Archer, Mr. Van Buren, all, in fact, who were worth knowing, with her own relatives, formed her brilliant coteries, which were really as historical as the most famous ones of French princesses. The youthful Jessie was often a listener to social and political discussions, by which unconsciously her opinions were shaped. The time-stained journal of her cousin, William C. Preston, kept during his tour abroad, and describing his stay as a guest at Abbottsford, &c., was eagerly read by her, and gave her the first actual impression of Scott's human existence. "Ivanhoe" was her first novel. Her studies were planned and superintended by her father, and aided by the splendid library which had been collected by her grandfather Benton. It was well selected, and rich not only in Latin, Greek, and English authors, but French. Jessie read her Shakspeare and Sevigné from the volumes read in the family in the days of the colonies. She learned to speak French in infancy from a French nurse, Mrs. Benton employing whites after giving freedom to her slaves. Her society experiences may be said to have commenced in early childhood. She was at a ball, with fire-works, given at the Russian Embassy, when she was ten years old, having been invited particularly because she could speak French and Spanish. English was not then generally understood by foreigners in Washington. Her first State dinner party was at the Presidential mansion, when she was not quite thirteen; Mr. Van Buren having collected a number of young girls and boys to introduce to his son, Smith Van Buren. At fifteen, Miss Benton was first bridesmaid to Madame Bodisco, a bride only a year her senior, while the bridegroom was over sixty. The partners were distributed on the same plan; Mr. Buchanan, then Secretary of State, being assigned to Miss Benton. This wedding was followed by dinners and balls at all the principal houses in Washington, from the White House through the diplomatic corps. The marriage caused a wide sensation. Madame Bodisco became a great favorite with the Emperor Nicholas.

Miss Benton was married to Mr. John C. Frémont, then Second Lieutenant of Engineers, in October, 1841. She did not, however, quit the delightful home of her family till eight years afterwards, her husband being often absent on long and dangerous expeditions. The record of Frémont's life and services is part of the country's history, and even the share in his labors taken by his wife, who was his private secretary and amanuensis, cannot be here adequately described. She would go to meet him at the frontier, in the country of the Delaware Indians, at the times appointed for his return, joining him sometimes in a tent, or a log cabin, and in various scenes of Western adventure. Familiar with almost every shade and grade of society, she has said that she found "as much grace of hospitality, though necessarily not of outward show, in a log cabin of the prairies, or a farm-house on a California ranche, as in the Faubourg Saint Germain, or at a prince's of the Bonaparte blood, or in the refined home of an English gentleman." At her dinner-table Delaware chiefs, in courtesy and deference to others, have rivaled the high-bred ease of men accustomed to the elegant culture of the best society. "A Mormon elder of much power and many wives" has been her guest, and she has entertained, and been entertained, as a friend remarked, "through not only the gamut but the chromatic scale of society."

General Frémont's first expedition to the Rocky Mountains terminated in October, 1842. His second, beyond that barrier, was accomplished in July, 1843. He arrived in the Valley of the Sacramento in May, 1846. There was imminent danger of the subjection of California to British protection, for during two centuries England had had her eye on that rich province, and now expected to seize it in the Mexican war then approaching. At the critical moment, General Frémont snatched the possession from the hands of Admiral Seymour, already stretched out to clutch it, and conquered the country, securing it forever to the United States. The result of this service was Mrs. Frémont's first experience in the agreeable flatteries of society. The Government was pleased at the acquisition of a new territory without the cost of a war, and pleased with the man who had taken it on his own responsibility. In Washington Mrs. Frémont received the tokens of this satisfaction—complimentary letters, the honored seat at dinners, from the President's house through the circle, &c. Then followed the quarrel between the land and water forces in California, which turned the class feeling of the army against Frémont, causing animosities and duels; till he came home to be subjected to a trial by court-martial. Resigning his place, he went overland in the winter to

California, where he had invested money in lands that now formed a magnificent estate. Mrs. Frémont followed him in March, but was detained seven weeks on the Isthmus of Panama by the want of a connecting steamer, and suffered severely from her experience of the tropics. She was hospitably received and attended by the family of General Herran, the minister from New Grenada, whom she had known in Washington; and on her return in the following year, when detained a month by illness, she was again received by them with the same large hospitality.

The fourth expedition to California was commenced in October, 1848. General Frémont wished to prepare for the reception of his family. Mrs. Frémont accompanied him as far as a Government post in Kansas, just out of Missouri. She remained here five or six weeks, and spent the days at her husband's encampment, her lodging being at the house of the Indian agent. A vast wilderness thence stretched westward, beyond the advancing march of civilization.

In California, in the rough days of 1849, when there was gold and nothing else in the land, Mrs. Frémont found a new experience. Society had no existence, and men were released from all forms and obligations except such as individual conscience might impose. Her experience confirmed her father's judgment, that there was more good than evil in human nature. Especially had she reason to be convinced of that native refinement and goodness of American men, which is so continually the subject of astonishment to foreigners traveling in this country.

The residence of Mrs. Frémont in California was at Monterey. Gold was not yet abundant, and the fullest tide of emigration had not set in. Provisions were usually obtained from the Sandwich Islands. Her only assistant in domestic labors was an English woman who had emigrated from Sidney. The liberal hospitality exercised in her house with such limited help excited the wonder of the residents. The convention for making a constitution for the State of California sat at Monterey, and many interests favored the introduction of slavery. No servants could be had where labor was so highly paid in other branches. The mines could not be worked at the tremendous price and uncertainty of labor; and to the owners it was the difference between vast fortunes and slow and precarious returns for certain and great expenditures. There was hesitation in the decision of the convention. Mrs. Frémont had the pleasure of being assured that the practical evidence of her example convinced many that home comfort and a liberal and cheerful hospitality were possible without servants. Her experience was within the sight and knowledge of those voting on the question, and largely aided in the decision for freedom in California.

Mrs. Frémont had her full share in the adventure of Western life. At one time, for six weeks she was not once in a house—sleeping in a traveling carriage, and moving about during the day. When lumps of gold and

bags of gold-dust were brought down from the mountains, there was no place for their deposit but under the carriage-seat, or in her trunks at Monterey. Some Spaniards from Sonora, who were working for General Frémont, received half the gold for their labors. Twenty of them wished to return to Sonora, and wrote to ask for their proportion. Mr. Frémont was at San Francisco, and could not conveniently go to Monterey; but sent an Indian with the key of the trunk—three days' journey by land—directing the Spaniards to open it, weigh out their part of the gold, and send back the key. This was done with perfect accuracy, not an ounce of the gold being taken beyond their share.

The name of General Frémont is enrolled among the most eminent explorers and geographers. When he returned to the east, it was with his share of the wealth of the new State he had first explored, and with political power, he having been chosen its first Senator. Of his years of trial and triumph, Mrs. Frémont could say, "All which I saw, and part of which I was." The negotiations to which his proprietorship of the Mariposas property gave rise, took him to Europe in the spring of 1852. His fame preceded him, and both he and Mrs. Frémont had a most flattering reception from men eminent in science and letters. They spent a year of unbroken content in Paris. At the English Court they were in the privileged list, including the diplomatic corps, on account of General Frémont's position at home, and his being one of the medalists of the Royal Geographical

Society. The medals are not given for services to government, but for expeditions conducted at private cost, involving sacrifices. For subsequent expeditions, Frémont received Austrian and Prussian medals and diplomas.

The death of Mrs. Frémont's only brother shortened their stay in London. Among other gratifications, they lost that of being present at the last dinner given in honor of the birthday of the Duke of Wellington, to which they were invited by Miss Coutts. The Duke always dined with her that day, selecting his own company. His death soon followed this celebration, at which some of the royal family were present.

In Paris, Mrs. Frémont saw the eagles of the Empire restored to the flags of the troops at the great review in the Champ de Mars, on the 10th of May, 1853. This was the era of the Republic headed by a President, and few anticipated the restoration of the Empire. She witnessed its proclamation, however, on the 2d of December of the same year; and admired the brave daring with which the new Emperor performed his part. A solitary figure passing on horseback through the crowded streets—no one within at least forty paces—holding his chapeau in his right hand, his breast and throat exposed to any deadly ball, his head bared and bending in acknowledgment of the popular greeting—his confidence in the people could not fail to inspire respect. Mrs. Frémont saw the Imperial nuptials, and had tickets for reserved places in all the fêtes succeeding. The picturesque aspect of the new court interested her, but she preferred the genuine royalty of "that dingy St. James." During the two hours she stood in the throne-room of that palace, a gallery of striking portraits was photographed on her mind. Nowhere is the beauty of noble English women excelled. Its expression of wholesome truth and unaffected goodness, with simplicity and dignity of manner, was most impressive to one who had been nurtured in the midst of English ideas, literature, and home ways, and saw all at the fountain-head. Near Mrs. Frémont stood the Duke of Wellington, with Mr. Gladstone, then Chancellor of the Exchequer, and on the wall above them hung a large picture of the battle of Waterloo; while at the head of the line of ladies belonging to the diplomatic corps stood the Countess Walewski, representing France as ambassadress of the empire of another Napoleon. The pearls she wore were the famous Cis-alpine pearls, which cost poor Josephine so dear; this association, with the wonderful resemblance of Count Walewski to his imperial father, added to the effect of the historical grouping.

After their return to America, Mrs. Frémont remained in Washington while her husband made an overland winter journey to California. Then came the political campaign of 1856, when General Frémont accepted the republican nomination for the Presidency; and his wife became severed from her past life, and associations linked to her by birth and education. It was a painful sacrifice to feel the alienation of valued friends;

but she accepted the trial with regret, sympathizing cordially in the plans of her husband, acting as his secretary, and aiding him by counsel as well as co-operation.

She was again in Paris in 1857, having had the large experiences of a political revolution, which made her even a more appreciative listener than before to one of her friends—the Count de la Garde, who had lived from childhood within court circles—the courts which made the history of Europe from the French Revolution to the present empire. He was naturally pleased to talk over such a life with a listener so deeply interested. He left her a collection of souvenirs of the Bonaparte family; the central figure Queen Hortense, whom he had known longest, their musical taste bringing them into constant correspondence. The album is a curious and valuable historical relic. It opens with a rare and exquisite miniature on ivory, by Isabey, of the first Napoleon, taken in 1804, in the uniform of the Old Guard. It was his love-gift to Josephine. The book contains other portraits in water-color, engravings, and lithographs, of Josephine, Hortense, the Marquis de Beauharnais, Prince Eugene, &c., with autograph letters from these and others related to the Bonapartes, original drawings and water-color sketches by Hortense, and music composed and written out by her. Among her letters is one to the Count, illustrating her heart as well as her mind, written as it was after such a tremendous reverse of fortune. It shows no bitterness or repining—only a certain gentle philosophy in recognizing society's estimate of a woman in power and out of power. I give an extract, printed as the original is written:—

"en arrivant chez moi, je trouve votre nouvelle romance monsieur le Compte, elle est bien jolie, et si je suis deja habituée aux choses aimables de votre part, je n'en suis pas moins etonnée de la promptitude avec laquelle vous faites de si jolis vers. On a un peu changé ma devise en vous la donnant, *moins connue moins troublée*, est celle que j'avais prise depuis bien longtems, elle convient tant à une femme! dans des temps plus brillants des amis y avoient ajouté *mieux connue mieux aimée* c'est qu'ils connoissaient toute mon ambition et voulaient me persuader que je possedais ce que j'envias le plus, ils ne le pensent peut-être plus à present? c'est donc la première devise qui seule peut me convenir.

* * * * * * * *
"Augsbourg ce 8 juin 1819. (signed) hortense."*

General Frémont had made arrangements in Paris to reside there with his family for some years; but the scheme was given up when impending war demanded his services at home. His California property was sold.

---

* TRANSLATION.—"On returning home, I find your new song, Monsieur le Comte. It is very beautiful, and although I am accustomed to these graceful acts of yours, I am not the less astonished by the rapidity with which you make such lovely verses. My device has been somewhat altered by those who gave it to you. '*Less known, less troubled,*' is the one I had chosen very long ago—it suits a woman so well! In more brilliant times, friends had added, '*Better known, better loved;*' this they did, knowing my chief ambition, and wishing to convince me that I possessed wnat I most desired. Perhaps now they no longer think so; only the first therefore can be suitable to me.

* * * * * * * *
"(Signed) HORTENSE.

"Dated Augsbourg, the 8th of June, 1819. Addressed to Monsieur le Comte de la Garde Messeull, at Munich."

During the war, the city of St. Louis was for a time the home of his family. They now reside in New York. In her beautiful country-seat on the Hudson—"Po-ca-ho" (the old Indian name), near Tarrytown, Mrs. Frémont has found congenial rest. The neighborhood has been described in the sketch of Mrs. Beekman. The region is associated with recollections of the manorial lords of colonial days, of wild adventures during the Revolutionary struggle, of quaint Dutch customs and curious traditions, some immortalized by the pen of Washington Irving.

Political life has never been the choice or the ambition of Mrs. Frémont; her preference has always been to live apart from it. The care and education of her children, who received all their instruction at home, more agreeably absorbed her attention. The cultivation of music was a part of her domestic life; all her children possessing musical talent. Flowers have always been her especial delight. A thorough system of reading has been pursued by the younger members of the household under her direction, and a splendid collection of rare books facilitated their studies. The library contains the greater part of Humboldt's among its treasures; with his diplomas, the signatures to which comprise the autographs of the distinguished literary and scientific men, and most of the sovereigns, in the civilized world, who have lived within sixty years. All the standard works, with others rare and valuable, some filled with annotations, are included. Mrs. Frémont has been the teacher of her daughter, who is accomplished in several modern languages, as well as in the other branches of a finished education. All these home employments have not been incompatible with energetic labors in the cause of charity. Mrs. Frémont is one of the active managers of the "Nursery and Child's Hospital," and of "The Soldiers' Orphan Home," of which association Mrs. Grant is President. She has been an efficient co-worker in the management of the "Ladies' Southern Relief Association." At her request to Congress, a ship was granted to convey the supplies to Charleston and other Southern ports. In her benevolent efforts, Mrs. Frémont obtains sympathy and aid from many with whom she has been associated in past years; for even political opponents remember her with respect and esteem. If in a railway station she has a moment of recognition and greeting from some statesman who has influenced the country's destiny, she is in no way surprised to receive afterwards a long letter from him referring to past events and the actors therein. She might go, with certainty of welcome, to homes in every State of the Union, and nearly every country in Europe.

The anxieties and trials—transcending woman's strength to bear—endured by Mrs. Frémont in the early part of the war, left their record on her luxuriant hair, which in a few days changed from glossy brown to silvery whiteness. The curious change was so sudden, her acquaintances thought she had covered her head with powder, and some did not recognize her. The blanched locks do not match her fresh and blooming face; but Mrs. Frémont prefers to wear her gray hair, regarding its hue as the sacred scars of a veteran.

Very few women in the United States have equaled Mrs. Frémont in brilliancy of conversation. Almost at all times her talk is sparkling—flashing, it may be said—with lively wit and picturesque illustration; ornament as unstudied, withal, as the play of a sunlit fountain. Her witticisms are continually repeated in society. It is the great charm of her humor and repartee, that they are perfectly spontaneous. In this kind of splendor she resembles William C. Preston, only her sarcasm is ever playful and good-humored. Had she been an orator, she would have beguiled "attent ears" with rich eloquence, and carried captive the judgment by the vivid force of her word-painting. New ideas start up as she speaks upon the most ordinary topic, and her fancy gives a fresh coloring to all things. She brings the stores of rare culture to enrich the lightest social gossip; but does it without effort or even consciousness. Her appearance and manner are those usually thought distinctive of an English woman, and strikingly like those of her father. Her form is rather above the ordinary height, splendidly proportioned, and her face is very handsome and full of intellectual expression; always lighted up with the glow of a bright spirit and the benevolence of a generous heart.

XXII.

Mrs. Henry W. Hills has long been celebrated in the society of New York for her rare musical attainments. She was Margaret Shellman; her mother, a Virginian of Huguenot descent. The daughter was born in Savannah, Georgia, where she continued to reside for twelve years after her early marriage. Her uncommon musical talents were displayed from childhood; at twelve she began to improvise, and composed waltzes, which were printed by her master; and from that time it has been her habit to express in music not only the emotions of her own heart, but current events of public or national interest. The poetess, Lydia Maria Child, when a young lady, was invited to hear Mrs. Hills play. She had never been able to appreciate or enjoy music, and fancied herself deficient in the faculty. But the brilliant touch and expression of Mrs. Hills awakened in her the sense of melody. In gratitude for the new-born joy, she addressed to the enchantress some impromptu verses, beginning, "Thanks, Orpheus, thanks;" expressive of her feelings. Mrs. Osgood wrote these impromptu lines on hearing Mrs. Hills' exquisite performance on the piano, in 1841:—

> "Of old the enchanted lyre,
> 'Neath Orpheus' touch of fire,
> Could charm, 'tis said, the very hills to joy;
> Could Orpheus come again,
> The *Hills* in magic strain
> Would now in turn bewitch and well reward the boy."

Mrs. Hills has lived many years in the city of New York, where her morning receptions were noted several years ago. This mode of entertainment was said to have been introduced, among the earliest, by Mrs. Girard, the eldest daughter of Governor Sumner, of Boston. The letters of Mrs. Hills, published in the Home Journal, contained excellent strictures on fashion and dress, and were extensively quoted. She described facetiously the competition of display among ladies who dressed for each other, in rivalry or emulation. But her great "mission" was the cultivation of music, and the promotion of a taste for the best and highest in the art. N. P. Willis wrote to her, in 1864: "I envy Gottschalk his being within reach of your ears and finger ends; you *think aloud* so deliciously."—"What happiness your harmony of soul and fingers might give!"

Unvisited in early years by affliction, and endowed with a gift in art which beautified all around her, Mrs. Hills' life passed joyously as a bird's. The fount was always flowing; every emotion gushed out in music. Her improvisation especially breathed airs that expressed her feelings. Her Lament for the loss of the Arctic uttered the very soul of tender sympathy and dolor. Melody is, in truth, the voice of her heart. This intense love of the art has had its beneficial effect among her acquaintances, and its influence can hardly be measured. It pervades Mrs. Hills' life so thoroughly that the ordinary pleasures of society have scarcely a charm for her, separated from the progress of music. She often superintends and directs concerts given in aid of charities. Several have been given under her auspices at Dr. Ward's private theatre, in New York, which he opens for charities every Easter week.

The daughter of Mrs. Hills, Mrs. John Schermerhorn, inherited her talent in music. Gottschalk was delighted with her playing of his compositions. Mrs. Hills' grand-daughter, Miss Minnie Parker, has not only the family gift in instrumental music, but a voice of rare sweetness and power. She has achieved brilliant triumphs in her singing for charities, and has been praised in the highest terms by connoisseurs.

Miss Hetty Carey, of Baltimore, was said to be the most beautiful girl in Virginia or Maryland. For ten years she was a reigning belle, especially noted in Richmond society. She married Major-General Pegram, of Richmond.

Miss Lillie Hitchcock was celebrated in San Francisco for brilliant accomplishments and personal graces. She would entertain at one time a circle of twenty gentlemen. She now resides in Paris, having married Mr. Thornton.

Mrs. Harvey, the wife of the Governor of Wisconsin, labored in hospitals and in aid of soldiers on the field, in the Southwest. She afterwards took some "orphans of the war" from Vicksburg, and established a Home for them in Wisconsin, which is under her superintendence.

Another, as benevolent, Margaret Breckenridge, the daughter of "the Ajax of orthodox Christianity in the Southwest," was educated by her grandfather at Princeton, and made her home with her brother-in-law, Colonel Porter, of Niagara. Her zeal and devotion in the cause of humanity took her to the West in 1862, where she gave her services to the soldiers in the hospitals.

Mrs. William Schermerhorn has given entertainments to the delight of the fashionables of New York. She was Miss Cotinet, and was remarkable for beauty and grace, and for the elegance of her reunions. She gave three of the most splendid receptions in the city in the winter of 1867. Her famous "*bal costumé de rigueur*," illustrating the reign of Louis XV., was not, as was said, the first fancy ball given; the first, or one of the first, was given about 1820, by Mrs. Brugiere, in her house near the Bowling Green. To that of Mrs. Schermerhorn six hundred guests were invited; all of whom came dressed in the prescribed costume. The dresses, exclusive of jewelry, were said to have cost between forty and fifty thousand dollars; the jewelry over half a million. The servants were dressed in the uniform of the period.

Mrs. Hamilton Fish, the wife of Governor Fish, who

was Miss Kane, has also been prominent in New York society.

In New York, Mrs. Auguste Belmont has obtained a celebrity for magnificent parties, attended by fashionables noted for gayety; and the same may be said of many ladies who have as yet no history.

Every aristocratic fête, every occasion for a fashionable assemblage in New York, has been for some years under the management of a person who may now be called historical, on that account. It is Brown—the portly sexton of Grace Church. Happy, fat, and sleek, with easy mien he salutes the belles as they alight, amiably conscious that—

> "Where Brown is found,
> To Fashion's eye is hallowed ground."

The poet chronicler of a midsummer fête given at "Woodland Hall," on Manhattan Island, thus apostrophized this manager of entertainments:—

> "Oh, glorious Brown! thou medley strange
>   Of churchyard, ball-room, saint and sinner;
> Flying by morn through Fashion's range,
>   And burying mortals after dinner!
> Walking one day with invitations—
> Passing the next at consecrations;
> Tossing the sod at eve on coffins;
> With one hand drying tears of orphans,
> And one unclasping ball-room carriage,
> Or cutting plum-cake up for marriage:
> Dusting by day the pew and missal;
> Sounding by night the ball-room whistle,
> Admitted free through Fashion's wicket,
> And skilled at psalms, at punch, and cricket."

The daughter of Hon. Josiah Quincy remarked: "Society is now almost entirely engrossed by very young people, who are often beautiful, accomplished, and pleasing; but there are no queens among them." It would scarcely interest the reader to have a mere list of the names of the present leaders of fashionable society in Boston. Now and then they appear in newspapers as patronesses of some State military ball or charity festival; for in Boston, as in New York, public entertainments are greatly in favor for such purposes. The same in other cities.

It may be seen from the brief history given in the foregoing pages, that the ladies most prominent in fashionable life—from the Republic's early days to the present time—have been noticeable for more than merely frivolous distinctions. They have been women of superior mind and culture. This intellectual element, with the benevolent activity and moral worth of our leaders, has given an elevated tone to the *best* society in New York, of which the country may be justly proud. This should be remembered when Europeans, or critics among ourselves, are disposed to sneer at American fashionable life and manners, confounding the really superior class with vulgar pretenders unworthy to be named with them.

At a ball given in Fifth Avenue, in the winter of 1867, "the German" was danced in the costumes in vogue from the twelfth to the eighteenth century. Fifteen hundred invitations were issued. In Washington, the same season, many receptions were given at which there were a thousand guests. At the White House, two separate entrances opened on a double roadway. The light from great globes over the portals fell on a mass of carriages, among which might be seen the "rattletrap" of the Virginia farmer, drawn by one horse and driven by an ancient "freedman." The brilliant though motley crowd emerging from the dressing-rooms met in the open sea of the "East Room." The President, in black, clean shaven, stood in his place, the picture of the severe respectability of the olden time. Mrs. Patterson and Mrs. Storr, who received the guests, were simply dressed; the cost of other dresses might be estimated by thousands. A prominent belle was the wife of the Chilian Minister; and in artistic array Mrs. Sprague bore away the palm. She is slender to fragility, with abundant brown hair and beautiful eyes, shadowed by long dark lashes. She is the daughter of Secretary Salmon P. Chase, and the wife of Senator Sprague, of Rhode Island. The wife of Senator Morgan wore the most valuable diamonds.

In the winter of 1867 was introduced in New York the fashion of giving balls at Delmonico's rooms, which had long been used by gentlemen for their dinner-parties. Balls for the "coming out" of young ladies were given there; the proprietor furnishing attendants, music, flowers, and supper, at a certain price per guest. There was a separate entrance to the rooms thus appropriated, and strict seclusion could be had; but one can hardly give the name of hospitality to such entertainments.

It is undeniable that changes, and changes not for the better, have taken place during the last few years in American social life in every quarter of the Union. They have been most perceptible in New York and at the most popular watering-places; chiefly Saratoga and Newport. There, to be "fast" has been to lead the ton. In 1864 the great feature of the season at Newport, among the lively folk thus designated by the grave and dignified, was the driving of "four-in-hands." One young lady drove a three-in-hand of tiny ponies, that looked like playthings. Another "took the wind out of all the female sails," by appearing in a "turn-out" with four black ponies; a groom riding a fifth in the rear. The Brazilian dames, said to have worn head-dresses composed of small gauze balls, each imprisoning a firefly, were outdone by a New York lady at a fancy ball given by her. She personated "Lyrus," wearing on her head a wreath of flowers, while over the forehead rose a lyre composed of tiny gas-lights, fed from a small reservoir concealed in the dress, and flashing as she moved her head.

Since the condition of things during the war enabled men to amass fortunes in an incredibly short time, and the discovery of oil in almost worthless lands gave them suddenly immense value, the "shoddy" and "petroleum" element has been prominent in circles composed of wealthy persons inclined to scatter their money profusely for the purpose of display. These leaders of gayety flutter in the admiring gaze of the stupid and ignorant masses, but they are not worthy to be named in the same category with those who can boast better claims to distinction than merely the possession of money. It is not worth our while to treasure the names of ladies of this order, who have made themselves conspicuous entirely by the extravagance of their entertainments, the excessive costliness of their dress, or their disregard of all feminine discretion. It is very easy to create a sensation in New York, or any large city. Where there is a display of unbounded wealth, such old-fashioned articles as morality and good taste are often despised. During the season of 1865–66, six hundred balls, more or less public, were given in that city, and it was estimated that seven millions of dollars were spent by the ball-goers; the average cost of a suitable dress being a thousand dollars, without jewelry. Frequently ten thousand dollars might be seen glittering on one fine form; the cost having increased since diamond dust became a necessity in a lady's toilet. Of course these public balls are not attended generally by fashionable people; but their extravagance shows the tendency in popular taste. The wildest stories are extant in current gossip about those dames of the gay world. One, who is building a splendid house near Central Park, is said to get herself up with hasheesh for dissipation. Another, overturned in a pony drive, and almost swooning, faintly exclaimed, "Take me to my children!"—"She'll have to be introduced to them," observed a cynical by-stander. To rise and reign among the money-worshiping idiots of this kind of fashion in New York—to hold the metropolis in admiration—it is only necessary to possess millions and scatter money lavishly for show. No matter how the riches are obtained; dishonesty, cruelty, repudiation of debts, even fraud, provided it comes not under the ban of law, are lost in the brightness with which wealth covers its possessor. But such worse than vulgar parvenues dare not aspire even to admission to the society ruled by ladies such as are illustrated in this volume. The really excellent will never mingle with them. Their day to shine must be short, even among the golden-calf idolaters of New York. That city, as well as others, may boast her pure-blooded, pure-mannered aristocracy, deserving respect as well as admiration, and exercising a healthy influence over all grades.

A few American ladies have become known in Paris for great powers of song, and as amateur actresses and vocalists have received attention at court and from connoisseurs. Mrs. Hills is pre-eminent in this country in instrumental music. Her talent and gift of improvisation were inherited from her father, who was highly cultivated in the classic school. He directed her musical studies in the works of the great 'German masters, accompanying her on the violin, when playing the sonatas of Haydn, Mozart, and other eminent composers.

Mrs. Henry J. Butterfield, an American lady whose beauty, grace and accomplishments not only gave her a prominent position in New York as a youthful belle, but as a celebrity in the court circles and with the noblesse of Paris, should be noticed among those who have added lustre to the society of this country.

She was Miss Mary Roosevelt Burke, daughter of the Hon. M. Burke, and niece of Judge Roosevelt, of New York. As a young lady, she passed much of her time in the family of her uncle, from whose house she was married to Mr. Henry J. Butterfield, an English gentleman of wealth and position. Soon after her marriage she went to Europe, and, finding the society of Paris much to her taste, made that city her home. Her personal beauty, her natural grace, her many accomplishments (being a fine linguist), and her exquisite taste in dress, added to her husband's wealth and liberality, soon gave her a prominent position in the court circles of that brilliant capital. She was much noticed by the Emperor and Empress, and was always a welcome guest at the private parties given at the Tuileries, where her faultless toilette was much admired by the Empress Eugenie, herself the queen of taste and fashion. Her house was the resort of distinguished foreigners and diplomats, who delighted in her society, while her own countrypeople, who had a claim to be received, were particularly welcome.

It was not alone in Paris that Mrs. Butterfield was admired. She was presented at the Court of Queen Victoria, and, amid the galaxy of beauty found at an English court drawing-room, attracted much attention. During one of her visits to London, she attended a ball given by a fashionable duchess, where her magnificent toilette and distingué appearance elicited universal admiration. A royal lady who was present was so much charmed with her exquisite taste that she sent one of her attendants to find out who the beautiful stranger was. On being told she was an American lady, she expressed surprise that any one but a Parisian could exhibit such a toilette or so much grace.

Mrs. Butterfield was presented to the late Empress of Russia at Nice, where she passed a winter; and that illustrious lady was so charmed with the young American, that she treated her in the most affectionate manner. She presented her to the other members of the Imperial family, who always manifested the greatest interest in Mrs. Butterfield.

Mrs. Butterfield was not spoiled by all this adulation, but retained the purity, sincerity, and charming simplicity of her early life. Elegant, cultivated, and refined, she was a true-hearted woman, loving her country and its institutions, loyal to her flag at all times and under all circumstances, and doing all in her power to make the name of America honored and respected abroad.

She was a faithful and affectionate wife and mother, a devoted daughter, a true Christian, loving and kind to all connected with her. Her death was mourned by many friends in the brilliant circle she adorned, while to her husband and relatives her loss was irreparable.

INDEX OF NAMES.

	PAGE
Adams, Abigail	108
Adams, Mrs. John Quincy	109
Adams, Miss (Mrs. Smith)	106
Letters, 68, 75, 138, &c.	
Acklen, Mrs.	417
Alexander, Lady Catherine	44
Allen, Mrs.	211
Allen, Miss	98
Ambler Family	19
Bal, Señora del	856
Barney, Miss	278
Barton, Mrs. Thomas	275
Beekman, Mrs.	171
Belmont, Mrs. Auguste	458
Benton, Miss Jessie	434
Benton, Mrs. Thomas H.	435
Bingham, Mrs.	137
Bingham, the Misses	147
Bledsoe, Sarah	195
Bodisco, Madame	436
Bonaparte, Madame	165
Bradford, Mrs.	84
Breckenridge, Mrs. Robert	297
Breckenridge, Margaret	452
Brehan, Marchioness de	23, 106
Brewton, Mrs.	184
Brown, Mrs. A. G.	888
Brown, Mrs. A. V.	889
Brown, Mrs. Jacob	226
Brugiere, Mrs.	452
Bruyn, Blandina	160
Bullitt, Miss Louisa	426
Burns, Marcia (Mrs. Van Ness)	264
Butt, Miss, of Norfolk	278
Butterfield, Mrs. H. J.	459

	PAGE
Cabell, Mrs.	828
Caldwell, Miss (Mrs. Gillam)	191
Calhoun, Mrs. Andrew	889
Calhoun, Mrs. John C.	191
Calhoun, Mrs.	191
Carey, Miss Hetty	451
Carneal, Miss Sallie	426
Carrington, Mrs. Edward	19
Carroll Family	85
Carroll, Mrs. Charles	85
Cass, Miss	285
Caton, Mrs.	86
Caton, the Misses	86
Chestnut, Mrs. James	340
Chew, the Misses	85
Clay, Mrs. Clement	340
Clay, Mrs. Henry	227
Clinton, Mrs.	106
Clinton, the Misses	91
Clinton, Cornelia	91
Combs, Mrs.	208
Costar, Mrs. John	808
Cranch, Mrs.	105
Crittenden, Mrs. J. J.	827
Crittenden, Miss	841
Cushing, Mrs.	98
Custis, Eleanor Parke	257
Custis Family	20
Custis, Mrs. Mary	260
Cutts, Mrs.	136
Dahlgren, Miss	839
Davis, Mrs.	340
De Lancey Family	198
De Peyster Family	175

INDEX OF NAMES.

Name	Page
Derby, Mrs. Richard	324
Douglas, Mrs.	340
Dubois, Mrs. Cornelius	359
Duer, Lady Catherine	108
Duval, Mrs.	340
Ellery, Miss	91
Elliott, Anne	190
Elliott, Mrs. Barnard	187
Elliott, Mrs. William	188
Elmendorf, Mrs.	160
Emmet, Mrs. Thomas Addis	358, 362
Fairfax Family	19
Faugeres, Margaretta	89
Fendall, Miss	336
Field, Mrs. Benjamin H.	175
Field, Mrs. Hickson	309
Field, Mrs. Hickson W.	308
Fish, Mrs. Hamilton	452
Fisher, Mrs. J. F.	227
Fitzhugh Family	17
Floyd, Mrs.	297
Foster, Miss Sally (Mrs. Otis)	88
Frankland, Lady Agnes	15
Franklin, Sarah (Mrs. Bache)	153
Franks, Rebecca (Lady Johnston)	156
Frémont, Mrs.	428
Gaines, Mrs. Myra Clark	341
Gaston, Mrs.	192
Gates, Mrs.	174
Genet, Madame	91
Gibbes, Mrs.	186
Gilpin, Mrs. Henry D.	376
Girard, Mrs.	450
Graeme, Elizabeth (Mrs. Ferguson)	152
Graydon, Mrs.	88
Greene, Mrs. Nathanael	131
Haight, Mrs.	308
Haley, Mrs.	89
Hamilton, Mrs. Alexander	163
Hampton, Miss	296
Hampton, Mrs. Wade	434
Hancock, Mrs. John	114
Hart, Miss Susan	195
Harvey, Mrs.	452
Harvey, the Misses	182
Hayes, Mrs.	417
Heald, Mrs.	209
Helm, Mrs.	210
Hills, Mrs. Henry W.	449
Hitchcock, Miss Lillie	451
Hunt, Mrs. Sallie Ward	285
Huntington, Mrs.	223
Innis, Mrs. Henry	208
Izard, Mrs. Ralph	192
Jackson, Mrs. Andrew	276
Jay Family	85
Jay, Mrs. John	44
Jefferson, Martha	88
Jefferson, Mrs. Thomas	87
Jeykell, Mrs.	14
Johnson, Mrs. Beverdy	340
Johnston, Mrs.	231
Johnston, Mrs. Albert Sidney	434
Jones, Mrs. Willie	192
Jones, Mrs. William	308
Kenton, Mrs.	204
King, Mrs. Rufus	159
Kinzie, Mrs.	210
Knox, Mrs.	96
La Fayette, Madame de	61, &c.
Lane, Miss Harriet	335
Leavenworth, Mrs.	310
Le Vert, Madame Octavia Walton	396
Le Vert, Miss Octavia	408
Livingston, Miss Cora	274
Livingston, Mrs. Edward	273
Livingston Family	41
Livingston, Governor, Daughters of	43
Livingston, Miss Kitty—Letters	50, &c.
Livingston, Miss Susan	43
Long, Mrs. Nicholas	192
Low, Mrs.	98
Macgregor, Mrs.	373
Mack, Mrs. John	355
Macubbin, Mrs. James	22
Madison, Mrs.	238
Marbois, Madame de	109
Marshall, Emily	324
Marshall, Mrs.	266
Mason, Miss Emily	422
McDowell, Mrs. James	296

INDEX OF NAMES. 463

Name	PAGE
McEvers, Eliza (Mrs. John R. Livingston)	274
McEvers, Mary	31, 274
McKinley, Mrs.	328
McLane, Mrs. Louis	272
McLean, Mrs.	336
Merrick, Mrs.	293
Montgomery, Mrs.	24
Morgan, Mrs.	455
Morgan, Eliza	336
Morris, Mrs. Lewis	189
Morris, Mrs. Robert	26, 31, 52, 147, &c.
Motte, Mrs.	186
Nelson, Mrs.	20
Ogden, Miss	109
Otis, Mrs.	83
Otis, Mrs. Harrison Gray	311
Ouseley, Lady	292
Page, Mrs.	20
Parish, Mrs. Henry	308
Parker, Miss Minnie	451
Patterson, Mrs. Robert	86
Payne, the Misses	239, 240
Peabody, Mrs.	105
Pendleton, Mrs.	308
Peters, Mrs.	160
Phelps, Paulina	182, 185
Philipse, Mary	14
Pleasants, Mrs.	226
Polk, Mrs. James K.	213
Preble, Miss Harriet	325
Prescott, Mrs. William H.	325
Preston Family	296
Preston, Mrs. William	297
Preston, Mrs. William C.	298
Pringle, Mrs.	340
Quincy Family	113
Quincy, Miss (Mrs. Asa Clapp)	272
Randolph, Edmonia	296
Randolph, Mrs.	83
Reed, Mrs.	17
Redfield, Mrs.	309
Renwick, Mrs.	302
Ritchie, Mrs. Montgomery	390
Ross Vertner Jeffrey	426

Name	PAGE
Rivington, Mrs.	162
Robertson, Mrs.	204
Robinson, Mrs.	14
Roosevelt, Mrs. J. J.	281
Roosevelt, Miss	292
Ross, Miss	84
Roupell, Mary	182, 186
Rush, Mrs. James	363
Sanders, Miss	338
Schaumburg, Miss Emilie	392
Schermerhorn, Mrs. John	451
Schermerhorn, Mrs. William	452
Schuyler, Catalina	15
Schuyler, Mrs. Philip	162
Scott, Miss Helen	427
Scott, Mrs. Winfield	295
Sears, Miss	108
Sedgwick, Mrs. Theodore	98
Sevier, Mrs.	197
Sevier, Ruth	202
Seymour, Julia	85
Shaw, Mrs.	105
Sheaffe, the Misses	107
Shippen, Margaret (Mrs. Arnold)	154
Sibley, Mrs.	209
Singleton, Mrs.	183
Sitgreaves, Mrs.	261
Slidell, Mrs.	336
Smith, the Misses	107
Sprague, Mrs.	455
Stannard, Mrs. Robert	420
St. Clair, Miss	306
Stevens, Mrs. John O.	307
Stewart, Mrs.	83
Stirling, Lady	44
Stockton, Mrs. Richard	159
Strangford, Lady	55
Talbot, Mrs.	206
Temple, Elizabeth	87
Temple, Lady	88
Thompson, Sarah (Countess Rumford)	133
Trask, Miss	212
Tryon, Lady	191
Van Cortlandt Family	171
Van Horne Ladies	155
Van Ness, Mrs.	264
Van Ness, Ann Elbertina (Mrs. Arthur Middleton)	267, 268

Name	PAGE
Van Ness, Miss Cornelia	282
Van Ness, Mrs. C. P.	281
Van Rensselaer, Mrs.	174
Vining, Miss	258
Von Berckel, Miss	108
Waddell, Mrs. Coventry	382
Wadsworth, Mrs. James S.	390
Wadsworth, Miss Elizabeth	391
Wake, Esther	191
Wallace, Mrs. E. F.	324
Wallace, Mrs. John Bradford	263
Wallace, Mrs. Mary Binney	263
Wallace, Mrs. Susan	263
Walworth, Mrs.	208
Ward, Miss Lillie	236
Ward, Mrs. Robert J.	228
Ward, Miss Sallie	228
Washington, Mrs.	17, 21, 23, 31, &c.
Washington, Mrs. (Jane Elliott)	189

Name	PAGE
Webster, Mrs. Daniel	374
Wheate, Lady	108
White, the Misses	89
White, Mrs. Florida	225
White, Mrs. James W.	342
Wickham, Mrs.	422
Wickham, the Misses	422
Wickliffe, Margaret	297
Willing Family	136
Wilson, Mrs.	167
Winthrop, Mrs.	88
Winthrop, Hannah	95
Wolcott, Mrs.	85
Wolcott, Miss Mary Ann	85
Woodbury, Mrs. Levi	272
Wooley, Mrs.	297
Wooster, Mrs.	132
Wortley, Lady Emmeline Stuart	404
Yrujo, de Casa, Marchioness	37, 283, 286

www.ingramcontent.com/pod-product-compliance
Lightning Source LLC
Chambersburg PA
CBHW051232300426
44114CB00011B/710